Mastering Arabic 2

Jane Wightwick &
Mahmoud Gaafar

Review Panel

Dr Otared Haidar (DPhil Oxford Univ. 2005), teaching at the Department of the Islamic World and the Middle East, University of Oxford, UK

Dr James Dickins, Professor of Arabic, School of Languages, University of Salford, UK

Ali Almakhlafi, Teacher of Arabic, Institute of Communication Sciences, University of Bonn, Germany

Sanaa Nounu, Lecturer in Arabic, UWE Language Programme, University of the West of England, UK; Head of Languages Department, Andalusia Academy Bristol, UK

Omsalama Ahmed, Teacher in Arabic, Joseph Chamberlain Sixth Form College, Birmingham, UK

palgrave
macmillan

Music composed by Leila Gaafar.

First published 2009 by
PALGRAVE MACMILLAN

Palgrave Macmillan in the UK is an imprint of Macmillan Publishers Limited, registered in England, company number 785998, of Houndmills, Basingstoke, Hampshire RG21 6XS.

Palgrave Macmillan in the US is a division of St Martin's Press LLC, 175 Fifth Avenue, New York, NY 10010.

Palgrave Macmillan is the global academic imprint of the above companies and has companies and representatives throughout the world.

ISBN-13: 978-0-230-22088-1
ISBN-13: 978-0-230-22086-7 book and CD pack
ISBN-13: 978-0-230-22087-4 CD pack

This book is printed on paper suitable for recycling and made from fully managed and sustained forest sources. Logging, pulping and manufacturing processes are expected to conform to the environmental regulations of the country of origin.

A catalogue record for this book is available from the British Library.

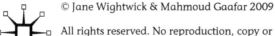

to Zeinah

Contents

Acknowledgements

We are grateful to the Review Panel for all their invaluable contributions. Their combined expertise has helped make this course more relevant and accurate. We would also like to thank everyone at Palgrave Macmillan, particularly Helen Bugler, Isobel Munday and Phillipa Davidson-Blake, for their continued support for our efforts.

We are grateful to the following for their help in recording samples of regional Arabic dialect: Emad Iskandar, Ahmed Meliebary, Najiba Keane, Mourad Diouri, Sami Dadi, Emilio Sawaya, Ali Basim Al Sawad, Radia Kesseiri, Eman and Mohammed Yafai, Adam Gargani and Abdul Rahim ibn Daw, Ashraf Abdelhay, Youssef Saadi.

The authors and publishers wish to thank the following who have kindly given permission for the use of copyright material: Otto Harrassowitz Verlag for material from Hans Wehr, *A Dictionary of Modern Arabic*, ed. J. Milton Cowan, 1991; Dar el-Shorouk and the estate of Naguib Mahfouz for an extract from www.shorouk.com; Beity Magazine for a schedule and home page from www.beitymagazine.com; Jobs for Arabs for an extract from the website www.jobs4Arabs.com; BBC Arabic Service for an article from their website www.bbcarabic.com; the World Economic Forum for a photo from Forum on the Middle East (2006), Sharm El Sheikh.

Every effort has been made to trace all the copyright holders but if any have been inadvertently overlooked the publishers will be pleased to make the necessary arrangement at the first opportunity.

Introduction

Mastering Arabic 2 is an intermediate course designed to work for a wide range of learners, including those studying for general interest or those following examination courses.

Mastering Arabic 2 follows on from *Mastering Arabic 1* and its companion books *Mastering Arabic Grammar* and *Mastering Arabic Script* (published in the US as *Easy Arabic Grammar* and *Easy Arabic Script*). However, it is also suitable for anyone with some prior knowledge of Arabic.

The course presents Modern Standard Arabic in an accessible and engaging way. A topic-based approach ensures that you will be given the opportunity to develop your skills and language within the framework of up-to-date themes relevant to the modern Arab world.

As in the first level course, when we present dialogues or situations in *Mastering Arabic 2* where the colloquial language would naturally be used, we have tried to use vocabulary, structures and pronunciation that are as close to the spoken form as possible.

In addition, we have included end-of-unit regional features that include samples of regional dialects. The purpose of including these is as much to emphasise the *similarities* between the different types of Arabic as it is to show their differences. An understanding of a particular dialect is often a case of accustoming your ear to pronunciation and some vocabulary variations. The dialects all have their positions within the spectrum of the Arabic language and we hope the samples will encourage you to view them this way.

How to use *Mastering Arabic 2*

This course has over two hours of accompanying audio and access to these recordings is essential, unless you are studying in a group where the tutor has the audio. Those parts of the book which are on the recording are marked with this symbol:

We are assuming when you start this book that you have a basic knowledge of the Arabic language and script, but that you may be working by yourself. *Mastering Arabic 2* is suitable for classroom or home use.

In this second level course, there is a particular emphasis on developing your ability to understand and produce more extended and sophisticated language. We have included extensive tips and exercises to help you achieve this end. It is possible for you to concentrate on the areas that are of particular interest to you, but you should not skip entire sections as there is a carefully built-in progression.

Review sections
These tinted sections review important points of grammar at appropriate points in the course. You will have met most of the grammar before, but here it is presented in a summary form that you can use as a checklist and refer to during your studies.

Conversation sections
These sections are designed to develop your conversational Arabic in social and everyday situations. You will usually be prompted to take part in a conversation related to the topic of the unit.

Additional notes
These occur at the end of some units and contain useful additional information. They are not essential but will be helpful to you in developing your study techniques and in recognising some of the finer points of Arabic.

The Arab world
These end-of-unit features focus on different regions of the Arab world. They include:
- a bilingual map of the area, showing the major cities and towns;
- an audio sample of authentic, unscripted regional dialect with notes, transcript and translation;
- a final article, many from authentic sources, with comprehension questions. The article links the theme of the unit with the focus region.

Review units
These occur at two points in the course. They will be very useful to you for assessing how well you remember what you have learnt. If you find you have problems with a particular exercise, go back and review the section or sections that deal with that area.

So now you're ready to continue learning with *Mastering Arabic 2*. We hope you enjoy the next leg of your journey.

part 1

Language units

unit 1

Myself and others
أنا والآخَرون

أنا وإبني على إبن عمّي... أنا وإبن عمّي على الغريب.

My son and I against my cousin... my cousin and I against the stranger.
(Arabic proverb)

Talking about yourself التكَلُّم عن نَفسك

Listen to these simple expressions you can use to talk about yourself:

(anā ismī) ...أنا اِسمي	My name is...
(uqīm fī/askun fī*) ...أُقيم في/أسكُن في	I live in...
(ɛunwānī) ...عُنواني	My address is...
(anā) ...أنا	I am... + *nationality/job*
(anā (aṣlan) min) ...أنا (أصلا) من	I am (originally) from...

**Tip:* أسكن (askun) is usually used in a more specific sense.
أقيم (uqīm) can be used more generally.

Remember that there is no equivalent of the English words 'am', 'is' or 'are' in this kind of simple, non-verbal sentence, nor are there separate words for 'a' or 'an' *(indefinite articles)*. In addition, if you are female you need to add the feminine ending ة (tā' marbūṭa) to most adjectives and nouns such as nationalities, jobs, etc., when you are talking about yourself.

أنا أمريكيّ/أمريكيّة. (anā amrīkīy/amrīkīyya)	I am American. *(masculine/feminine)*
أنا طالب/طالبة. (anā ṭālib/ṭāliba)	I am a student. *(masculine/feminine)*
عنواني ٦ شارع الملك، عمّان. (ɛunwānī sitta shāriɛ al-malik, ɛammān)	My address is 6 Al-Malik Street, Amman.

Exercise 1 تمرين ١

Look carefully at the speech bubbles below. Then put each of the statements into the correct category, as shown in the example:

الجنسيّة (*nationality*)	المهنة (*profession*)	مكان الإقامة (*place of residence*)	العنوان (*address*)	الاسم (*name*)
٣	٢ ٦	١		٥

١ أسكن في لُندُن.

٢ أنا نجّار.

٣ أنا أصلا من تُركيا.

٤ أقيم في دُبي مع أمّي.

٥ أنا اسمي فرانكو روسي.

٦ أنا تونسيّة.

٧ أنا طبّاخ في مطعم كبير.

٨ أنا سامي خوري.

٩ عنواني ٢٥ شارع المَسرَح.

١٠ أنا مُهرِّج!

Asking others سُؤال الآخَرين

هل... هل أنتَ طالب؟	*(question marker)*... are you a student?
ما... ما عمَلك؟	what? *(+ noun)* ... what's your job?
ماذا... ماذا تَدرُس؟	what? *(+ verb)* ... what are you studying?
أين... أين تَسكُن؟	where?... where do you live?
كَيف... كَيف الحال؟	how?... how are you?
لماذا... لماذا تعمل في الليل؟	why?... why do you work at night?
مَن... مَن هذا؟	who?... who's this?
أيّ (أيّة) ... أيّ وَلَد اِبنك؟	which? *(fem.)*... which boy is your son?

Exercise 2 تمرين ٢

Fill in the correct question word to match the answers, as in the example.

١ ـــماـــ اسمك؟ أنا اسمي نور.

٢ ــــــــ هذه؟ هذه زوجتي سميرة.

٣ ــــــــ حال أمّك؟ هي بخير.

٤ ــــــــ جنسيّتك؟ أنا سوري.

٥ ــــــــ بنت اِبنتك؟ هذه البنت ابنتي.

٦ زوجك من ــــــــ؟ هو أصلا من السعوديّة.

٧ ــــــــ أنت مُهندس؟ لا، أنا نجّار.

٨ ــــــــ تدرس في الجامعة؟ أدرس اللُغة العربيّة.

٩ ــــــــ تَذهَبون إلى المدرسة؟ نذهب بالقِطار.

١٠ ــــــــ تدرُس العربيّة؟ لأنّ أبي أصلا من فلسطين.

Talking about nationality التكلُّم عن الجِنسيّة

There are two main ways of expressing where you are from in Arabic, as there are in most languages:

I'm + *nationality* أنا + الجنسية

I'm from + *country* أنا من + البَلَد

***Nationality* الجنسية ← *Country* البلد**

(How to form nisba adjectives)

1 Remove الـ al- *(the)* from the word;

2 Remove any ة a, ا ā , or يا yā from the end of the word;

3 Add ـيّ -īy (or ـيّة -īyya for feminine).

Lebanese (masc./fem.)	←	Lebanon
(lubnānīyya) لبنانيّة/(lubnānīy) لبنانيّ	←	(lubnān) لُبنان
Sudanese (masc./fem.)	←	Sudan
(sūdānīyya) سودانيّة/(sūdānīy) سودانيّ	←	(as-sūdān) السودان
American (masc./fem.)	←	America
(amrīkīyya) أمريكيّة/(amrīkīy) أمريكيّ	←	(amrīkā) أمريكا

Note this important exception:

English (masc./fem.)	←	England
(ingilīzīyya) إنجليزيّة/(ingilīzīy) إنجليزيّ	←	(ingiltarā) إنجلترا

Exercise 3 تمرين ٣

Rephrase the sentences and questions, as shown in the examples:

أنا من العراق. I'm from Iraq → أنا عراقيّ/عراقيّة. I'm Iraqi

هِيَ فَرَنسيّة. She's French → هِيَ من فرنسا. She's from France

١ أنا من البَحرَين.

٢ هل أنتِ فلسطينيّة؟

٣ أنا كُويتيّ.

٤ هي من إيطاليا.

٥ هو يَمَنيّ.

٦ هل أنتَ من سوريا؟

٧ هو من انجلترا.

٨ هل هي مصريّة؟

Greetings التَحيّات

Arabic greetings are many and varied and could fill up an entire book in their own right.

There are universal greetings such as أهلاً (ahlan), hello; مرحباً (marḥaban), welcome; السلام عليكم (as-salāmu ع alaykum), peace be on you; and صباح/مساء الخير (ṣabāḥ/masā' al-khayr), good morning/evening. The universal greetings also have a large number of regional alternatives.

In addition, there are more elaborate greetings used in formal situations, such as at the beginning of news broadcasts. For example أسعد الله صباحكم بكلّ خير (asع ad allāh ṣabāḥakum bi-kulli khayr), which literally means 'May God make your morning happy with every goodness'.

Special occasions often have their own greetings. For example, on someone's birthday or for the New Year you might say كلّ عام وأنت بخير (kull ع ām w-anta/anti bi-khayr), 'every year and you are well'; on a religious feast day, عيد مبارك (ع īd mubārak), 'blessed Eid'; or at a wedding, مبروك (mabrūk), congratulations.

Other events are also worthy of their own greetings. For example you can send someone off on a journey with رحلة سعيدة (riḥla saع īda), 'happy journey', and greet them on arrival with الحمد لله على السلامة (al-ḥamdu lillāh ع ala s-salāma) 'thank God for the safe [arrival]'.

Exercise 4 تمرين ٤

Listen to two people talking about themselves and fill in the information on the forms below.

الاسم ...... خالد نور ......

مكان الإقامة ......

العنوان ......

الجنسية ......

المهنة ......

الاسم ......

مكان الإقامة ......

العنوان ......

الجنسية ......

المهنة ......

Exercise 5 تمرين ٥

Complete these two paragraphs using the information from Exercise 4.

أنا اسمي خالد ______ و______ أصلا من ______ .

أقيم الآن ______ ______ و______ مُراسِل

هُناك. عنواني ١٠٥ ______ الخليفة، الدوحة.

أنا ______ سامية ______ وأنا ______ من ______ .

______ الآن في ______ وأنا ______ هناك.

______ ٧٥ شارع ______ ، الدار البيضاء.

Exercise 6 تمرين ٦

Fill out this form with your own details.

الاسم ....

مكان الإقامة ....

العنوان ....

الجنسية ....

المهنة ....

Now write a paragraph about yourself using the models in Exercise 5 as a guide.

Conversation المحادثة

You're going to meet someone for the first time and talk about yourself. Prepare what you might say, using the information in the form above and thinking about the corresponding questions. Note that you will also need the phrases تشرّفنا (tasharrafnā), 'pleased to meet you', and عظيم! (ʿaẓīm), 'great!'.

Then take part in the conversation on the recording, following our prompts. You can try this several times until you feel confident.

Tip: In some phrases an *active participle* (fāʿil) can be used instead of a verb, although this is generally less formal:

Active participle	*Verb*	*Meaning*
(anā sākin) أنا ساكن	(askun) أسكُن	I am living/I live
(anā khārij) أنا خارج	(akhruj) أخرُج	I am going out

Active participles behave like adjectives and you need to add the usual feminine and plural endings:

أنا ساكنة في شقّة. (anā sākina fī shaqqa) I (fem.) live in an apartment.

هم خارجون. (hum khārijūn) They are going out.

My family عائلتي

Arabic is very precise in how it expresses family relationships. A vague concept such as 'my cousin' is replaced by an exact relationship, for example 'daughter of my paternal aunt' (i.e. my father's sister's daughter) or 'son of my maternal uncle', and so on; 'my brother-in-law' is replaced by 'husband of my sister' or 'brother of my wife'.

Listen first to the core vocabulary for family members:

أب/والد (ab/wālid) father	حَفيد (ḥafīd) grandson
أمّ/والدة (umm/wālida) mother	حَفيدة (ḥafīda) granddaughter
أخ (akh) brother	خال (khāl) maternal uncle
أخت (ukht) sister	خالة (khāla) maternal aunt
ابن (ibn) son	عمّ (ɛamm) paternal uncle
ابنة (ibna) daughter	عَمّة (ɛamma) paternal aunt
جَدّ (jadd) grandfather	حَم (ḥam) father-in-law
جَدّة (jadda) grandmother	حَماة (ḥamā) mother-in-law

Other family relations

To create family relationships outside the core terms, you need to use an إضافة iḍāfa construction to combine two or more nouns. Remember:

- Words in an iḍāfa are put directly together.
- ة (tā' marbūṭa) needs to be pronounced when followed by another noun in an iḍāfa or by a possessive ending such as ي (-ī, my).
- Only the final word in an iḍāfa can have الـ (al-, the) or a possessive ending.

زوج أختي (zawj ukhtī)	the husband of my sister (my brother-in-law)
ابنة عمّي (ibnat ɛammī)	the daughter of my paternal uncle (my cousin)
ابن أخت المدرّس (ibn ukht al-mudarris)	the son of the sister of the teacher (the teacher's nephew)

Tip: و (-ū) is added to أب (ab), father, أخ (akh), brother and حم (ḥam), father-in-law when they are the first nouns in an iḍāfa: أبو خالد Khalid's father, أخو نادية Nadia's brother, حمو خالي my uncle's father-in-law.

Exercise 7 تمرين ٧

Look at the family tree below and decide what relationship each of the people shown are to the main character (أنا 'me'). For example:

my niece ('daughter of my brother') :(ibnat akhī) ١ ابنة أخي

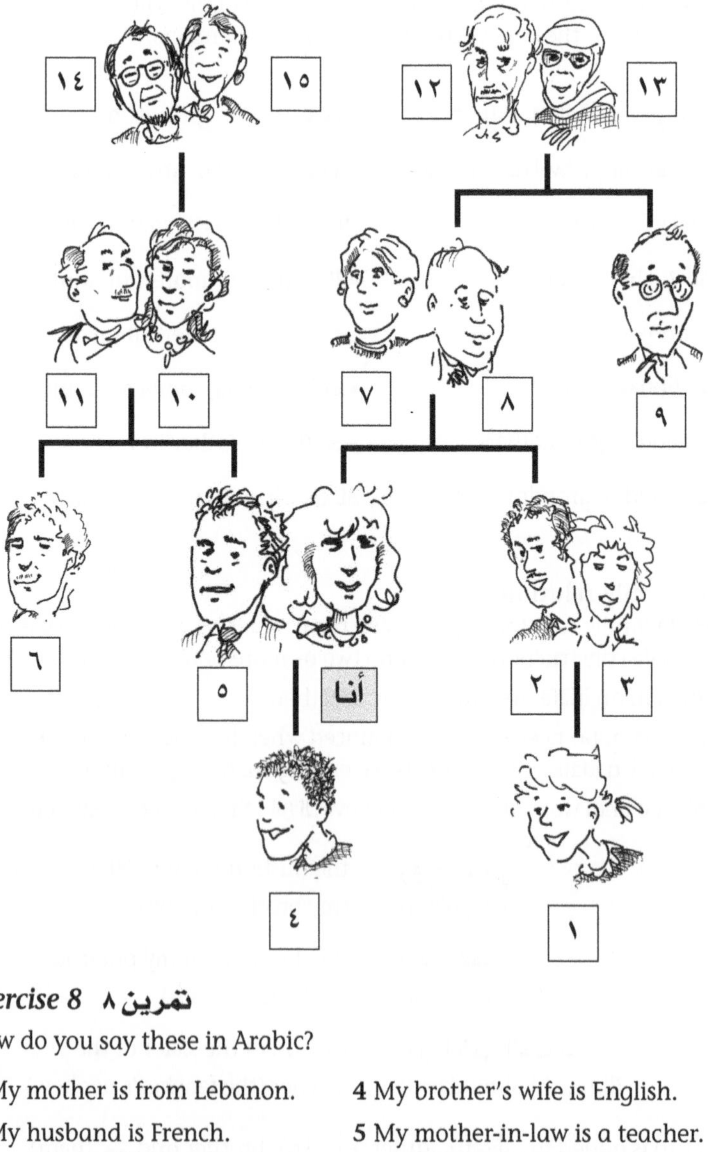

Exercise 8 تمرين ٨

How do you say these in Arabic?

1 My mother is from Lebanon.

2 My husband is French.

3 My grandfather is originally from Egypt.

4 My brother's wife is English.

5 My mother-in-law is a teacher.

6 My nephew (sister's son) is a correspondent in Qatar.

Pronouns الضمائر

You have met the two types of Arabic pronoun: subject pronouns (equivalent of 'I', 'he', 'we', etc.) and attached pronouns (equivalent of 'my/me', 'his/him', 'our/us', etc.). The attached pronouns are joined to the end of the word – as their name suggests. With one small exception for 'my' and 'me', the same attached pronoun is used for both possession and the object of a verb.

Subject pronoun		*Attached pronoun*	
I	أنا anā	my, me	ـي ī = my / ـني nī = me
you *(m.)*	أنتَ anta	your, you	ـك -ka (-ak)
you *(f.)*	أنتِ anti	your, you	ـك -ki (-ik)
he/it *(m.)*	هُوَ huwa	his, him/its, it	ـه -hu (-uh)
she/it *(f.)*	هِيَ hiya	her/its, it	ـها -hā
we	نَحنُ naḥnu	our, us	ـنا -nā
you *(m. pl.)*	أنتُم antum	your, you	ـكُم -kum
you *(f. pl.)*	أنتنَّ antunna	your, you	ـكُنَّ -kunna
they *(m.)*	هُم	their, them	ـهُم -hum
they *(f.)*	هُنَّ	their, them	ـهُنَّ -hunna

Arabic also has a 'dual' form for talking about two people or things, made by adding -ā (ā) to the masculine plurals: أنتُما (antumā) you, ـكُما (-kumā) your/you, هُما (humā) they, ـهُما (-humā) their/them.

Exercise 9 تمرين ٩

Replace the underlined words with the correct pronoun, as in the example:

(He's my son) هو ابني. ← (This boy is my son) هذا الولد ابني.

١ المدرّسة أصلا من كندا.

٢ المراسلون في المكتب.

٣ هذا هو مكتب المحاسبين.

٤ أين وجدتَ حقيبة جدّتك؟

٥ الممرّضات في المستشفى.

٦ سيّارة ابن خالتي جديدة.

٧ أنا وهو في البنك.

٨ هل سمير وزوجته في البيت؟

Describing character التكلّم عن الشخصيّة

Look at the following words that describe appearance and character.

وفيّ (wafī) loyal

حكيم (ḥakīm) wise

رشيق (rashīq) graceful

مضحك (muḍḥik) funny

عنيد (ʿanīd) stubborn

مكّار (makkār) cunning

رقيق (raqīq) delicate

موهوب (mawhūb) talented
محبوب (maḥbūb) popular
كريم (karīm) generous
كسول (kasūl) lazy
نشيط (nashīṭ) active
ذكيّ (dhakī) intelligent

Exercise 10 تمرين ١٠

Listen and fill in the missing words according to the descriptions you hear.

1 My mother is very *graceful*.

2 Her father is ____________ and ____________.

3 Our uncle is ____________ and ____________.

4 Your mother-in-law is ____________.

5 My brother is ____________ and ____________.

6 Their grandfather is very ____________.

7 Your cousin is ____________.

Improving your written Arabic

Now you have mastered the basics of Arabic, you can find ways to improve your style. One of the most important ways of achieving this improvement is through the use of 'connectors' such as فـ (fa-, and so) and ثمّ (thumma, then). Short, unconnected sentences are not considered good style in written Arabic. *Mastering Arabic 2* will introduce you to a variety of connectors and stylistic devices you can use to improve understanding and written style.

inna/wa-lākinna إنّ / ولكنّ

The Arabic particle إنّ does not have any specific meaning, although historically it has been translated as 'verily'. It is used to introduce a sentence and is usually followed by a noun or an attached pronoun. Starting a written sentence with هو or أنتَ can be considered ungainly in Arabic, whereas إنّه (innahu) or إنّك (innaka) are more graceful. ولكنّ (wa-lākinna) works in a similar way, carrying the meaning of 'but'.

إنّ جدّي حكيم ولكنّه عنيد. (inna jaddī ḥakīm wa-lākinnahu ع anīd)	My grandfather is wise but he's stubborn.
إنّ قطّتي رشيقة ولكنّها كسولة. (inna qiṭṭatī rashīqa wa-lākinnahā kasūla)	My cat is graceful but she's lazy.

Tip: إني / ولكنّي (innī/wa-lākinnī) and إنّني / ولكنّني (innanī/wa-lākinnanī) are alternatives when joining the attached pronoun for 'I'.

Exercise 11 تمرين ١١

Make sentences about the characters of family members, as in the example. (Take care to use the feminine if necessary.)

١ خالي ذكيّ/عنيد إنّ خالي ذكيّ ولكنّه عنيد.

٢ أختي محبوب/مكّار ....

٣ ابن عمّي موهوب/كسول ....

٤ جدّتي فقير/كريم ....

٥ حفيدي قَصير/نشيط ....

٦ ابنة خالتي طويل/رشيق ....

Can you use similar sentences to describe yourself and other members of your family?

Talking about childhood التكلّم عن الطُفولة

Listen to these phrases you can use to talk about your childhood.

وُلِدْتُ في ٧ مارس عام... (wulidtu fī sabع a māris ع ām)	I was born on March 7 in the year...
أمضَيْتُ طُفولتي في قرية صغيرة. (amḍaytu ṭufūlatī fī qarya ṣaghīra)	I spent my childhood in a small village.
كان أبي طبيب أسنان. (kāna abī ṭabīb asnān)	My father was a dentist.
كانت أمّي مغنّية. (kānat ummī mughanniya)	My mother was a singer.
اِنتَقَلْتُ إلى العاصمة عام... (intaqaltu ilā l-ع āṣima ع ām)	I moved to the capital in the year...

Notice that in Arabic you add في ('in') in front of the date but not the year. In Arabic the years are expressed as whole numbers using ألف (alf), a thousand, or ألفين (alfayn), two thousand. This is in contrast to English where years are generally expressed as pairs of numbers ('nineteen eighty-five', 'twenty twelve', etc.).

عام ١٩٨٥	ع ām alf wa-tisع mi'a wa-khamsa wa-thamanīn
عام ٢٠١٢	ع ām alfayn wa-ithnaعashar

Tip: there are two common words for 'year' in Arabic: عام ع ām and سنة sana: سنة ٢٠١٢ (sanat alfayn wa-ithnaعashar), the year 2012.

Exercise 12 تمرين ١٢

Write down the dates of birth you hear on the recording, for example.

١٤ فبراير عام ١٩٧٥

Exercise 13 تمرين ١٣

Use the example sentences above to give details of your date of birth and childhood. Try saying them out loud initially, and then write them down as a paragraph, using as many connectors as you can.

Omm Kalthoum, 'Star of the East' أمّ كلثوم، «كوكب الشرق»

Read the paragraph below about the famous Egyptian singer, Omm Kalthoum, using the additional vocabulary and tables to help you.

- شهير (shahīr) famous
- دلتا النيل (daltā an-nīl) the Nile Delta
- غنّى/يغنّي (ghannā/ yughannī) to sing
- ملابس (malābis) clothes
- صبيّ (ṣabīy) young boy
- بدويّ (badawīy) bedouin
- حفلة (ḥafla) concert, party
- مات/يموت (māta, yamūt) to die
- جنازة (jināza) funeral
- شخص (shakhṣ) person

وُلِدَت أم كلثوم، المغنية العربيّة الشهيرة، في قرية مصرية صغيرة عام ١٩٠٤ وأمضت طُفولتها في دلتا النيل، وكانت تُغنّي بـمَلابِس صَبيّ بَدَوي.

انتقلَت أم كلثوم إلى القاهرة عام ١٩٢٠، وكان لها حفلة في الخميس الأوّل من كلّ شهر.

إنّها كانت موهوبة ومحبوبة، رقيقة وقويّة في نَفس الوقت.

ماتَت «كَوكب الشَرق» في ٣ فبراير عام ١٩٧٥ وحضر جنازتها أربعة ملايين شخص.

(read table from right to left)

كان/كانَت (kāna/kānat) he/she was		وُلِدَ / وُلِدَت ... (wulida/wulidat) he/she was born
كان له/كان لها ... (kāna lahu/kāna laḥā) he/she had	عام/سنة ... (ʕām/sanat) (in) the year	مات / ماتَت ... (māta/mātat) he/she died
أمضى/أمضَت ... (amḍā/amḍat) he/she spent		انتقل / انتقلَت إلى ... (intaqala/intaqalat ilā) he/she moved to

Exercise 14 تمرين ١٤

Now find out details about the life of a famous singer you know and write a similar article about him or her.

العالم العربي ... نظرة على مصر

(The Arab World... A look at Egypt)

Arabic in Egypt العربيّة في مصر

'Egyptian' dialect usually refers to the spoken language of Cairo and the north of Egypt. Dialects in other regions will vary more or less.

Egypt has traditionally exported films, popular television programmes and songs to the rest of the Arab world. The advent of pan-Arab satellite channels has exposed people to a greater variety of accents, but the Egyptian dialect can still claim to be the most widely understood.

Egyptian dialect shares some features with other dialects, e.g.:

- replacement of ق with a glottal stop ('), e.g. وقت (time) as wa't
- pronunciation of ث as 't', e.g. كثير (many/a lot) as kitīr

Features particular to Egyptian dialect include:

- pronunciation of ج as a hard 'g', e.g. الجمعة (Friday) as ig-gumعa
- use of specifically Egyptian expressions, e.g. دلوقتي dilwa'tī (now), قوي 'awī (a lot, literally 'strong'), عربيّة عarabīyya (car)
- extensive use of foreign loan words, e.g. موبايل mobāyil (mobile)

Listen to Emad talking about himself in his Egyptian dialect. You will find a transcript and translation in the Answers section.

- وُلد في ١١ ديسمبر عام ١٩١١
- أمضى طفولته في حي الجمّالية، ثم انتقل إلى العبّاسية ثمّ الحسين
- بدأ كتابة القصّة القصيرة عام ١٩٣٦ ونشر ثلاثيته الشهيرة عام ١٩٥٦
- حصل على جائزة نوبل للآداب عام ١٩٨٨
- مات نجيب محفوظ في مستشفى بالقاهرة عام ٢٠٠٦

سيرة
أعمال
جوائز وأوسمة
أفلام
نوبل
في حب نجيب محفوظ
كتابات أولى
صور
أخبار
اتصال

(adapted from www.shorouk.com)

حيّ، أحيـ (ḥayy, aḥyā') district, ea
بدأ، يبـ (bada'a, yabda') to begin
قصّة، قصـ (qiṣṣa, qiṣaṣ) story
نشر، ينشـ (nashara, yanshur) to publish
ثلاثيـّ (thulāthīyya) trilogy
حصل، يحصل على (ḥaṣala, yaḥṣul ʿala) to obtain, to win (a prize, etc.)

Note: al-gammālīyya, al-ʿabbāsīyya and al-ḥusayn are all districts of Cairo.

In 1988, at the age of 76, the Egyptian writer Naguib Mahfouz won the Nobel prize for literature. He was the first Arab author to win this prestigious award.

His most famous work is the 'Cairo Trilogy', following the story of a family in Egypt from World War I to the 1950s.

As well as writing extensive short stories, novels and film scripts, Naguib Mahfouz worked in a variety of government positions, retiring from the Ministry of Culture in 1972.

Naguib Mahfouz died in 2006 at the age of 94.

الأَسئِلة (Questions)

١ متى وُلد نجيب محفوظ؟

٢ متى بدأ الكتابة؟

٣ متى نشر الثُلاثيّة الشهيرة؟

٤ أين مات؟

Vocabulary in Unit 1

Nouns الأسماء

address	عُنوان (عَناوين)
residence	إقامة (ات)
apartment	شَقّة (شُقَق)
village	قَرية (قُرىً)
district/area	حَيّ (أحياء)
family	عائِلة (ات)
childhood	طُفولة (ات)
father	أَب (آباء)/ والِد (ون/ ين)
mother	أُمّ (أُمّهات)/ والِدة (ات)
brother	أَخ (إخوَة)
sister	أُخت (أَخَوات)
son	اِبن (أَبناء)
daughter	اِبنة (ات)
grandfather	جَدّ (أَجداد)
grandmother	جَدّة (ات)
grandson	حَفيد (أَحفاد)
granddaughter	حَفيدة (ات)
maternal uncle	خال (أَخوال)
maternal aunt	خالة (ات)
paternal uncle	عَمّ (أَعمام)
paternal aunt	عَمّة (ات)
father-in-law	حَم (أَحماء)
mother-in-law	حَماة (حَمَوات)
husband	زَوج (أَزواج)
wife	زَوجة (ات)
year	عام (أعوام)/ سَنة (سِنين)
thousand	أَلف (آلاف)
singer	مُغَنٍ (ون/ ين)
dentist	طَبيب (أطِبّاء) الأسنان
clown	مُهَرِّج (ون/ ين)
young boy	صَبيّ (صُبيان)
concert/party	حَفلة (ات)
funeral	جِنازة (ات)
person	شَخص (أشخاص)
clothes	مَلابِس
story	قِصّة (قِصَص)
trilogy	ثُلاثيّة (ات)

Adjectives الصفات

loyal	وَفيّ
cunning	مَكّار
graceful	رَشيق
funny	مُضحِك
wise	حَكيم
delicate	رَقيق
stubborn	عَنيد
talented	مَوهوب
popular	مَحبوب
generous	كَريم
lazy	كَسول
active	نَشيط
intelligent	ذَكيّ

famous شَهير

bedouin بَدَويّ

Verbs الأفعال

live/reside سَكَنَ، يسكُن

أقامَ، يُقيم

spend (time) أَمضى، يُمضي

move (house, etc.) انتَقَلَ، يَنتَقِل

sing غَنَّى، يُغَنِّي

begin بَدَأَ، يبدأ

publish نَشَرَ، يَنشُر

obtain/win (a prize, etc.) حَصَلَ، يحصُل على

die ماتَ، يموت

Other phrases العبارات الأخرى

originally أصلاً

Nile Delta دَلتا النيل

I was born وُلِدتُ

he/she was born وُلِدَ / وُلِدَت

Additional note: Vocabulary

Vocabulary lists appear at the end of each unit, and there is also an English–Arabic glossary at the end of the book on page 281.

English equivalents are given according to usage in this course. Other meanings may also be possible for individual words.

As a general rule only vocabulary new to *Mastering Arabic 2* will be listed. Refer to *Mastering Arabic 1* for vocabulary already covered in the first level. The main exception will be if a word is part of a wider vocabulary set, where there may be some repetition for the sake of completeness.

Nouns are listed with their (most common) plurals in brackets and verbs are shown in both the past and present tenses.

You should make learning vocabulary part of your routine. You can just try to learn from a list but consider also these different ideas:

- Write out new vocabulary on bi-lingual cards and use the cards to test yourself (see *Mastering Arabic 1*).
- Make yourself a presentation on your computer (see *Mastering Arabic 1* for tips on keying Arabic). You can illustrate the words with clipart to help you remember them.
- Use one of the language learning sites on the internet that enable you to key in your own words to create virtual flashcards and vocabulary learning activities.
- Challenge yourself to make sentences using as many new words as possible from a list.

unit 2

House and home
الدار والبيت

الجار قَبلَ الدار.

The neighbour before the house[hold]. (Arabic proverb)

Talking about rooms التكلّم عن الغُرَف

Look at the illustration below while you listen to the recording.

Tip: غُرفة مَعيشة (living room) can also be called غُرفة جُلوس (sitting room).

Exercise 1 تمرين ١

An estate agent is showing you around an apartment. Put the places in the order that he shows them, as in the example.

صالة ١	غرفة جلوس ___
حمّام ___	مطبخ ___
غرفة نوم ___	شرفة ___
سفرة ___	حديقة ___

Exercise 2 تمرين ٢

Do you remember these items you can find in or around a house? Match the English with the Arabic.

a bed	١ خزانة
b car	٢ كمبيوتر
c chair	٣ شَجَر
d clock	٤ مائدة
e cupboard/wardrobe	٥ مكتب
f desk	٦ تليفزيون
g picture	٧ صورة
h table	٨ ساعة
i television	٩ سرير
j bicycle	١٠ سيّارة
k computer	١١ كرسيّ
l trees	١٢ درّاجة

Here are some more useful words for items around the house:

ستائر (satā'ir) curtains	دش (dush) shower
سجّاد (sajjād) carpets	عشب (ɛushb) grass/plants
مرآة (mir'āt) mirror	ورد (ward) flowers
مصعد (miṣɛad) lift/elevator	كنبة/أريكة (kanaba/arīka) sofa
غسّالة (ghassāla) washing machine	ثلاّجة (thallāja) fridge
حوض (ḥawḍ) sink	فرن (furn) cooker

Exercise 3 تمرين ٣

Use the vocabulary in the box on page 21 and in Exercise 2. Decide on the most likely place for each item, as in the example. (You can put an item in more than one place and you do not need to include مصعد lift/elevator.)

الحديقة/ الجراج	المطبخ	الحمّام	السفرة/ غرفة الجلوس	غرفة النوم/ مكتب
				سرير

Describing your home وصف مَنزِلك

Here are some adjectives you can use to describe your home:

حديث (ḥadīth) modern	فاخر (fākhir) luxurious
تقليديّ (taqlīdīy) traditional	بسيط (basīṭ) simple/basic
هادئ (hādi') quiet	مريح (murīḥ) comfortable
مزدحم (muzdaḥim) crowded	مناسب (munāsib) suitable
واسع (wāsiع) spacious	خاصّ (khāṣṣ) private

جراج خاصّ garāj khāṣṣ *(Private Garage)*

عفواً ممنوع الانتظار ۶afwan mamnūع al-intiẓār *(Sorry No Waiting)*

Tip: There are many different words to describe dwellings in Arabic. Common words for 'house' or 'home' are بيت (bayt), and دار (dār) – familiar through place names such as Darussalaam (دار السلام 'house of peace') and, less obviously, Bethlehem (بيت لحم 'house of meat'). Casablanca is a Spanish translation of the Arabic name الدار البيضاء (ad-dār al-bayḍā'), 'the white house' – not to be confused with the US presidential building which is translated as البيت الأبيض (al-bayt al-abyaḍ).

Other terms for dwellings include منزل (manzil, 'place of staying') and مسكن (maskan, 'place of residing'). شقّة (shaqqa, pl. shuqaq) refers to an apartment or flat, and عمارة (ع imāra, pl. -āt) to an apartment building.

Listen to Sherif describing where he lives.

أنا اسمي شريف سرور وأسكن في شقّة في الطابق الرابع من عِمارة حديثة. إنّ شقّتي بسيطة ولكنّها مريحة. أمّا الشارع فهو هادئ وليس هناك سيّارات كثيرة.

تَتكَوّن شقّتي من غرفة نوم، مطبخ صغير، غرفة معيشة وحمّام وتوجد أيضاً شرفة تُطِلّ على حديقة. الشقّة مفروشة بستائر فاخرة وسجّاد تقليديّ. لا يوجد مِصعَد في العمارة ولذلك فهي مناسبة للنشيطين فَقَط!

[ليس] هناك ...
([laysa] hunāka)
there is, are [not]...

[لا] يوجَد/توجَد ...
([lā] yūjad/tūjad)
... can[not] be found *(masc./fem.)*

[ليس] لَهُ/لَها ...
([laysa] lahu/lahā)
it *(masc./fem.)* has [doesn't have]...

يتكوّن/تتكوّن من ...
(yatakawwan/tatakawwan min)
it *(masc./fem.)* consists of...

يطلّ/تطلّ على ...
(yuṭill/tuṭill ع alā)
it *(masc./fem.)* looks onto...

في الطابق الـ... من
(fīṭ-ṭābiq il... min)
on the ... floor of

Exercise 4 تمرين ٤

Look back at the description of Sherif's apartment on page 23 and decide if these statements are true (✔) or false (✘).

١ يسكن شريف في عمارة قديمة.

٢ الشقّة في الطابق الثالث.

٣ الحيّ هادئ.

٤ توجد حديقة بجانب العمارة.

٥ لا توجد سفرة في الشقّة.

٦ الشقّة واسعة وكبيرة.

٧ تتكوّن الشقّة من غرفتَين ومطبخ وحمّام.

٨ إنّها مفروشة بالستائر.

٩ السجّاد تقليديّ.

١٠ الشقّة مناسبة للكبار في السِنّ.

أمّا ammā/لذلك lidhālik

The description of Sherif's apartment contains two more useful connectors:

أمّا الشارع فهو هادئ. (ammā sh-shāriع fa-huwa hādi')	As for the street, it's quiet.
لذلك فهي مناسبة للنشيطين فقط! (lidhālik fa-hiya munāsiba lin-nashīṭīn faqaṭ)	For that reason it's suitable for active people only!

أمّا ('as for') is used when you are moving on to a different aspect of the same topic; لذلك ('for that (reason)') is used to connect cause and effect. Both are usually followed by فـ ('and so').

Exercise 5 تمرين ٥

Rephrase these sentences using ... فـ ...أمّا, as in the example.

١ الشقّة في الطابق الرابع. أمّا الشقّة فهي في الطابق الرابع.

٢ السجّاد تقليديّ. ____________

٣ العِمارة حديثة. ____________

٤ الشرفة تُطِلّ على حديقة. ____________

٥ المطبخ صغير. ____________

ṭābiq li-ghayr il-mudakhkhinīn *(floor for non-smokers)*

Exercise 6 **تمرين ٦**

Listen to Sherif telling us who lives on the other floors of his apartment block. Write the correct names on the name plates, as in the example.

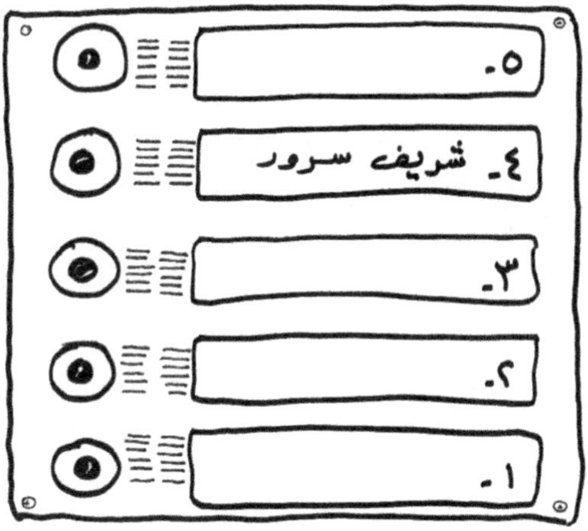

Conversation المحادثة

Describe your new apartment in the prompted audio conversation. Prepare the Arabic to describe these features:

- 3rd floor
- spacious living room
- small but modern kitchen
- no lift
- 2 bathrooms
- modern and comfortable
- large hall
- 3 bedrooms
- balcony overlooking street

The plural الجَمع

There are three different methods of making words plural in Arabic and these methods in turn have variations. This summary will help you to consolidate your knowledge of how Arabic plurals are made.

You need to try and remember a word together with its plural. Gradually you will find that you get a more instinctive grasp of the patterns and are able to 'feel' which plural might be right for a particular word.

Sound (external)

1 *Sound masculine plural (SMP)* ـون/ـين (-ūn/-īn)

- Used almost exclusively with words referring to groups of people of whom at least one is male.
- Commonly used for nationalities, jobs, attributes derived from forms of the verb (beginning with مُـ mu-).
- ـون (-ūn) is the 'default' ending in Standard Arabic. ـين (-īn) is used in particular structures – see additional note on page 55.

(murāsilūn/-īn) مراسلون/ين ← correspondent (murāsil) مُراسِل

(muslimūn/-īn) مسلمون/ين ← Muslim (muslim) مُسلِم

(lubnānīyūn/-īn) لبنانيّون/ين ← Lebanese (lubnānīy) لُبنانيّ

2 *Sound feminine plural (SFP)* ات (-āt)

- Probably the most common Arabic plural.
- Used for words referring to groups of people *all of whom* are female.

(mumarriḍāt) ممرّضات ← nurse *(fem.)* (mumarriḍa) ممرّضة

(muṣrīyyāt) مصريّات ← Egyptian *(fem.)* (muṣrīyya) مصريّة

- Used for some other masculine and feminine non-human words, especially longer words derived from forms of the verb and imported words of foreign origin.

(ḥammāmāt) حمّامات ← bathroom (ḥammām) حمّام

(ijtimāع āt) اجتماعات ← meeting (ijtimāع) اجتماع

(tilīfizyūnāt) تليفزيونات ← television (tilīfizyūn) تليفزيون

Broken (internal)

- Plural made by identifying the root of a word and changing internal vowel sounds (similar to English 'goose/geese' or 'mouse/mice').
- About twelve common different patterns, plus a few other less common.
- Patterns defined using root letters فعل (e.g. أقلام 'pens' = أفعال pattern).

- Broken plural is used with many words referring to non-humans:

(*pattern* = أفعال) (afrān) أفران ← cooker (furn) فُرن

(*pattern* = فُعَل) (ghuraf) غُرَف ← room (ghurfa) غُرفة

(*pattern* = فُعول) (buyūt) بُيوت ← house (bayt) بيت

(*pattern* = فُعُل) (kutub) كُتُب ← book (kitāb) كتاب

(*pattern* = فِعال) (diyār) ديار ← house/home (dār) دار

(*pattern* = مَفاعِل) (makātib) مكاتب ← office/desk (maktab) مكتب

- Broken plural can also be used with words referring to groups of males (in preference to the SMP):

(*pattern* = فِعال) (rijāl) رِجال ← man (rajul) رَجُل

(*pattern* = فُعَلاء) (wuzarā') وُزَراء ← minister (wazīr) وَزير

(*pattern* = أفعال) (aḥfād) أحفاد ← grandchild (ḥafīd) حَفيد

Collective

- Collective nouns are masculine singular but have a plural meaning.
- Add ة to make a feminine singular noun referring to one of the group.
- Natural features that come in groups (plants, animals, etc.) are often collective nouns.

a cow (baqara) بَقَرة ← cows (baqar) بَقَر

a tree (shajara) شَجَرة ← trees (shajar) شَجَر

- Other items that come in groups can be collective (e.g. carpets):

a carpet (sajjāda) سجّادة ← carpets (sajjād) سجّاد

Plurals in the dictionary

منظر *manẓar* pl. مناظر *manāẓir*[2] sight; view, panorama; look(s), appearance, aspect; prospect, outlook, perspective	نظيف *naẓīf* pl. نظفاء *nuẓafā'*[2], نظاف *niẓāf* clean, neat, tidy; well-groomed, well-tended
ناظر *nāẓir* pl. نظار *nuẓẓār* observer, viewer, spectator, onlooker; overseer, supervisor; inspector; manager, director	انظف *anẓaf*[2] cleaner, neater
	تنظيف *tanẓīf* pl. *-āt* cleaning, cleansing | تنظيف الاظفار manicure

Plurals are shown after the singular in the most popular English–Arabic dictionary (*A Dictionary of Modern Arabic*, Hans Wehr). Note that the entry above for نظيف (clean) has alternative plurals. A few words have these alternatives; the most common is used in *Mastering Arabic*.

Exercise 7 **تمرين ٧**

(You will need a dictionary to complete this exercise.)

Find the plurals of these words you have met in this unit, as in the example. You could also try and guess at the plural before looking it up.

Meaning المَعنى	Plural الجَمع	Word الكَلمة
pictures	صُوَر	صورة
....	....	ثَلّاجة
....	....	مَطبَخ
....	....	حَوض
....	....	شُرفة
....	....	كمبيوتر
....	....	خَزانة
....	....	طابق
....	....	سرير

Now check your answers in the answer section before moving on.

Tip: In some spoken dialects you may only hear the ـين (-īn) ending for groups of people , even when the group consists entirely of females. So البنات مشغولين (al-banāt mashgūlīn) could be used to mean 'the girls are busy', rather than the more grammatically correct البنات مشغولات (al-banāt mashghūlāt).

Exercise 8 تمرين ٨

Listen to Samya describing where she lives and put a tick next to the features of her home, as in the example.

apartment	small house	villa ✔
garden	garage	view of sea
hall	dining room	two bathrooms
flowers	trees	grass
old couch	mirrors	desk

Exercise 9 تمرين ٩

Complete this description of Samya's villa using the words in the box.

جديدة تتكوّن غُرَف واسع ليس حديقة كراسي يوجد الصالة

أقيم في فيلاّ في مدينة ______ قريبة من العاصمة. الفيللاّ
تطلّ على الجبال و ______ من صالة، غرفة جلوس، ثلاث
______ نوم، مطبخ ______ وحمّامين. الفيللا لها ______
خاصّة فيها شجر ليمون ولكن ______ هناك ورد أو عشب.
غرفة الجلوس فيها ______ مريحة وأريكة قديمة... هَدِية
من أمّي ... ووراء الأريكة ______ مكتب عليه كمبيوتر لابني.
أما ______ فهي بطراز تقليديّ.

Tip: بطراز (bi-ṭirāz) = in the style of

You can check your description by listening to Samya in Exercise 8 again and by looking at the Answers section.

Exercise 10 تمرين ١٠

Now describe *your* home using the vocabulary and models you have met so far. Remember to vary the phrases you use and try to include some of the connecting words you have met.

Adjectives and plurals الصفة والجَمع

There is not really a grammatical difference between nouns and adjectives in Arabic. Adjectives such as active (نشيط nashīṭ) or popular/loved (محبوب maḥbūb) can also be used to mean 'an active person' or 'a popular/loved one'.

Adjectives need to be made plural when referring to groups of people. Some adjectives use a *sound* plural, others use a *broken* plural. The plural of an adjective may follow a different plural pattern from the word it is describing.

(awlād ṭiwāl) **أولاد طِوال**	tall boys
(al-kuramā') **الكرماء**	the generous (ones)
(an-nās al-mashghūlūn) **الناس المشغولون**	the busy people
(innahum nashīṭūn jiddan) **إنّهُم نشيطون جداً.**	They are very active.

For an all-female group, the adjective can be made plural by using the Sound Feminine Plural.

(al-banāt aṭ-ṭawīlāt) **البنات الطويلات**	the tall girls
(mumarriḍāt mashghūlāt) **ممرّضات مشغولات**	busy nurses

Plurals of non-human objects and ideas are grammatically a single female!

Non-human plurals

Remember that plurals not referring to people are treated as *feminine singular* in Arabic. So an adjective describing a group of objects, such as 'chairs' or 'pictures' needs ة as for a single feminine object.

(al-karāsī al-ḥadītha) الكراسي الحديثة	the modern chairs
(aṣ-ṣuwar jamīla). الصور جميلة.	The pictures are beautiful.

Exercise 11 تمرين ١١

Make these descriptions plural as in the examples. You may need to use your dictionary to look up some of the plurals.

هو مشغول. (He is busy.) ← هم مشغولون. (They are busy.)

المائدة جديدة. (The table is new) ← الموائد جديدة (The tables are new.)

١ الولد نشيط.

٢ هناك شرفة واسعة.

٣ الكرسي مريح.

٤ البيت له حديقة خاصّة.

٥ الشارع مُزدَحِم.

٦ إنّها بنت موهوبة.

٧ إنّ حفيدي طويل.

٨ هناك سجّادة تقليديّة في الغرفة.

For rent للإيجار

Look at the four notices advertising property to rent.

فيللا للإيجار في حيّ هادئ. . .
٤ غرف نوم و٤ حمامات. تكييف
هواء، مطبخ أمريكي، سفرة،
حديقة صغيرة وجراج لسيّارتين.
سلّم داخلي من الرخام الإيطالي.
سطح كبير مناسب للحفلات.

kareem@msarabic.eg

شقة حديثة بإيجار مناسب
قريبة من الشاطئ. الطابق
السابع (٣ مصاعد ألمانيّة).
يوجد حمام سباحة وملعب
تنس لسكّان العمارة. شرفة
كبيرة تطلّ على البحر.
تليفون: ٠٣ ٤٥٦٧٨٦

شقة كبيرة في موقع جميل
طابق أرضي، مدخل خاصّ.
تتكوّن من ٣ غرف واسعة -
تكييف هواء - حمّامات فاخرة.
جراج خاصّ. مناسبة لمكتب
محامٍ أو محاسب.
هاتف محمول: ٠٩٦٧٨١١١٤٧٦

منزل تقليديّ في الريف
بحديقة كبيرة
٧ غرف مريحة وحمامين. منظر
جميل، يطلّ على الحقول والنهر.
مفروش بالطراز العربيّ -
سجّاد إيرانيّ. ساعة بالسيّارة
من وسط المدينة.

هاتف: ٨٧٩٤٠٥
فاكس: ٨٧٩٤٥٦

شاطئ (shāṭi') beach

حمام سباحة (ḥammām sibāḥa) swimming pool

ملعب تنس (malعab tennis) tennis court

ساكن، سكّان (sākin, sukkān) resident

رخام (rukhām) marble

موقع (mawqiع) location

مدخل (madkhal) entrance

تكييف هواء (takyīf hawā') air-conditioning

الريف (ar-rīf) the countryside

منظر (manẓar) view

حقل، حقول (ḥaql, ḥuqūl) field

هاتف (محمول) (hātif (maḥmūl)) (mobile) phone

Exercise 12 تمرين ١٢

Decide which property would suit the following:

1 Family with four children and a dog. Prefer rural setting but must be within 60-75 minute commute from town for husband's work.

2 Young professional couple working in the hotel business in a popular resort. Prefer modern apartment. Keen on sports.

3 American diplomat looking for quiet, spacious upmarket villa with entertainment potential. Parking essential. Garden a bonus.

4 Businesswoman - currently working from home - looking for offices for her accountancy business.

Exercise 13 تمرين ١٣

Now complete the chart showing the facilites of each property, as in the example.

شقة كبيرة	منزل تقليدي	فيللا هادئة	شقة حديثة	
✗	✗	✗	✔	مصعد
				حديقة
				جراج
				منظر
				شرفة
				حمّامان أو أكثر
				سجاد
				سفرة
				تكييف هواء
				رخام
				حمام سباحة
				ملعب تنس

Exercise 14 تمرين ١٤

Write an advertisement for a property to rent with these features:
• large furnished apartment • third floor • two elevators • four bedrooms
• three luxurious bathrooms • balcony overlooking countryside
Add two more features of your own and a mobile telephone number.

العالم العربي ... نظرة على السعودية

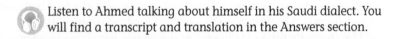

Arabic in Saudi Arabia اللغة العربيّة في السعوديّة

The Arabian peninsula, which now forms part of modern Saudi Arabia, was where the Arabic language originated and where the prophet Mohammed was born in the 7th century AD. Arabic spread with the rapid Islamic conquests, but the spoken language of the Arabian peninsula can still claim to be closer to the Classical than that of other more distant regions that were open to diverse linguistic influences.

Features of Saudi Arabic include:

- pronunciation of ق as a hard 'g', e.g. قهوة (coffee) as gahwa
- pronunciation of ك as 'ch', e.g. سمك (fish) as simich
- use of feminine plural in spoken language
- less use of imported foreign words

Listen to Ahmed talking about himself in his Saudi dialect. You will find a transcript and translation in the Answers section.

توجّه، يتوجّه (نحـ (tawajjah, yatawajjah (naḥwa) to face towards)
باحـ (bāḥa) courtyard
نافور (nāfūra) fountain
اختلف يختلف (ikhtalafa, yakhtalif) to vary
يُستخدم (yustakhdam) is used
سرداب (sirdāb) cellar
نهار (nahār) day(time)
خزن (khazn) storage

البيت العربيّ التقليديّ

يتوجّه البيت العربيّ التقليديّ نحو الداخل، وله باحة تتوجّه نحوها الشبابيك وأبواب الغرف. إن هذه الباحة هي قلب البيت، وفي وسطه يوجد حوض ماء أو نافورة.

يختلف عدد الطوابق في البيوت التقليديّة. البيوت في الريف لها طابق واحد وأما المنازل القديمة في المُدُن، في مَكّة وجَدّة مثلاً، فلها أربعة أو خمسة طوابق - مثل بيت نصيم الشهير في جدّة.

يُستَخدِم السِرداب للجلوس في نهار الصيف، والباحة للجلوس لَيلاً والسطح للنوم. وأما في الشتاء فتُستخدم الباحة للجلوس في النهار والغرف الداخليّة للنوم والسرداب للخزن.

الأَسئِلة (Questions)

١ ما هو قلب البيت العربيّ التقليديّ؟
٢ ماذا يوجد في وسط الباحة؟
٣ كم طابقاً في بيوت الريف؟
٤ ما هو اسم البيت القديم الشهير في جَدّة؟
٥ أين يجلسون في الشتاء في النهار؟

Better known these days for its ultra-modern skyscrapers, Saudi Arabia also retains some fine examples of traditional buildings, particularly in the older towns such as Jeddah and Mecca. These tall town houses generally look inwards to a central courtyard and can consist of several floors.

Vocabulary in Unit 2

Nouns الأسماء

house/home	دار (دِيار/دور)
	منزِل (منازِل)
house/residence	مَسكَن (مَساكِن)
location	موقع (مَواقِع)
apartment building	عِمارة (ات)
floor/storey	طابِق (طَوابِق)
entrance	مَدخَل (مَداخِل)
hall	صالة (ات)
stairs	سُلَّم (سَلالِم)
roof	سَطح (سُطوح)
room	غُرفة (غُرَف)
bedroom	غرفة نَوم
living room	غرفة مَعيشة
sitting room	غرفة جُلوس
dining room	سُفرة (ات)
kitchen	مَطبَخ (مَطابِخ)
bathroom	حَمّام (ات)
toilet	دَورة (ات) مِياه
balcony	شُرفة (ات)
garage	جَراج/كَراج (ات)
cellar	سِرداب (سَراديب)
garden	حَديقة (حَدائِق)
mirror	مِرآة (ات)
lift/elevator	مِصعَد (مَصاعِد)
washing machine	غَسّالة (ات)
sink	حَوض (أَحواض)
sofa	كَنَبة (ات)/أَريكة (أَرائِك)
fridge	ثَلّاجة (ات)
cooker	فُرن (أَفران)
curtains	سَتائِر
shower	دُش
carpets	سَجّاد
grass/plants	عُشب
flowers	وَرد
smoker	مُدَخِّن (ون/ين)
swimming pool	حَمّام سِباحة
tennis court	مَلعَب تنس
air-conditioning	تَكييف هَواء
resident	ساكِن (سُكّان)
marble	رُخام
beach	شاطِئ (شَواطِئ)
countryside	ريف
view	مَنظَر (مناظِر)
field	حَقل (حُقول)
courtyard	باحة (ات)
fountain	نافورة (ات)
storage	خَزن
phone	هاتِف (هَواتِف)
mobile phone	هاتف محمول

Adjectives الصفات

modern	حَديث
traditional	تَقليديّ
quiet	هادِئ

crowded	مُزدَحِم
spacious	واسِع
luxurious	فاخِر
simple/basic	بَسيط
comfortable	مُريح
suitable	مُناسِب
private	خاصّ
forbidden	مَمنوع

Verbs الأفعال

consist (of)	تَكَوَّن، يَتَكَوَّن (من)
look (onto)	أَطَلَّ، يُطِلّ (على)
face (towards)	تَوَجَّه، يَتَوَجَّه (نَحو)
vary	اِختَلَف، يَختَلِف

Other phrases العبارات الأخرى

ground floor	الطابق الأرضيّ
first floor	الطابق الأوّل
can be found	يوجَد/توجَد
is used	يُستَخدَم/تُستَخدَم
for rent	لِلإيجار
in the style of...	بِطِراز...
in the day(time)	في النهار
as for...	أمّا
for that reason	لِذالِك
non-/not	غَير

Additional note: Case endings

You will probably be aware that formal standard Arabic includes case endings added to nouns and adjectives. You may hear these endings in scripted news bulletins, formal speeches and similar situations.

As a general rule, the case endings do not affect the spelling and you need only recognise them when you see or hear them. The most common exception to this is the additional alif known as alif tanwīn which is added to the indefinite accusative:

	indefinite ('a boy')	*definite* ('the boy')
nominative	وَلَدٌ walad<u>un</u>	الوَلَدُ al-walad<u>u</u>
accusative	وَلَداً walad<u>an</u>	الوَلَدَ al-walad<u>a</u>
genitive	وَلَدٍ walad<u>in</u>	الوَلَدِ al-walad<u>i</u>

Note that alif tanwīn is not added to a word ending with tā marbūṭa: غرفةً ghurfatan.

Mastering Arabic 1 Structure Note sections give more details about how the individual cases are formed and when they are used. Alternatively you can consult a good reference grammar.

unit 3

Work and routine
العَمَل والعادة

مَن جَدَّ وَجَدَ.

Whoever strives, finds (what he wants). (Arabic proverb)

Talking about work التكلّم عن العمل

Exercise 1 تمرين ١

How many of these professions do you remember? Write the meaning and the plural (using a dictionary if necessary). Then check your answers.

Meaning المَعنى	Plural الجَمع	Word الكَلمة
teacher	مدرّسون/ين	مدرّس
....	....	محاسب
....	....	طالب
....	....	مراسل
....	....	ممرّضة
....	....	مهندس
....	....	خَبّاز
....	....	مُغَنٍّ
....	....	تِلميذ
....	....	طَبّاخ
....	....	نجّار

Here are some more professions with their plurals. Notice how many of the words are formed either with the faععāl pattern or with an active participle (fāعil or mu-).

(ṣuḥufīy, -ūn/-īn)	صحفيّ، ـون/ـين	journalist
(ṭabīb, aṭibbā')	طبيب، أطبّاء	doctor
(muḥāmin, muḥāmūn/-īn)	محامٍ، محامون/ـين	lawyer
(muṣammim, -ūn/-īn)	مصمّم، ـون/ـين	designer
(mandūb, -ūn/-īn)	مندوب، ـون/ـين	representative
(fannān, -ūn/-īn)	فنّان، ـون/ـين	artist
(bannā', -ūn/-īn)	بنّاء، ـون/ـين	builder
(sā'iq, -ūn/-īn)	سائق، ـون/ـين	driver
(ḥāris, ḥurrās)	حارس، حرّاس	guard
(mudīr, mudarā')	مدير، مدراء	manager
(musāعid, -ūn/-īn)	مساعد، ـون/ـين	assistant
(عāmil, عummāl)	عامل، عمّال	worker

رجال وسيّدات أعمال rijāl wa-sayyidāt aعmāl *(business men and women)*

Exercise 2 تمرين ٢

ما عملهم؟ What do they do? Make sentences as in the example.

١ هو فنّان. ٢ ٣

٤ ٥ ٦

٧ ٨

Tip: There are a few Arabic words that end with -in, written with two kasras: مغنٍّ (mughanin, singer), محامٍ (muḥāmin, lawyer). When these words are made definite or have alif tanwīn added, the ending becomes ī, written with yā': المغنّي (al-mughannī), محامياً (muḥāmīyan). The yā' also appears in the feminine: مغنية (mughannīya, female singer); but *not* in the masculine plural: محامون (muḥāmūn, lawyers).

We have already seen how you can use a simple, non-verbal, sentence to talk about occupations:

أنا مصمّم. (anā muṣammim)	I'm a designer.
أختي طبيبة. (ukhtī ṭabība)	My sister is a doctor.
هو مندوب في شركة كبيرة. (huwa mandūb fī sharika kabīra)	He's a representative in a large company.
إنّهم حرّاس في السفارة. (innahum ḥurrās fīs-sifāra)	They are guards at the embassy.

You could also use the verb يعمل (yaعmal), meaning 'to work', followed directly by the job. As a verb is used, the job needs the (accusative) tanwīn, or the sound plural -īn ending (see pages 37 and 55):

أعمل مهندساً في مصنع كبير. (aعmal muhandisan fī maṣnaع kabīr)	I work [as] an engineer in a large factory.
تعمل والدتي صحفيّةً (taعmal wālidatī ṣuḥufīyyatan)	My mother works [as] a journalist.
يعمل والدي محامياً لدى الحكومة. (yaعmal wālidī muḥāmiyan ladā l-ḥukūma)	My father works [as] a lawyer with the government.
يعملون مصمّمين لبرامج الكمبيوتر. (yaعmalūna muṣammīn li-barāmij il-kumbyūtar)	They work as designers of computer programmes.

Exercise 3 **تمرين ٣**

Make sentences using يعمل (yaعmal), as in the example. Remember to make the occupation and the verb feminine or plural as necessary.

طبيب/مستشفى أمريكيّ (أختي) ←

تعمل أختي طبيبةً في مستشفى أمريكي.

(My sister works as a doctor in an American hospital.)

١ حارس/فندق كبير (أخي)

٢ محامٍ/وزارة الزراعة (سميرة)

٣ مهندس/مصنع سوريّ (أحمد)

٤ بنّاء/شَرِكة صغيرة (أنا)

٥ سائق/السفارة البريطانيّة (هم)

٦ مراسل/الكويت (خالتي)

A day in the life of... يوم في حياة...

Listen to Nadim talking about his daily routine (read from right to left).

أنا مُساعد المدير في
فندق ثلاث نجوم.

كلّ يوم أعمل طوال
الليل وأنام في النهار.

أبتدئ دائماً بالإشراف على
عمّال الليل وهم ينظّفون.

ثمّ أجلس مع المحاسب
ونُعدّ معاً فواتير النُزَلاء.

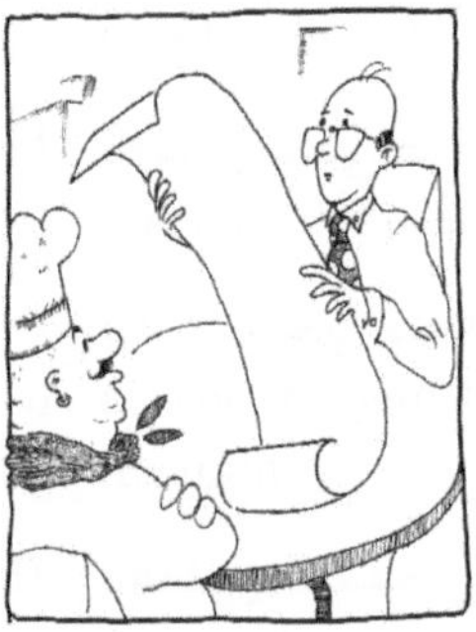

بعد ذلك أعدّ مع الطبّاخ
قائمة لسوق الجملة.

عادة آكل شيئا، ولكن
أحياناً أنسى أن آكل!

أعمل حتى الساعة
السادسة، ثم أرتّب
أوراقي وأغلق مكتبي.

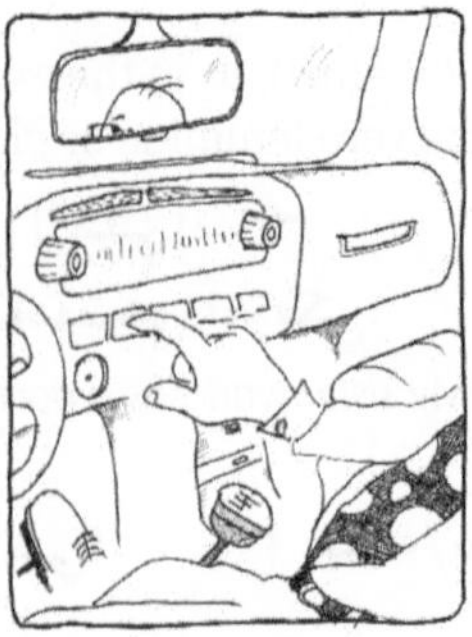

أقود سيّارتي إلى
منزلي وأنا استمع
إلى الراديو.

عادة أستيقظ من
نومي بعد الظهر وأعدّ
العشاء لعائلتي.

when?	← *what?*	← *how often?*
في الـ... (fil...) in the ...	أعمل (aعmal) I work	كلّ يوم... (kull yawm) every day
طوال الـ... (ṭawāl al...) all ... [long]	أستيقظ (astayqiẓ) I get up	دائماً... (dā'iman) always
قبل (qabla) before *(+ noun)*	أنام (anām) I sleep	عادةً ... (عādatan) usually
بعد (baعda) after *(+ noun)*	أبتدئ (بـ) (abtadi' (bi-)) I begin (by)	أحياناً ... (aḥyānan) sometimes
قبل أن (qabla an) before *(+ verb)*	أعدّ (uعidd) I prepare	نادراً ... (nādiran) rarely
بعد أن (baعda an) after *(+ verb)*	أنظّف (unaẓẓif) I clean	لا... أبداً (lā ... *(verb)* abadan) never
حتّى (ḥattā) until	أرتّب (urattib) I tidy	
الساعة... (as-sāعa) at ... o'clock	آكل (ākul) I eat	
	أغلق (ughliq) I close/lock	
	أقود سيّارتي (aqūd sayyāratī) I drive	

Tip: The position in a sentence of the frequency words in the right-hand column is somewhat flexible and depends on what sounds natural in a particular context. You'll develop an ear for this over time.

Exercise 4 تمرين ٤

Match the English to the Arabic phrases in Nadim's routine.

a the guest's invoices	١ أحياناً أنسى أن آكل
b supervising the night workers	٢ استمع إلى الراديو
c sometimes I forget to eat	٣ فواتير النزلاء
d a list for the wholesale market	٤ ينظّفون
e I tidy my papers	٥ الإشراف على عمّال الليل
f I listen to the radio	٦ قائمة لسوق الجملة
g they clean	٧ أرتّب أوراقي

Exercise 5 تمرين ٥

Now try to fill in the gaps in Nadim's routine *without* looking at page 42. Then listen again to check your answers.

Tip: Notice that to express 'while/as', for example 'I drive while listening...', 'I supervise as they are cleaning', Arabic uses وأنا ('and I'), وهم ('and they'), and so on.

أنا مساعد المدير في ______ ثلاث نجوم.

كلّ يوم ______ طوال الليل و ______ في النهار.

أبتدئ دائماً بالإشراف على ______ الليل وهم ينظّفون.

بعد ذلك أعدّ فواتير ______.

ثم ______ والمدير نعدّ معاً ______ لسوق الجملة.

عادةً آكل الغداء، ولكن ______ أنسى أن آكل!

أعمل ______ الساعة السادسة، ثم أرتّب أوراقي وأغلق ______.

أقود سيارتي إلى منزلي وأنا ______ إلى الراديو.

عادة ______ من نومي بعد الظهر و ______ العشاء لعائلتي.

Exercise 6 تمرين ٦

Make sentences with these meanings, using the table on page 43 to help you.

1 Sometimes I get up before seven o'clock.
2 I rarely sleep in the day.
3 Every day I clean the table before dinner.
4 I usually prepare the invoices before six o'clock.
5 I always lock my house before I drive to the office.
6 I never eat in the morning.

Talking about housework التكلّم عن الأعمال المنزليّة

يرتّب الفراش

يكوي الملابس

يغسل الأطباق

يساعد في الطبخ

ينظّف السيّارة

Exercise 7 تمرين ٧

Fill in the chart below depending on how frequently you carry out these tasks. Then make sentences to match your answers. For example, أحياناً أغسل الأطباق. Sometimes I wash the dishes.

					دائماً
					عادةً
				(✔)	أحياناً
					نادراً
					لا... أبداً

You can also complete the chart for a friend or a member of your family:
لا تكوي أختي الملابس أبداً. My sister never irons the clothes.

Talking about your CV (resumé) التكلّم عن سيرَتك الذاتية

Exercise 8 تمرين ٨

Look at the CV and find the equivalents of these headings:

1 Qualifications **2** Nationality **3** Address **4** Gender/Sex

5 Skills **6** Work experience **7** Date of Birth

السيرة الذاتية

الاسم: نادية الحسيني الجِنس: أُنثَى

تاريخ الميلاد: ١٨/٥/١٩٨٣ الجنسيّة: عراقيّة

العُنوان: ٦٤ شارع المطار، البصرة

المُؤَهّلات:

كلّية الهَندَسة، جامعة بغداد – التقدير: جيِّد

المعهد البريطاني – شهادة "First Certificate"

الخِبرة العمليّة:

٢٠٠٩ – : مساعدة المدير العامّ – شركة كوكب للبناء

٢٠٠٦–٢٠٠٧: سكرتيرة – وزارة الصناعة

المَهارات:

اللغة الإنجليزيّة: جيّد جدًّا اللغة الفرنسيّة: جيِّد

إجادة برامج ويندوز و"CorelDraw"

Exercise 9 تمرين ٩

Dina is going over a CV that arrived today, with her manager, Mr Farouk. Listen to them talking about the CV and fill in the details of the candidate opposite.

You may need to listen several times in order to note all the details for the CV.

السيرة الذاتية

الاسم:	الجِنس: ذَكَر
تاريخ الميلاد:	الجنسيّـة:
العُنوان:	

المُؤَهّلات:

الخِبرة العمليّـة:

٢٠٠٧- :

المَهارات:

Conversation المـحادثة

Talk about your daily routine, whether at work, college or in the home. Prepare the following information in Arabic and then take part in the interview on the recording.

what time you usually get up and go to sleep

what you usually do after breakfast (بَعدَ الإفطار)

2–3 things you usually or sometimes do in the day (at work, college, etc.)

a household task you always do/you never or rarely do

Note that it is common in spoken Arabic to express times by using the regular (cardinal) numbers: as-sāʿa sitta ('the hour six'), rather than the more formal as-sāʿa as-sādisa ('the sixth hour').

Present verbs المُضارِع

Arabic verbs can generally be classified into 'basic' and 'derived'. Basic verbs are those that carry the root meaning and have a stem using the three root letters vowelled only with short vowels.

Derived forms have different, but predictable, patterns with long vowels, non-root consonants or doubled root letters interposed between the basic root. A detailed summary of the derived forms is in Units 4 and 6.

Here is a table showing all the parts of the present verb, using the basic verb يَفتَح yaftaḥ (open). The present stem is فتَح ftaḥ and the prefixes and endings are arranged around this stem. The less commonly used feminine plurals and duals are in lighter type.

example	*ending*	*prefix*	
(I open) aftaḥ(u*) أَفتَح	—	a- أَ	أنا
(you *m.* open) taftaḥ(u) تَفتَح	—	ta- تَـ	أنتَ
(you *f.* open) taftaḥīna تَفتَحينَ	-īna ينَ	ta- تَـ	أنتِ
(he/it opens) yaftaḥ(u) يَفتَح	—	ya- يَـ	هو
(she/it opens) taftaḥ(u) تَفتَح	—	ta- تَـ	هي
(we open) naftaḥ(u) نَفتَح	—	na- نَـ	نَحنُ
(you *m. pl.* open) taftaḥūna تَفتَحونَ	-ūna ونَ	ta- تَـ	أنتُم
(you *f. pl.* open) taftaḥna تَفتَحنَ	-na نَ	ta- تَـ	أنتُنَّ
(you *dual* open) taftaḥān تَفتَحان	-ān ان	ta- تَـ	أنتُما
(they *m.* open) yaftaḥūna يَفتَحونَ	-ūna ونَ	ya- يَـ	هُم
(they *f. pl.* open) yaftaḥna يَفتَحنَ	-na نَ	ya- يَـ	هُنَّ
(they *dual* open) yaftaḥān يَفتَحان	-ān ان	ya- يَـ	هُما

* *The full pronunciation includes a final u, but this is not normally heard except in formal contexts.*

Notice that the prefix for 'you' verbs is ta- and the prefix for 'he' and 'they' is ya-. The additional endings show the gender and number: -ūna for masculine plural, -na for feminine plural and -ān for dual.

The prefix for some of the derived forms of the verb is vowelled with a damma rather than a fatha (e.g. ursil, I send, yursil, he sends, etc.), but otherwise the prefixes and endings are standard for all verbs.

Negative

You can make a present verb negative by putting لا in front.

عادةً لا أعمل يوم السبت. (ع ādatan lā aعmal yawm as-sabt)	Usually I don't work on Saturday.
لا يطبخ ابني أبداً. (lā yaṭbukh ibnī abadan)	My son never cooks. ("doesn't cook ever")

Irregular verbs: general notes

Some verbs behave somewhat differently due to features of the root. Here is a reminder of the three ways in which a root can be irregular:

1 one of the root letters is a hamza (ء)
2 the root is "doubled", i.e. the second and third root letters are the same
3 one of the root letters is "weak", i.e. و or ي

The main consideration with *hamzated verbs* is how to write the hamza (أ/ آ/ ؤ/ ئ/ ئـ). Other than this, they mainly behave as regular verbs.

نأكل العشاء الساعة الثامنة. (na'kul al-عashā' as-sāعa ath-thāmina)	We eat dinner at eight o'clock.
تُؤلّف هذه السيّدة كتباً للأطفال. (tu'allif hādhihi s-sayyida kutuban lil-aṭfāl)	This woman writes books for children.

Doubled verbs generally follow a simple rule: if the stem is followed directly by a consonant (non-vowel), the second and third root letters are written and pronounced separately. If not, they become a doubled letter written together with a shadda. Looking at the table opposite, you can see that the only ending in the present tense beginning with a consonant is -na, associated with the two relatively uncommon feminine plurals. Excluding these, present tense doubled verbs in most forms are characterised by a doubled letter written together with a shadda.

تطلّ الشرفة على البحر. (tuṭill ash-shurfa عalā l-baḥr)	The balcony looks onto the sea.
أعدّ الفواتير للنزلاء. (uعidd al-fawātīr lin-nuzalā')	I prepare the invoices for the guests.

That leaves the third, and trickiest, category: *weak verbs*. The 'weak' letters و or ي can appear as any of the three roots and are very fickle in how they behave. Depending on the pattern and the position of the weak root, the و or ي can be pronounced 'w' or 'y', become a long or short vowel, or disappear altogether! Gradually you will become more familiar with the various possibilities. For the moment we can generalise that weak "assimilated" verbs (with the weak letter, almost always و, as the first root) lose the و altogether in the present tense. 'Hollow' verbs (with و or ي as the middle root) and weak 'defective' verbs (with و or ي as the final root) are characterised by a long vowel in the middle or at the end respectively.

يصل القطار الساعة التاسعة. (yaṣil al-qiṭār as-sāعa at-tāsiعa)	The train arrives at nine o'clock.
عادةً أقود سيّارتي إلى المكتب. (عādatan aqūd sayyāratī ilā l-maktab)	I usually drive my car to the office.
هل تقيمون في شقّة؟ (hal tuqīmūna fī shaqqa?)	Do you *(pl.)* live in an apartment?
نشتري الخضار من سوق الجملة. (nashtarī al-khuḍār min sūq il-jumla)	We buy the vegetables from the wholesaler.

Exercise 10 تمرين ١٠

Complete these sentences with the correct verb, as in the example.

١ كلّ يوم تقود سميرة السيّارة إلى مكتبها. (يقود)

٢ إن العمّال ______ المطبخ بعد العشاء. (ينظّف)

٣ أنا ومساعدي ______ الفواتير كلّ يوم خميس. (يعدّ)

٤ ______ أخي محامياً لدى الحكومة. (يعمل)

٥ أنا لا ______ أبداً جريدة في الصباح. (يشتري)

٦ هل أنتَ ______ غرفتك كلّ يوم؟ (يرتّب)

٧ إن البنات ______ دائماً الساعة السابعة. (يستيقظ)

٨ هل أنتم ______ مكتبكم قبل الخروج؟ (يُقفل)

٩ عادةً أمّي وأبي ______ العشاء معاً. (يُعدّ)

١٠ هل أنتِ ______ قبل الساعة التاسعة ليلاً؟ (ينام)

Situations vacant وظائف شاغرة

مدير عامّ لشركة تجاريّة

الوظيفة: مدير عامّ للمكتب الرئيسي في الرياض. راتب عالٍ، بيت فاخر، تذاكر من وإلى السعودية، تأمين صحّي.

مطلوب في بغداد

نائب لمدير شركة هندسية في بغداد. خبرة في مجال الهندسة لا تقلّ عن ٣ سنوات. اللغة الإنجليزيّة مطلوبة.

مندوب مبيعات

في مجال الكمبيوترات. خبرة لا تقلّ عن ٥ سنوات. طموح في عمله. متخرج من الجامعة. راتب حسب الخبرة.

مطلوب

في المكتب المصري لمجلة ألمانية، مصمّم ومساعد للمديرة. راتب حسب الخبرة. إجادة الألمانية تحدّثًا وكتابةً

طبّاخ فرنسي

في وسط مدينة عمّان.

... أعوام

- مطلوب (maṭlūb) wanted, sought
- وظيفة، وظائف (waẓīfa, waẓā'if) position, (job) situation
- مجال، ات (majāl, āt) field, sphere
- مبيعات (mabīʿāt) sales
- هندسة (handasa) engineering
- راتب (rātib) salary
- تأمين صحّيّ (ta'mīn ṣiḥḥīy) health insurance
- تذكرة، تذاكر (tadhkira, tadhākir) ticket
- حسب (ḥasaba) according to
- لا يقلّ/تقلّ عن (lā yaqill/taqill ʿan) not less than
- طموح (ṭamūḥ) ambitious

Exercise 11 تمرين ١١

1 Which of the vacancies above would be most suitable for the applicant with the CV on page 46? Give reasons.

2 Which would be most suitable for applicant with the CV on page 47?

3 Which would <u>you</u> prefer and why?

Exercise 12 تمرين ١٢

Using the above as models, write a notice advertising the following position: *assistant to head accountant/five-star hotel/Damascus/not less than three years' experience/university graduate/fluent English spoken and written/ambitious*

العالم العربي ... نظرة على سوريا

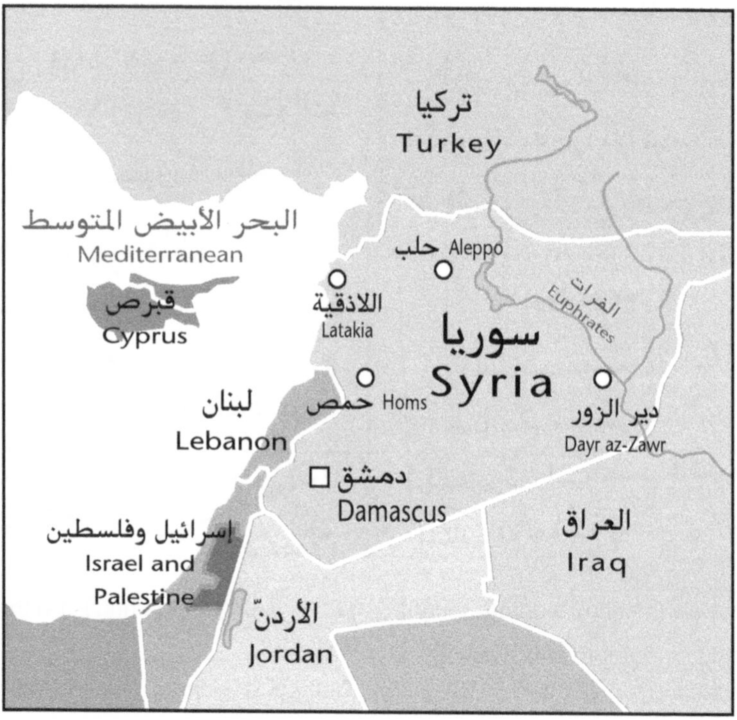

Arabic in Syria اللغة العربيّة في سوريا

Syria forms part of the 'Levant', an area to the East of the Mediterranean that today also includes Lebanon, Jordan and Palestine. The dialects of the Levant share characteristics and are mutually comprehensible, although there are local differences. Features of Levantine Arabic include:

- softer, non-gutteral sounds and lyrical intonation
- pronunciation of ة as 'eh' or 'ee', e.g. مدينة (town) as medineh/-ee
- pronunciation of ذ as 'd', e.g. هذا (this) as hādā
- use of particular expressions, e.g. بدي biddī (I want, derived from بودّي bi-waddī, 'by my wish')

Listen to Sahar talking about herself in her Syrian dialect. You will find a transcript and translation in the Answers section.

أخر الوظائف

، فقدتَ كلمة المرور؟

؛؛ طالب عمل جديد، سجّل هنا !

قدم سيرتك الذاتية

مندوب مبيعات

مابكو

سوريا

MABCO

الوظائف المتاحة

البحث السريع

[ابحث]   [... كلمة البحث ...]

البحث حسب مجال العمل

-- اختر واحدة --

مطلوب مصمم غرافيك و فلاش

SAWA ISP

سوريا

مزود خدمة الانترنت
sawa.cec.sy
خيارات أوسع

إحصائيات الوظائف حسب الدول

مندوب مبيعات وتنسيم

SAWA ISP

سوريا

بحث (baḥth) search
إحصائيات (iḥṣā'īyāt) statistics
كلمة مرور (kalimat murūr) password
طالب عمل (ṭālib ʿamal) job seeker

مندوب مبيعات

نبع الكومبيوتر

الإمارات

سوريا [125] ★★
السعودية [69]
لبنان [16]
مصر [14]

(www.jobs4arabs.com)

A number of online recruitment sites specialise in the Arab World. The site above advertises vacancies primarily in Syria and Saudi Arabia. Arabic and English scripts and terminology are often mixed together on this kind of site. Can you spot the English words 'graphic' and 'flash' written phonetically in Arabic script in one of the job titles?

الأَسئِلة (Questions)

١ أي شركة تطلب مصمّماً؟

٢ ما هي الوظيفة في الإمارات؟

٣ هناك كم وظيفة في سوريا؟

٤ وكم في لبنان؟

Vocabulary in Unit 3

Nouns الأسماء

life	حَياة (حَيَوات)
routine, habit	عادة (ات)
position (job)	وَظيفة (وَظائِف)
sphere/field	مَجال (ات)
journalist	صُحُفيّ (ون/ين)
doctor	طَبيب (أَطِبّاء)
lawyer	مُحامٍ (ون/ين)
designer	مُصَمِّم (ون/ين)
representative	مَندوب (ون/ين)
artist	فَنّان (ون/ين)
builder	بَنّاء (ون/ين)
driver	سائِق (ون/ين)
guard	حارِس (حُرّاس)
manager	مُدير (مُدَراء)
assistant	مُساعِد (ون/ين)
worker	عامِل (عُمّال)
businessman	رَجُل (رِجال) أعمال
businesswoman	سَيِّدة (ات) أعمال
company/business	شَرِكة (ات)
engineering	هَندَسة
experience	خِبرة
salary	راتِب (رَواتِب)
qualification	مُؤَهِّل (ات)
skill	مَهارة (ات)
invoice	فاتورة (فَواتير)
list	قائِمة (ات)
ticket	تَذكِرة (تَذاكِر)
paper	وَرَق (أوراق)
guest (hotel, etc.)	نَزيل (نُزَلاء)
(some)thing	شَيء (أشياء)
supervision	إشراف
cooking	طَبخ
search	بَحث (بُحوث)

Adjectives الصفات

wanted/sought	مَطلوب
ambitious	طَموح

Verbs الأفعال

get up	اِستَيقَظ، يَستَيقِظ
begin	اِبتَدَأ، يَبتَدِئ
prepare	أعَدَّ، يُعِدّ
tidy	رَتَّبَ، يُرَتِّب
make the beds	رَتَّبَ، يُرَتِّب الفِراش
iron	كَوَى، يَكوي
lock	أغلَقَ، يُغلِق
drive	قاد، يَقود (السيّارة)
forget	نَسِيَ، يَنسَى
listen	اِستَمَعَ، يَستَمِع

Other phrases	**العبارات الأخرى**	gender/sex	الجِنس
CV/resumé	سيرة ذاتيّة	date of birth	تاريخ الميلاد
computer programmes	بَرامِج الكُمبيوتر	not less than	لا يَقِلّ/تَقِلّ عَن
wholesale market	سوق الجُملة	according to	حَسَبَ
sales/retail	مَبيعات	all ... long	طَوال...
health insurance	تأمين صِحّي	always	دائِماً
job seeker	طالِب عَمَل	usually	عادَةً
statistics	إحصائيات	sometimes	أحياناً
password	كَلِمة مُرور	rarely	نادِراً
		never	لا... أبَداً

Additional note: Sound Masculine Plural (SMP)

Unlike the most common case endings, those for the Sound Masculine Plural behave in a way that affects the spelling and basic pronounciation of the word:

- The nominative case ending ون (-ūn) changes to ين (-īn) in the accusative and genitive cases:

هم مصمّمون. (hum muṣammimūn)	They are designers.
هل هناك طابق للمدخّنين؟ (hal hunāka ṭābiq lil-mudakhkhinīn)	Is there a floor for smokers?

- The final ن (n) of the SMP is dropped when combined with a following noun in an iḍāfa construction:

هم مراسلو الحرب (hum murāsilū l-ḥarb)	They are war correspondents.
هذه الغرفة لمراسلي الحرب. (hādhihi l-ghurfa li-murāsilī l-ḥarb)	This room is for the war correspondents.

unit 4

Sport and leisure
الرياضة والترفيه

العَقل السليم في الجِسم السليم.
A sound mind in a sound body.

Talking about sport التكلّم عن الرِياضة

Here are some popular sports:

كرة القدم (kurat al-qadam)
football (soccer)

الملاكمة (al-mulākama)
boxing

السباحة (as-sibāḥa)
swimming

الإسكواش (al-iskwāsh)
squash

التنس (at-tanis)
tennis

كرة اليد (kurat al-yad)
handball

الجولف (al-gūlf)
golf

الجودو (al-jūdū)
judo

ألعاب القوى (alɛāb al-quwa)
athletics

الكرة الطائرة (al-kura aṭ-ṭā'ira) volleyball ('flying ball')

كرة السلّة (kurat as-salla)
basketball

تنس الطاولة (tanis aṭ-ṭāwila) table tennis

General concepts

Unlike English, Arabic often uses a definite noun (the swimming, the health, etc.) when referring to a general concept:

السباحة مفيدة للصحّة. (as-sibāḥa mufīda liṣ-ṣiḥḥa)	[the] Swimming is beneficial for [the] health.
الإسكواش محبوب في الشرق الأوسط. (al-iskwāsh maḥbūb fī sh-sharq il-awsaṭ)	[the] Squash is popular in the Middle East.

Exercise 1 تمرين ١

Write the sports on page 56 in the correct column depending on whether they are team sports (رياضات جماعيّة riyāḍāt jamāɛīyya) or individual sports (رياضات فرديّة riyāḍāt fardīyya). An example has been done for you.

رياضات جماعيّة	رياضات فرديّة
	السباحة

Talking about preferences التكلّم عن التفضيل

You can use these phrases to ask about and express preferences:

هل تحبّ/تحبّين...؟ (hal tuḥibb/tuḥibbīna)	Do you *(masc./fem.)* like...?
ما رأيك في...؟ (mā ra'yak/-ik fī)	What's your *(masc./fem.)* opinion of...?
(لا) أحبّ... ((lā) uḥibb...)	I (don't) like...
أفضّل... (ufaḍḍil...)	I prefer...
لا أهتمّ بـ... (lā ahtamm bi-...)	I'm not interested in...
أكره... (akrah)	I hate...

Tip: Remember that you don't need to use a pronoun such as أنا (anā, I) with a verb since the prefix (and ending) of the verb shows the subject. However, sometimes the pronoun is used, especially for emphasis: أنا أحبّ الرياضة (anā uḥibb ar-riyāḍa, I like sport).

Exercise 2 تمرين ٢

Listen to two friends, Jamal and Nura, discussing what sports they like. Fill in the chart below depending on whether they are positive (☺), negative (☹) or neutral (😐) about each sport, as in the example.

Tip: مثير= exciting; مُمِل = boring; ممتِع = enjoyable; مُسَلٍّ = entertaining

						☺	جمال
						😐	نورة

Giving reasons التكلّم عن الأسباب

li'anna/bi-sabab لأنّ/بسبب

The Arabic word لأنّ (li'anna), meaning 'because', is followed by an attached pronoun in the same way as ولكنّ (wa-lākinna, but) – see page 13. Alternatively you can use the phrase بسبب (bi-sabab) meaning 'due to', or more literally 'by reason [of]'.

أحبّ كرة السلّة لأنّها مسليّة. (uḥibb kurat as-salla li'annahā musalīyya)	I like basketball because it's entertaining.
أكره الملاكمة بسبب العنف. (akrah al-mulākama bi-sabab il-ɛunf)	I hate boxing due to the violence.
لا أشاهد الجولف لأنّه لا فائدة منه. (lā ushāhid al-golf li'annahu lā fā'ida minuh)	I don't watch golf because there's no point to it.

Exercise 3 تمرين ٣

Here are some of the reasons Jamal and Nura gave as to why they liked or disliked certain sports. Listen again to their discussion in Exercise 2 and note whether it was Nura or Jamal (or both) who expressed the opinion, as in the example.

١ أحبّ التنس لأنّه ممتع. ___جمال___

٢ أفضّل كرة القدم لأنّها لعبة مثيرة جدّا. ______

٣ أكره كرة القدم لأنّها لا فائدة منها. ______

٤ أحب ألعاب القوى لأنها مسلية جداً. ______

٥ لا أشاهد الجولف لأنه لعبة طويلة ومملّة. ______

٦ أكره الملاكمة بسبب العنف. ______

Exercise 4 تمرين ٤

In the first row of the chart write five sports in Arabic about which you have varying opinions. Then put ☺, 😐 or ☹ in the second row, depending on *your* preferences.

					الرياضة:
					☺؟ 😐؟ ☹؟

Now talk about your preferences, giving reasons. You can use what Jamal and Nura said as models. For example:

لا أشاهد تنس الطاولة لأنه مُملّ.

I don't watch table tennis because it's boring.

Read this paragraph about Jamal.

يهتمّ جمال بالتنس ولكنّه يفضّل كرة القدم لأنها مثيرة جدًّا في رأيه. يحبّ جمال أيضاً الجولف ولكنّه لا يشاهد السباحة ولا تنس الطاولة لأنّها ليست رياضات مسليّة. كما أنّه لا يحبّ الملاكمة بسبب العُنف. وأما ألعاب القُوى فهو يَكره هذه الرياضة لأنّها في رأيه مملّة جدًّا ولا فائدة منها.

kamā anna كما أنّ

كما أنّ (kamā anna, and also/just as) is another way of connecting your ideas and improving your style. The use of كما أنّ kamā anna avoids having to repeat و wa (and) too many times. It is often followed by an attached pronoun as in the paragraph above.

Exercise 5 تمرين ٥

Write a similar paragraph about what sports Nura likes and dislikes and mention why she feels that way. Don't forget to change the verbs and pronouns to the feminine and to make use of connecting words and phrases.

لا تحبّ نورة التنس كثيراً ولكنّها ...

Now write about your own sporting likes and dislikes, using your answers in Exercise 4 to guide you. You could start like this:

أهتمّ بـ... ولكنّي أفضّل ...

Verbal nouns & participles المصدر والفاعل والمفعول به

The key to progressing in Arabic is a knowledge of how to use different root patterns to form related words and recognise unfamiliar vocabulary. You can think of every verb as a door to a complete set of inter-related words. With the exception of the verbal nouns for basic verbs, most of these patterns are entirely predictable. For example, if you know the word for teacher is مدرِّس (mudarris), you will be able to predict with confidence that the verb 'to teach' would be يدرِّس (yudarris) and that the noun meaning 'teaching' would be تدريس (tadrīs).

Probably the three most useful patterns are the verbal noun (known in Arabic as المصدر al-maṣdar), the active participle (الفاعل al-fāعil), and the passive participle (المفعول به al-mafعūl bihi).

verbal noun = action carried out by verb, e.g.

لَعِب (laعib) *playing*

ملاكمة (mulākama) *boxing*

تدريب (tadrīb) *training*

active participle = (the one) carrying out the action, e.g.

لاعب (lāعib) *player*

ملاكِم (mulākim) *boxer*

مدرِّب (mudarrib) *trainer, coach*

passive participle = (the one that is) the object of the action, e.g.

مشغول (mashghūl) *(the one) occupied, busy*

مفضَّل (mufaḍḍal) *(the one) preferred, favourite*

مدرَّب (mudarrab) *(the one) trained, coached*

Nouns and participles from basic verbs

Verbal nouns from basic (form I) verbs cannot be predicted, although there are common patterns. You will need to check in a dictionary for the pattern associated with a particular verb. However, the participles are predictable: the active is formed by putting the root into the pattern فاعل (fāعil) and the passive by putting the root into the pattern مفعول (mafعūl).

Nouns and participles from derived forms

Nouns and participles formed from derived verbs are almost completely predictable. The main exception is the form III verbal noun which has alternative patterns (see table on page 63).

The active and passive participles are simple to form from derived forms: take the present verb of the derived from and replace the prefix with مُـ (mu-). For the active participle, make the final vowel kasra (i); and for the passive change this final vowel to fatḥa (a).

Here is a summary of the patterns for forms I–IV. The other derived forms will be covered in later units.

Form	*Present verb*	*Verbal noun*	*Active Part.*	*Passive Part.*
I	يَفعل	varies	فاعِل	مَفعول
II	يُفَعِّل	تَفعيل	مُفَعِّل	مُفَعَّل
III	يُفاعِل	مُفاعَلة/فِعال	مُفاعِل	مُفاعَل
IV	يُفعِل	إفعال	مُفعِل	مُفعَل

Exercise 6 تمرين ٦

Fill in the gaps in the table below. Use a dictionary if you need to check the correct pattern for the verbal noun.

Form	*Present verb*	*Verbal noun*	*Active Part.*	*Passive Part.*
___	يُصَوِّر *(photograph)*	________	________	________
___	يَذهَب *(go)*	________	________	________
___	يُشاهِد *(view/watch)*	________	________	________
___	يَركَب *(ride)*	________	________	________
___	يُرسِل *(send)*	________	________	________
___	يُفَضِّل *(prefer)*	________	________	________
___	يَقرَأ *(read)*	________	________	________
___	يُخَيِّم *(camp)*	________	________	________

When you've completed the table, check your answers and then say them out loud so that you begin to hear the patterns.

Tip: Not every verb will have an active and passive participle in common use, although it is theoretically possible to form both. For example, the form IV verb يُسلِم (yuslim, to submit [to God]) gives us the verbal noun إسلام (islām, submission) and the active participle مُسلِم (muslim, one who submits). However, the passive participle مُسلَم muslam, theoretically meaning 'submitted', is not commonly used.

Talking about free time التكلّم عن وَقت الفراغ

صيد السمك ṣayd as-samak (*fishing*)

ركوب الخيل rukūb al-khayl (*horse riding*)

Exercise 7 تمرين ٧

Listen to eight people talking about what they like to do in their spare time. Write the correct number next to each illustration, as in the example.

You can follow a verb such as يحبّ (yuḥibb, like) or يفضّل (yufaḍḍil, prefer) with either a verbal noun or with أن (an, 'that') plus another verb.

Arabic makes extensive use of verbal nouns where in English we might use an infinitive ('to go', 'to play', etc.). Verbal nouns are considered good style and are often used in preference to a second verb.

Notice that if the first verb is followed by a second verb, then the second verb must also match the subject:

أحبّ القراءة. (uḥibb al-qirā'a)	I like reading.
إن هوايتي هي التصوير. (inna hiwāyatī hiya t-taṣwīr)	My hobby is photography.
تحبّ أن تذهب إلى النادي. (tuḥibb an tadh-hab ilā n-nādī)	She likes to go to the club.
يفضّلون الذهاب الى المسرح. (yufaḍḍilūna dh-dhahāb ilā l-masraḥ)	They prefer going to the theatre.

Exercise 8 تمرين ٨

Make sentences about what the people opposite like doing, based on what you heard them say in Exercise 7, for example:

He likes reading. ١ **يحبّ القراءة.**

I hate to love like [other] people	أَكرَهُ أن أُحِبَّ مِثلَ الناس
I hate to write like [other] people	أَكرَهُ أن أَكتُبَ مِثلَ الناس
I wish that my mouth were a church	أَودُّ لَو كانَ فَمي كَنيسة
... and my letters bells	... وأَحرُفي أجراس

From كتاب الحبّ *(Book of Love)* by Nizar Qabbani (Syrian Poet, 1923–1998)

Talking about going out التكلُّم عن الخروج

هل نَذهَب إلى...
Shall we go to...

هل نلتَقي ...
Shall we meet...

هل تريد/تريدينَ...
Do you want to...

يَوم الـ...
on ...day

الساعة...؟
at... o'clock

✗

آسِف/آسِفة، لا أستَطيع.
Sorry, I can't.

شكرًا ولكنّي مَشغول/مَشغولة.
Thank you but I'm busy.

متى يُناسِبك؟
When would suit you ?

✓

فِكرة جَيِّدة!
Good idea!

هذا مُمتاز!
That's excellent!

سَيُشَرِّفني.
I'd love to.
('I'll be honoured')

Days of the week أيّام الأسبوع

Remind yourself of the days of the week.

Sunday	يوم الأحد (yawm al-aḥad)	Thursday	يوم الخميس (yawm al-khamīs)
Monday	يوم الاثنين (yawm al-ithnayn)	Friday	يوم الجمعة (yawm al-jumعa)
Tuesday	يوم الثلاثاء (yawm ath-thulāthā')	Saturday	يوم السبت (yawm as-sabt)
Wednesday	يوم الأربعاء (yawm al-arbiعā')		

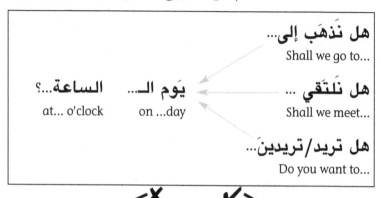

Tip: It is optional to include the word يوم (yawm, day) when talking about days of the week: السبت as-sabt, Saturday; الخميس al-khamīs, Thursday.

Exercise 9 تمرين ٩

Listen to two sets of friends arranging to meet, and make notes about when and where they decide to meet and what they will be doing.

النشاط	المكان	الساعة	اليوم	
_____	_____	_____	_____	محمود وجاك
_____	_____	_____	_____	نجيبة ولوسي

Conversation المحادثة

An invitation

Put all you've learnt in this unit to good use by inviting a (male) friend to the club. You'll need to think about how to say the following in Arabic:

– Good morning. How are you?

– Do you want to go to the club on Friday?

– Does Thursday suit you?

– Shall we play golf?

– Shall we meet at my house at six o'clock?

– Good idea.

– Goodbye. See you. (إلى اللقاء)

Now join in the conversation on the recording, saying your part in the pauses.

رزنامة (ruznāma) calendar, schedule
فنّ، فنون (fann, funūn) art
فنّان، ـون/ـين (fannān, -ūn/-īn) artist
مركز، مراكز (markaz, marākiz) centre
معرض، معارض (maɛrid, maɛārid) exhibition, show
مكتبة، ـات (maktaba, -āt) library
حديقة، حدائق (ḥadīqa, ḥadā'iq) garden, park
طائر، طيور (ṭā'ir, ṭuyūr) bird

Exercise 10 تمرين ١٠

Look at the calendar adapted from the Jordanian magazine *Beity* ("My house"). It shows activities planned for the first days of Ramadan.

Fill out the chart opposite, as in the example. You can use the additional vocabulary on the left to help you.

Activity	Day	Venue	Suitable for
Ramadan tent	*Thursday 12*	*Palace hotel*	*family*
Horse riding			
Exhibition of Iraqi artist			
Children's library			
Exhibition of drawings from children's books			
Comic play			
Children's Ramadan party			
History of European art			
Bird Show			
Yoga			

العالم العربي ... نظرة على المغرب

Arabic in Morocco العربيّة في المَغرِب

Morocco lies at the western extreme of the Arabic-speaking world. It is from here that the Muslim 'Moors' crossed the Mediterranean and occupied southern Spain for most of the Middle Ages. The spoken language has been greatly influenced by the local Berber language, Andalusian dialect and European languages, especially French which is a second language for almost the entire population. Moroccan Arabic can be difficult to understand, even for other native Arabic speakers. Features of Moroccan Arabic include:

- disappearance of short vowels resulting in many consonants pronounced together (also a feature of Berber)
- 'k' sound in front of some present verbs (k-yikūn = is)
- extensive use of Berber, French and Spanish vocabulary (listen for the French word 'té' (tea) in the extract)

Listen to Mourad talking about himself in his Moroccan dialect. You will find a transcript and translation in the Answers section.

طباعة حفظ ارسال

الأربعاء 24 صفر 1428هـ - 14 مارس2007م

الحكومة المغربية تدعم ألعاب القوى بمبلغ 65 مليون دولار

دعم، يدعم (daعama, yadعam) to support

مبلغ، مبالغ (mablagh, mabāligh) sum (of money)

عدّاء، ون/ين (عaddā', -ūn/-īn) runner

وقّع، يوقّع (waqqaعa, yuwaqqiع) to sign

اتّحاد، ات (ittiḥād, -āt) union, association

اتّفاق، ات (ittifāq, -āt) agreement

ما يعادل (mā yuعādil) equivalent to

صورة أرشيفية للعداء المغربي هشام الكروج (أرشيف)

الرباط - رويترز

وقعت الحكومة المغربية والاتحاد المغربي لألعاب القوى مساء الثلاثاء 13-3-2007 اتفاقا تدعم الحكومة بموجبه رياضة العاب القوى في البلاد خلال السنوات الخمس القادمة بمبالغ مالية تصل إلى 550 مليون درهم مغربي ما يعادل (65 مليون دولار).

(www.alarabiya.net)

Morocco has a long tradition of success in athletics, particularly middle and long-distance running. Olympic gold medalists include Said Aouita (5000m, 1984), Nawal el-Moutawakel (400m hurdles, 1984) and Hisham el-Karrouj (1500m/5000m, 2004). Training is supported by the government and the athletes are treated as national heroes.

الأَسئِلة

١ ما هو تاريخ المقالة؟

٢ مَن هو العدّاء في الصورة؟

٣ متى وقّعت الحكومة الاِتّفاق؟

٤ ما هو اسم الاتّحاد؟

٥ كَم المبلغ بالدولار؟ وبالدِرهَم؟

Vocabulary in Unit 4

Nouns الأسماء

leisure	تَرفيه
free time	وَقت الفِراغ
activity	نَشاط (أنشِطة)
hobby	هِواية (ات)
health	صِحّة
ball	كُرة (ات)
football (soccer)	كُرة القَدَم
basketball	كُرة السَلّة
handball	كُرة اليَد
volleyball	الكُرة الطائِرة
tennis	تَنِس
table tennis	تَنِس الطاوِلة
swimming	سِباحة
athletics	ألعاب القُوَى
training	تدريب
boxing	مُلاكَمة
squash	إسكواش
judo	جودو
golf	جولف
horse riding	رُكوب الخَيل
fishing	صَيد السَمَك
photography	تَصوير
player	لاعِب
runner	عَدّاء (ون/ين)
boxer	مُلاكِم (ون/ين)
coach/trainer	مُدَرِّب (ون/ين)
artist	فَنّان (ون/ين)
library	مكتَبة (ات)
centre	مَركَز (مَراكِز)
park	حَديقة (حَدائِق)
club	نادٍ (نَوادٍ)
union/association	اِتِّحاد (ات)
show/exhibition	مَعرِض (مَعارِض)
calendar/schedule	رُزنامة (ات)
art	فَنّ، (فُنون)
bird	طائِر (طُيور)
sum (of money)	مَبلَغ (مَبالِغ)
agreement	اِتِّفاق (ات)
violence	عُنف

Adjectives الصفات

beneficial/useful	مُفيد
individual	فَرديّ
team/collective	جَماعيّ
exciting/moving	مُثير
boring	مُمِلّ
enjoyable	مُمتِع
entertaining	مُسَلٍّ
favourite	مُفَضَّل
busy/occupied	مَشغول
sorry	آسِف
excellent	مُمتاز

Verbs الأفعال

like	أحَبَّ، يُحِبّ
prefer	فَضَّلَ، يُفَضِّل

hate	كَرِهَ، يكرَه
watch/view	شاهَدَ، يُشاهد
train/coach	دَرَّبَ، يُدَرِّب
photograph	صَوَّرَ، يُصَوِّر
camp	خَيَّمَ، يُخَيِّم
ride	رَكِبَ، يَركَب
send	أرسَلَ، يُرسِل
meet	اِلتَقَى، يلتَقي
be able to/can	اِستَطاعَ، يَستَطيع
suit	ناسَبَ، يُناسِب
support	دَعَمَ، يَدعَم
sign	وَقَّعَ، يُوَقِّع

Other phrases العبارات الأخرى

I'm not interested in	لا أهتَمّ بـ
due to	بِسَبَب
no point to it	لا فائِدة منه/منها
good idea	فِكرة جَيِّدة
I'd love to ('I'd be honoured')	سَيُشَرِّفني
and also/just as	كَما أنّ
equivalent to	ما يُعادِل

Additional note: Subjunctive

A modified version of the present tense, known as the *subjunctive*, is used after أن (an, 'that') and other similar particles. The most significant modification is that the final nūn disappears from the feminine 'you', the masculine plural and the dual:

subjunctive	ending	prefix	
(you *f.* open) taftaḥī تَفتَحي	ي -ī	ta- تَـ	أنتِ
(you *m. pl.* open) taftaḥū تَفتَحوا	وا -ū	ta- تَـ	أنتُم
(you *dual* open) taftaḥā تَفتَحا	ا -ā	ta- تَـ	أنتُما
(they *m.* open) yaftaḥū يَفتَحوا	وا -ū	ya- يَـ	هُم
(they *dual* open) yaftaḥā يَفتَحا	ا -ā	ya- يَـ	هُما

Tip: Many spoken Arabic dialects use this modified subjunctive form of the present tense in all contexts, for example تشربين tashrabīna (you *fem.* drink) becoming tashrabī, and يشربون yashrabūna (they drink) becoming yashrabū.

Another feature of some dialects is that the masculine plural verb is employed for all plural or dual subjects regardless of gender. This means that the feminine plural and dual verbs are a consistent feature only of Standard Arabic.

unit 5

Travel and tourism
السَفَر والسِياحة

رِحلة الألف ميل تَبدأ بِخَطوة.

A journey of a thousand miles starts with one step. (Arabic proverb)

Around town حَول المدينة

Look at these places downtown and listen to the recording:

مركز الرياضة (markaz ar-riyāḍa) sports centre

مركز التسوّق (markaz at-tasawwuq) shopping centre

مركز الشرطة (markaz ash-shurṭa) police station ('centre')

مكتب السياحة (maktab as-siyāḥa) tourist office

مكتب الطيران (maktab aṭ-ṭayrān) airline office

مكتب البريد (maktab al-barīd) post office

محطّة البنزين (maḥaṭṭat al-banzīn) petrol station

محطّة القطار (maḥaṭṭat al-qiṭār) train station

محطّة الباص (maḥaṭṭat al-bāṣ) bus station

مركز (markaz, centre) and مكتب (maktab, office) both make their plurals using the pattern مفاعل (mafāʿil): مراكز التسوّق (marākiz at-tasawwuq, shopping centres), مكاتب الطيران (makātib aṭ-ṭayrān, airline offices).

The plural of محطّة (maḥaṭṭa, station) is محطّات (maḥaṭṭāt): محطّات القطار (maḥaṭṭāt al-qiṭār, train stations).

Exercise 1 تمرين ١

Complete these sentences using one of the places opposite, as in the example.

١ نشتري تذاكر القطار في محطّة القطار.

٢ نشتري البنزين في ________.

٣ نلعب الاِسكواش في ________.

٤ نشتري تذاكر الطائرة من ________.

٥ نَستَفسِر عَن *(enquire about)* المَتاحِف في ________.

٦ نشتري الملابس في ________.

٧ نَستَفسِر عَن المَسروقات *(stolen items)* في ________.

٨ نُرسِل البِطاقات البريديّة *(postcards)* من ________.

٩ نأخذ الباصات من ________.

الخطوط التونسيّة al-khuṭūṭ at-tunisīyya *(Tunisian airlines)*

Asking the way السُؤال عن الطريق

You can use these phrases to ask for directions:

أين ...؟ (ayna)/	Where's ...?
... من أين؟ (min ayna)	(*lit: '... from where?'*)
كيف أصل إلى ...؟ (kayfa aṣil ilā ...)	How do I get to ...?
أين أقرب ... ؟ (ayna aqrab ...)	Where's the nearest ...?
هل هذا هو الطريق إلى ...؟ (hal hādhā huwa ṭ-ṭarīq ilā ...)	Is this the way to ...?

Exercise 2 تمرين ٢

Test yourself by asking these questions.

1 Where's the train station?
2 Is this the way to the sports centre?
3 How do I get to the theatre?
4 Where's the nearest shopping centre?
5 How do I get to the tourist office?
6 Where's the nearest bus station?

I'll show you the way أنا أدُلّك على الطريق

عند الناصية (ع inda n-nāṣiya) at/on the corner	على طول (ع alā ṭūl) straight on	اذهب/اذهبي ... (idh-hab/idh-habī) Go (*masc./fem.*)
عند إشارة المرور (ع inda ishārat al-murūr) at the traffic lights	يمين (yamīn) right	اتَّجه/اتَّجهي... (ittajih/ittajihī) Turn (*masc./fem.*)
قبل المحطَّة (qabla l-maḥaṭṭa) before the station	يسار (yasār) left	خذ/خذي ... (khudh/khudhī) Take (*masc./fem.*)
بعد الميدان (baع da l-maydān) after the square	أوّل/ثاني شارع (awwal/thānī shāriع) the first/second street	اعبر/اعبري ... (uع bur/uع burī) Cross (*masc./fem.*)

Exercise 3 تمرين ٣

Listen to five people asking for directions and decide what the numbered features are on the map below. The first is completed for you.

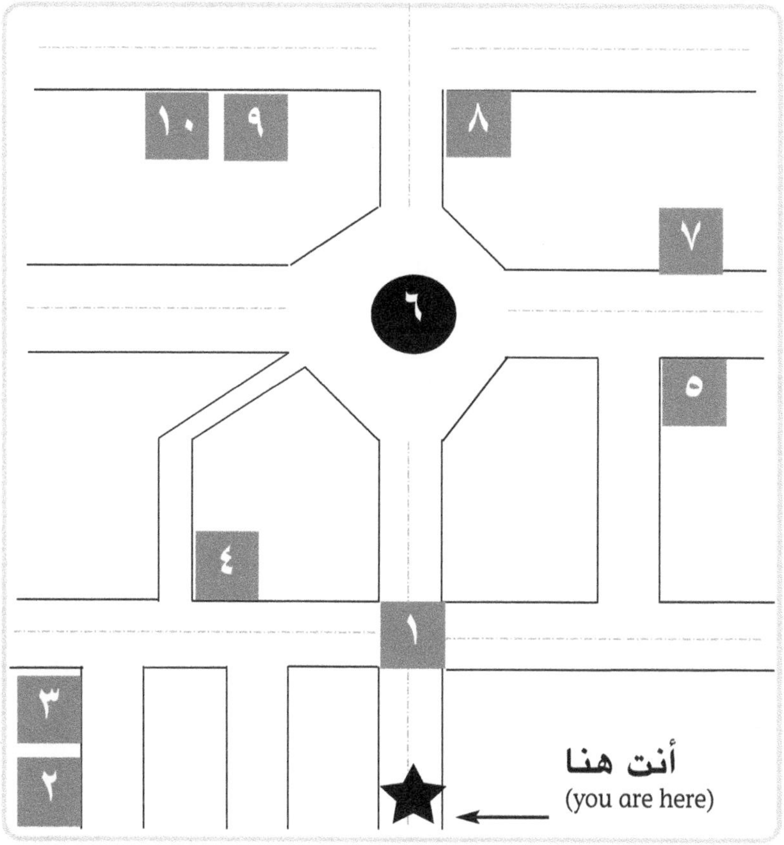

١ إشارة المرور . ٦ ________ .

٢ ________ . ٧ ________ .

٣ ________ . ٨ ________ .

٤ ________ . ٩ ________ .

٥ ________ . ١٠ ________ .

Conversation المحادثة

You are going to direct a *man* to the cinema and a *woman* to the nearest hotel. Prepare for the conversation by looking at the table on page 76 to work out how you would say:

Go straight on at the traffic lights.
Turn right at the square ('in the square').
The cinema is on the corner, opposite the airline office.

Turn left at the traffic lights.
Take the second street on the left.
There's a hotel on the right after the train station.

Means of transportation وَسائل النقل

Exercise 4 تمرين ٤

How many of these means of transportation do you know?
Match the Arabic with the pictures, for example **a**١٠.

١ درّاجة
٢ طائرة
٣ سيّارة
٤ باص/أوتوبيس
٥ جمل
٦ مركب
٧ قطار
٨ قطار الأَنفاق
٩ حمار
١٠ تاكسي
١١ سفينة

a

b

c

d

e

f

g
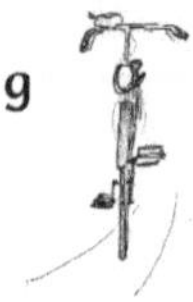
h

i

j

k

Remember that bi- ('with') is used with means of transportation to mean 'by'. When directly before al-, the combination is pronounced bil-:

كلّ يوم يذهب إلى المدرسة بالباص. (kull yawm yadh-hab ilā l-madrasa bil-bās)	Every day he goes to school by bus.
كيف أصل إلى مركز الرياضة بالسيّارة؟ (kayfa aṣil ilā markaz ir-riyāḍa bis-sayyāra)	How do I get to the sports centre by car?

To say 'on foot' or 'walking' you can use the expression ماشياً (māshiyan):

كيف أصل إلى مكتب البريد ماشياً؟ (kayfa aṣil ilā maktab il-barīd māshiyan)	How do I get to the post office on foot?

The Transportation Game لعبة النقل

Here is a game to help you remember places and means of transportation. You can play by yourself or with others. The board is on page 80.

You will need:

- one regular dice
- transportation dice below (cut out, stick onto card and make into a cube)
- one or more small counters or buttons

How to play:

- Put your counter on البداية (the start).
- Roll the regular dice and move the number of squares indicated.
- Roll the transportation dice and ask the appropriate question. For example, if you land on the picture of the tourist office and the transportation dice lands on the underground, you should ask:
  كيف أصل إلى مكتب السياحة بقطار الأنفاق؟
  (How do I get to the tourist office by underground train?)
- If you can't ask the question, go back to the square you came from.
- You must roll an exact number to reach النهاية (the finish).

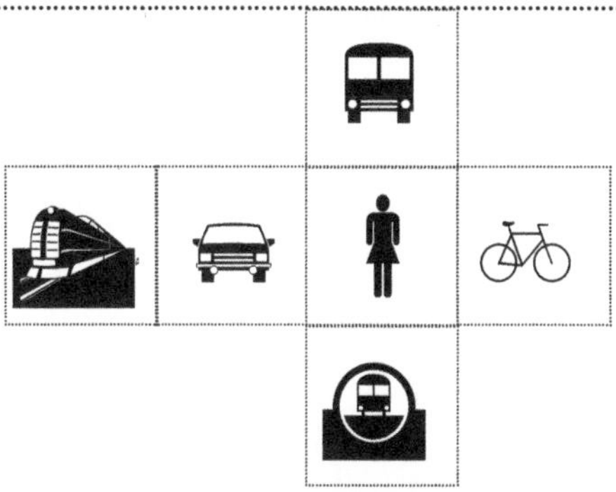

The Transportation Game لعبة النقل

See page 79 for instructions on how to play the game.

Travel in the Arab World السفر في العالم العربيّ

There are many reasons to travel to the Middle East. With the Red Sea, the Mediterranean, and the Gulf all on offer, beach resorts have sprung up in the region at a phonomenal rate in the past few decades. In addition, the Middle East has a huge wealth of sites of historical interest, from the ancient Egyptian monuments, to the Islamic sites and Crusader castles.

The Hajj الحجّ

The most significant journey in terms of sheer numbers of people is the annual pilrimage (الحجّ al-ḥajj) to "Revered Mecca" (مكّة المكرّمة makka al-mukarrama) in Saudi Arabia.

One of the five pillars of Islam is the duty of every Muslim who is able to "perform the obligation of the Hajj" (يؤدّي فريضة الحجّ yu'addī farīḍat al-ḥajj) at least once in his or her lifetime.

Millions of pilgrims converge on Mecca for a few days where they perform a series of rituals. These include circling seven times the ancient black stone known as the Ka'ba (الكعبة al-kaعba) inside the al-Haram Mosque (المسجد الحرام al-masjid al-ḥarām), running between two hills, drinking the waters of the Zamzam well (بئر زمزم bi'r zamzam), visiting Mount Arafat (جبل عرفات jabal عarafāt), and throwing stones at a symbolic devil.

Exercise 5 تمرين ٥

Anwar has just returned from the pilgrimage. Look at the various stages in his journey, and think about in which order they might have occurred. Then listen to Anwar and write the correct number, as in the example.

— رَجَعتُ ومعي ثلاث زجاجات ماء من بِئر زمزَم.	— أَخَذنا الباص من جدّة إلى مكّة المكرّمة.
— ذَهَبتُ إلى السِفارة السَعوديّة لآخذ تأشيرة (*visa*).	— اِشتَرَينا تذاكر السَفَر من مكتب السياحة.
— أَدَينا فريضة الحجّ وَزُرنا الكَعبة والمَسجِد الحَرام.	١ قَرَّرنا أنا وأبي وأمّي أن نُؤَدّي فريضة الحجّ هذا العام.
— أَعدَدتُ حقائِبي للسَفَر.	— رَكِبنا المركب إلى جدّة.

Past verbs الفعل الماضي

Arabic has only two basic tenses: the present (or imperfect) and the past, although there are variations on and combinations of these tenses.

The past tense is used for completed events. Endings are added to a past stem to show the subject. There are no prefixes as there are for the present tense. Here is a table showing all the parts of the past verb. The less commonly used feminine plurals and duals are in lighter type.

example	*ending*	
(I opened) fataḥtu فَتَحتُ	-tu تُ	أنا
(you *m.* opened) fataḥta فَتَحتَ	-ta تَ	أنتَ
(you *f.* opened) fataḥti فَتَحتِ	-ti تِ	أنتِ
(he/it opened) fataḥa فَتَحَ	-a ـَ	هو
(she/it opened) fataḥat فَتَحَت	-at تْ	هي
(we opened) fataḥnā فَتَحنا	-nā نا	نَحنُ
(you *m. pl.* opened) fataḥtum فَتَحتُم	-tum تُم	أنتُم
(you *f. pl.* opened) fataḥtunna فَتَحتُنَّ	-tunna تُنَّ	أنتُنَّ
(you *dual* opened) fataḥtumā فَتَحتُما	-tumā تُما	أنتُما
(they *m.* opened) fataḥū * فَتَحوا	-ū وا	هُم
(they *f. pl.* opened) fataḥna فَتَحنَ	-na نَ	هُنَّ
(they *dual* opened) fataḥā فَتَحا	-ā ا	هُما

* *The extra alif is a spelling convention and is not pronounced.*

Most basic verbs have past stems vowelled with two fatḥas (فَتَح fataḥ, opened; كَتَب katab, wrote), but a few are vowelled fatḥa/kasra (شَرِب sharib, drank), or less commonly fatḥa/ḍamma (كَبُر kabur, to be big).

Derived verbs have their own distinctive past stems but, as for the present tense, the subject endings are standard for all verbs:

غادرت طائرتنا. وتوجّهنا نحو الغرب. (ghādarat ṭā'iratnā wa-tawajjahnā naḥw al-gharb)	Our plane left and we headed towards the west.

Irregular verbs: general notes

Each type of irregular verb will be looked at in more detail in later units, but here are some general guidelines on what to look out for.

Hamzated verbs

As with the present, the main consideration in the past tense is how to write the hamza. Other than this, hamzated verbs behave mainly regularly.

Doubled verbs

Doubled verbs in the past follow the same general rule as present verbs (see page 48). Subject endings starting with a consonant (non-vowel) result in the second and third root letters being written and pronounced separately. Subject endings beginning with a vowel generally result in the doubled letter being written together with a shadda:

(aعdadtu ḥaqā'ibī) **أعدَدتُ حقائبي.**	I prepared my bags.
(ḥallū al-mashākil) **حلّوا المشاكل.**	They solved the problems.

Weak verbs

Assimilated verbs (weak letter as first root) are almost entirely regular in the past. *Defective verbs* (weak letter as last root) are generally characterised by a long ā, ay, ū or aw replacing the final root letter.

(ishtaraynā at-tadhākir) **اشترينا التذاكر.**	We bought the tickets.
(mashā bi-surعa) **مشى بسرعة.**	He walked quickly.

Hollow verbs have two stems – one 'open' stem with a long ā in the middle for subject endings starting with a vowel; and one 'closed' stem with a short vowel for subject endings starting with a consonant.

(zurnā al-qalعa) **زرنا القلعة.**	We visited the fort.
(zārū l-matḥaf) **زاروا المتحف.**	They visited the museum.

Negative

The most common way of making a past verb negative in Standard Arabic is using لم (lam) + *present verb*:

(lam yaعmal al-furn) **لم يعمل الفرن.**	The cooker didn't work.
(lam najid thaljan) **لم نَجد ثلجاً.**	We didn't find ice.

The present verb used after lam is a modified form known as the *jussive* (see Additional Note page 91).

Sohair's blog مُدَوَّنة سهير

Sohair is on a four-day university trip to Al-Qusair (القصير), an Egyptian town on the Red Sea south of Hurghada (الغردقة al-ghardaqa). The trip also takes in the desert to the west. Every night she writes her blog on the web.

http://www.arabicblog fisahra.html

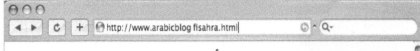

سُهير في القُصير

<u>الخميس</u>: غادَرَت طائرتنا الساعة الخامسة صباحاً ووصلنا إلى الغردقة بعد ساعة. كانت ساعة من العَذاب!! الريح كان شديداً جدّاً ولذلك كنتُ خائفة و شَعَرتُ بالعَصَبيّة طوال الرِحلة. أخيراً رَكِبنا الباص من مطار الغردقة إلى مدينة القصير. زُرنا القَلعة القديمة هناك وذهبنا إلى الفندق.

<u>الجمعة</u>: غُرفتنا كانت صغيرة وحارّة جدّاً! تكييف الهواء كان مضحكاً : كان أكبر من الخزانة القديمة ولكنّه لم يعمل أبداً! الكافيتريا أيضاً كانت مضحكة... الشاي كان بارداً ولكن الكولا كانت دافئة ولم نجد ثَلجاً! في المساء أعددتُ حقائبي لرحلة الصحراء غداً.

<u>السبت</u>: غادرنا الفندق المضحك في الفَجر وتَوَجَّهنا نَحو الصحراء. في الطريق شاهَدنا بعض المَناجِم القديمة المَهجورة والجِبال وكُثبان الرِمال الجميلة. زرنا واحة خَضراء في الصحراء. شربنا من ماء البئر وأكلنا مع البَدو تحت النَخيل – البَدو كانوا كِراماً. ركبتُ جملاً ولكنّ حركة الجمل ذَكَّرَتني بِرحلة الطائرة! نِمنا في خيام والنُجوم كانت عَجيبة ... لامِعة جداً في ليل الصحراء.

<u>الأحد</u>: أحبَبتُ الصحراء ولا أريد الرجوع إلى المدينة وركوب الطائرة مرّة ثانية...

إلى اللِقاء يا صحراء، مع السلامة يا نجوم!

عذاب (ع adhāb) torture

خائف (khā'if) afraid

شعر، يشعر بـ (sha ع ara, yash ع ur bi-) to feel

عصبيّة (ع aṣabīyya) nervousness

رحلة، ات (riḥla, āt) journey

قلعة، قلاع (qal ع a, qilā ع) fort

فجر (fajr) dawn

منجم، مناجم (manjam, manājim) mine

مهجور (mahjūr) abandoned

كثيب، كثبان الرمال (kathīb, kuthbān ar-rimāl) sand dune

واحة، ات (wāḥa, āt) oasis

نخلة، نخيل (nakhla, nakhīl) palm tree

ذكّر، يذكّر (dhakkara, yudhakkir) to remind

عجيب (ع ajīb) wonderful, amazing

لامع (lāmi ع) shining, bright

Exercise 6 تمرين ٦

Tick the pictures representing features mentioned in Sohair's blog, as in the example.

Exercise 7 تمرين ٧

Now identify all the past verbs you can find in the blog and say what they mean, for example غادَرَت – it [our plane] left.

Describing the past وصف الماضي

Simple descriptions in the present do not need an equivalent of the verb 'am', 'are' or 'is' in Arabic. However, in the past you do need to use كان (kān) in the appropriate form to mean 'was' or 'were'. كان (kān) is a hollow verb with the stem changing to كُن (kun) when you add an ending beginning with a consonant, e.g. كُنتُ (kuntu, I was) - see page 83.

An adjective following كان (kān) will have the accusative ending -an. In most cases this is written on alif tanwin (اً) if the adjective doesn't end with tā' marbūṭa. Compare these descriptions in the present and in the past:

(in the past) في الماضي		(now) الآن
كان الفيلم مثيراً. The film was exciting.	←	الفيلم مثير. The film is exciting.
كانَت خائفة. She was afraid.	←	هي خائِفة . She is afraid.
كُنتُ سعيداً. I was happy.	←	أنا سَعيد. I *(masc.)* am happy.
كانَت القِلاع عَجيبة. The forts were wonderful.	←	القِلاع عَجيبة. The forts are wonderful.

Tip: In Modern Standard Arabic the usual word order is *verb* + *subject* + *rest of sentence* (كان الفيلم مثيراً The film was exciting). However, in less formal contexts you may see the subject first (الفيلم كان مثيراً), reflecting the usual order in spoken dialects. Remember: the verb will be singular if it comes *before* a plural subject: الرجال كانوا كراماً. but كان الرجال كراماً (The men were generous).

Exercise 8 تمرين ٨

Find these past descriptions in Sohair's blog, as in the example.

1 The tea was cold. الشاي كان بارداً .

2 The cola was warm.

3 The Bedouin were generous.

4 The air-conditioning was laughable.

5 I was afraid.

6 The stars were amazing.

7 Our room was small and very hot.

8 The wind was very strong.

Letter of complaint شكوى في خطاب

Sohair has decided to write a letter of complaint to the hotel manager in Al-Qusair about the problems (المشاكل, al-mashākil) she and her fellow students encountered during their recent stay.

تحية طيّبة (taḥiya ṭayyiba): literally 'fine greeting' – a common way to open a letter

للأسف (lil-asaf): unfortunately

رغم أنّ... (raghma anna): in spite of [the fact] that...

أردتُ أن أخبرك حتى... (aradtu an ukhbirak ḥatta): I wanted to inform you so that ...

> السيّد مدير فندق الشمس، القصير
>
> تحية طيّبة،
>
> نزلنا في الفندق في الأسبوع الماضي في رحلتنا مع الجامعة. للأسف غرفتنا رقم ٢٠٥ في الدور الثاني كانت صغيرة جدّاً وتطلّ على محطّة التاكسي.
>
> كان الطقس حاراً، ولكن التكييف لم يعمل أبداً، رغم أنه كان كبيراً جدّاً!
>
> في الصباح ذهبنا إلى الكافيتريا ولكن للأسف كان الشاي بارداً وكان الخبز قديماً، وبعد الظهر رجعنا إلى الكافيتريا ولكن الكولا كانت دافئة ولم نجد ثلجاً.
>
> أرَدتُ أن أُخبرك حتى تحَلّ هذه المشاكل،
>
> وشكراً،
>
> سهير عبد اللطيف

Exercise 9 تمرين ٩

You stayed last month in the same hotel with your family (in room 512 on the fifth floor). You were also unhappy because:

- the room was cold and overlooked the bus station
- the weather was cold and the heater (مدفأة midfa'a) never worked
- the coffee in the cafeteria was cold and the pizza was small
- you didn't find any soap in the bathroom

Write a letter of complaint to the hotel manager, using Sohair's letter as a model.

العالم العربي ... نظرة على تونس

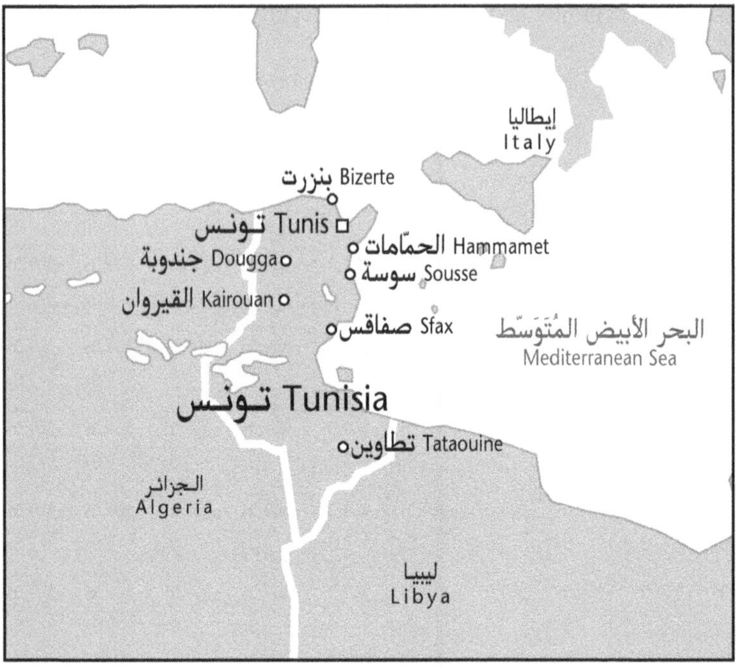

Arabic in Tunisia العربيّة في تونس

Tunisia is the smallest of the North African countries, lying between Algeria and Libya. As in its two neighbours to the west, Morocco and Algeria, in Tunisia there is a very strong French influence on both the culture and the language. As well as using French and Italian words such as 'piscine' (swimming pool) and 'cucina' (kitchen) within spoken Tunisian Arabic, Tunisians might also switch entirely between speaking French and Arabic, sometimes in mid-sentence.

Some of the features of Tunisian dialect are:

- Use of the verb يخدم ('to serve') with the meaning of 'to work'
- Use verbal prefix نـ n- to refer to 'I': نخدم nikhdim (I work)
- Use of specifically Tunisian expressions such as برشة barsha and and ياسر yaaser, both meaning 'very' or 'a lot'
- Dropping the 'd' sound in عند, e.g. ƹanina ('we have')

Listen to Abdelhaq talking about himself in his Tunisian dialect. You will find a transcript and translation in the key.

صابر الرباعي يصوّر أغنيته في تونس

اختار الفنّان صابر الرباعي الجنوب التونيسي لِتصوير كليب أغنية «خلّوني». في واحات وبين كثبان الرمال والنخيل تمّ التقاط مشاهد الكليب.

استمرّ التصوير ثلاثة أيام وتمّ تصوير مشاهد زفاف تقليدي في الجنوب التونسي.

وسيُقيم صابر حفلة في تونس في ٢١ يونيو القادم في قصر القُبة بالمنزه.

كليب (kleeb) video 'clip'

تمّ، يتمّ (tamma, yatimm) to be completed, to end

التقاط (iltiqāṭ) shooting

مشهد، مشاهد (mash-had, mashāhid) scene

استمرّ، يستمر (istamarr, yastamirr) to continue

زفاف (zifāf) wedding party

(Adapted from Sayyidati magazine, 17/5/2008)

Tunisia, with its long sandy beaches, has long been a popular tourist destination. It is also an attractive location for film and music video producers, with pristine desert and green oases. The extract above reports on a music video being shot amongst the dunes and palm trees of a Tunisian oasis.

الأَسئِلة

١ ما هو اسم المغنّي؟

٢ ما هو اسم الأغنية؟

٣ أين يصوّر الكليب ؟

٤ متى سيقيم صابر الحفلة؟

٥ أين الحفلة؟

Vocabulary in Unit 5

Nouns الأسماء

travel	سفَر
tourism	سِياحة
journey	رِحلة (ات)
visa	تأشيرة (ات)
centre	مَركَز (مَراكِز)
sports centre	مركز الرِياضة
shopping centre	مركز التَسَوُّق
police station	مركز الشُرطة
office	مكتَب (مكاتِب)
tourist office	مكتب السِياحة
airline office	مكتب الطَيران
post office	مكتب البَريد
station	مَحَطّة (ات)
train station	محطّة القِطار
bus station	محطّة الباص
petrol station	محطّة البَنزين
square	ميدان (مَيادين)
corner	ناصِية (نَواصٍ)
traffic lights	إشارة (ات) المُرور
fort/castle	قَلعة (قِلاع)
way/road	طَريق (طُرُق)
sand dune	كَثيب (كُثبان) الرِمال
oasis	واحة (ات)
palm tree	نَخلة (نَخيل)
well (water)	بِئر (آبار)
mine	مَنجَم (مَناجِم)
transportation	نَقل
(air)line	خَطّ (خُطوط)
underground train	قِطار الأَنفاق
pilgrimage	حَجّ
postcard	بِطاقة (ات) بَريديّ
problem	مُشكِلة (مَشاكِل)
torture	عَذاب
stolen items	مَسروقات
ice	ثَلج (ثُلوج)
nervousness	عَصَبيّة
dawn	فَجر
wedding party	زِفاف
shooting (film, etc.)	اِلتِقاط
scene (film, etc.)	مَشهَد (مَشاهِد)
clip (video, etc.)	كليب (ات)

Adjectives الصفات

afraid/frightened	خائِف
abandoned	مَهجور
wonderful/amazing	عَجيب
shining/bright	لامِع
happy	سَعيد

Verbs الأفعال

enquire	استَفسَر، يَستَفسِر
show (the way)	دَلّ، يَدُلّ (الطريق)
leave/depart	غادَر، يُغادِر
head (towards)	تَوَجَّه، يَتَوَجَّه (نَحوَ)

undertake/perform	أدّى، يُؤدّي
solve	حَلَّ، يَحِلّ
buy	اِشتَرَى، يَشتَري
feel	شَعَرَ، يَشعُر بِـ
remind	ذَكَّرَ، يُذَكِّر
inform/tell	أخبَرَ، يُخبِر
finish/complete	تَمَّ، يتِمّ
continue	اِستَمَرَّ، يَستَمِرّ

Other phrases **العبارات الأخرى**

straight on	على طول
go! *(m/f)*	اِذهَب/اِذهَبي
take! *(m/f)*	خُذ/خُذي
turn! *(m/f)*	اِتَّجِه/اِتَّجِهي
cross! *(m/f)*	اُعبُر/اُعبُري
towards	نَحوَ
on foot/walking	ماشِياً
unfortunately	لِلأسَف
despite	رَغمَ أنَّ
'fine greeting' (*opening for letter*)	تَحِية طَيِّبة

Additional note: Jussive with the past negative

A modified version of the present tense, known as the *jussive*, is used for the past negative after لم (lam). The jussive is very similar to the subjunctive in that the final nūn disappears from the feminine 'you', the masculine plural and the dual (see page 73). For regular verbs, this is the only significant difference.

However, if fully pronounced the other parts of the jussive end with a sukūn: يكتبْ (yaktub) rather than يكتبُ (yaktubu). This has the effect of shortening the long vowels in weak verbs. For example, يزور (yazūr, he visits) becomes يزُر (yazur) in the jussive; أمشي (amshī, I walk) becomes أمشِ (amshi).

Look at these examples of negative sentences in the past:

لم يذهبوا. (lam yadh-habū)	They didn't go.
ألم تعدّي الحقائب؟ (a-lam tuعiddī al-ḥaqā'ib)	Didn't you *(f.)* prepare the bags?
لم نزر تونس. (lam nazur tūnis)	We didn't visit Tunisia.
لم أشترِ التذاكر. (lam ashtari at-tadhākir)	I didn't buy the tickets.

unit 6

Food and cooking
الطَعام والطَبخ

بَصَلة المُحِبّ خروف.

The loved one's onion is [like a whole] lamb.

Talking about food التكلّم عن الطعام

Exercise 1 تمرين ١

How many of these items of food and drink do you remember? Write the English next to the Arabic, as in the example.

______	جُبن	*milk*	حليب
______	لَحم	______	تُفّاح
______	زَيت	______	زُبدة
______	بُنّ	______	أَرُزّ
______	خُبز	______	بُرتُقال
______	مَوز	______	بَطاطِس
______	لَيمون	______	كَعك
______	بِطّيخ	______	سَمَك
______	تين	______	طَماطِم
______	دَجاج	______	زَبادي
______	سُكَّر	______	بَيض
______	بَسكويت	______	عَصير

Now check your answers by listening to the recording. You could also replay the recording *without* looking at your list, pausing after the Arabic for each item to see if you can remember what it means.

Food shops محلات الطعام

مخبز (makhbaz) bakery

جزّارة (jazzāra) butcher shop

بقّالة (baqqāla) grocery

خُضَرِيّ (khuḍarīy) greengrocer

سمّاك (sammāk) fishmonger

لَبّان (labbān) dairy/milkman

Exercise 2 تمرين ٢

Write the items of food and drink from the list in Exercise 1 below the place you would buy it, as in the example.

				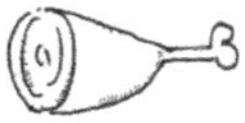	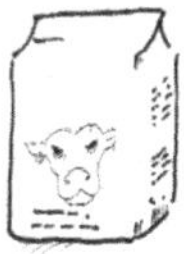
					حليب

Now make a sentence for each item following this model:

نشتري الحليب من اللبّان. We buy [the] milk from the dairy.

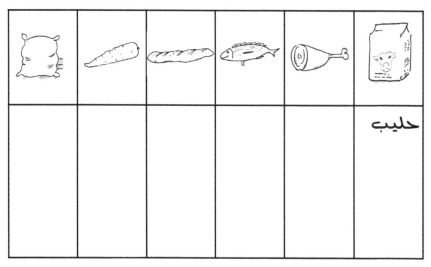

Exercise 3 تمرين ٣

Match the Arabic to the correct picture, for example **a٥**.

١ زجاجة
٢ عُلبة
٣ كيلو
٤ كوب
٥ ١٠٠ جرام
٦ كيس
٧ مِلعَقة
٨ نصف كيلو
٩ أنبوبة
١٠ رُبع كيلو
١١ مِلعَقة شاي
١٢ رغيف

Talking about measure التكلّم عن الكمّية

Remember that to express the concept of 'a ... of ...' you simply put the measure word directly in front of the food word in an iḍāfa construction. If the measure word ends with tā' marbūṭa, this should be pronounced -at:

(kīlū tuffāḥ) كيلو تفّاح	a kilo of apples
(kīs sukkar) كيس سكّر	a packet of sugar
(zujājat miyāh) زجاجة مياه	a bottle of water

An adjective describing the measure follows the *complete* iḍāfa:

(kīs milḥ saghīr) كيس ملح صغير	a small packet of salt
(zujājat kolā kibīra) زجاجة كولا كبيرة	a large bottle of cola

If you want to say '*the* bottle of ...', '*the* small packet of ...', etc., you add al- to the *final* word in the iḍāfa construction (i.e. the food item), and also to any following adjective.

(kīs al-aruzz)	كيس الأرزّ	the packet of rice
(ɛulbat at-tīn aṣ-ṣaghīra)	علبة التين الصغيرة	the small box of figs

Exercise 4 تمرين ٤

How do you say these in Arabic?

1 a packet of coffee beans
2 a can of tomatoes
3 1/4 kilo of figs
4 a glass/cup of yoghurt
5 a kilo of chicken
6 a loaf of bread
7 a small tin of fish
8 the large bottle of juice

Exercise 5 تمرين ٥

ذهبَت ليلى إلى المحلات اليوم وأخذَت هذه القائمة معها.

Leila went to the shops today and took this list with her.

Look at the shopping Leila came home with and tick off the items you can see. Then describe what she remembered, as in the example.

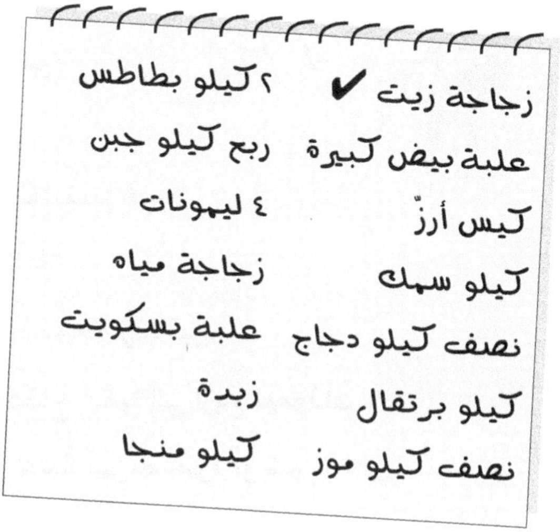
زجاجة زيت ✔
علبة بيض كبيرة
كيس أرزّ
كيلو سمك
نصف كيلو دجاج
كيلو برتقال
نصف كيلو موز
٢ كيلو بطاطس
ربع كيلو جبن
٤ ليمونات
زجاجة مياه
علبة بسكويت
زبدة
كيلو منجا

تذَكّرت ليلى الزيت ولكنّها نَسِيَت البيض.

Leila remembered the oil but she forgot the eggs.

At the greengrocer عند الخضري

Leila has gone back to the greengrocer to buy the fruit and vegetables she forgot. Listen to the conversation.

ـ مساء الخير. أنا رجعتُ... نسيتُ بَعض الأشياء.

ـ مساء النور يا مدام. أهلا بكِ في أيّ وَقت!

ـ أريد ٢ كيلو بطاطس من فضلك.

ـ تحت أمرك يا مدام. شيء ثاني؟

– نعم. هل عندكم منجا؟

– أنا آسف يا مدام. ليس عندنا منجا اليوم.

ـ وعُلَب التين هذه... بكم العلبة؟

– التركي بعشرين والتونسي بخمسة وثلاثين.

– طيّب. سآخذ التونسي... وأحتاج أيضاً إلى أربع ليمونات .

– أربع ليمونات ... تفضّلي.... علبة تين صغيرة أو كبيرة؟

ـ صغيرة من فضلك... كم الحساب؟

(hal ɛindakum...) هل عندكم...؟	Do you have ...?
((laysa) ɛindana...) (ليس) عندنا...	We (don't) have ...?
(sa-ākhudh...) سآخذ...	I'll take ...
(aḥtāj ilā...) أحتاج إلى...	I need ...
(shay' thānī) شيء ثاني؟	Anything else?
(bikām al-...) بكم الـ...؟	How much is/are the ...?
(kām al-ḥisāb) كم الحساب؟	How much is the bill?

Tip: If you want to say *'this* ... of ...' or *'these* ... of ...', you need to put هذا or هذه *after* the iḍāfa construction: كوب العصير هذا (kūb al-asīr hādhā, this glass of juice); زجاجة الزيت هذه (zujājat az-zayt hādhihi, this bottle of oil); علب التين هذه (ɛulab at-tīn hādhihi, these boxes of figs).

Exercise 6 تمرين ٦

Decide if these sentences about Leila's visit to the greengrocer are true or false, as in the example.

1 Leila went back to the greengrocer in the morning. ☒
2 She forgot three things from the greengrocer. ☐
3 Leila asked for two kilos of tomatoes. ☐
4 The greengrocer didn't have any mangos. ☐
5 The Turkish figs cost less than the Tunisian figs. ☐
6 Leila took a box of Turkish figs. ☐
7 She took the small box. ☐
8 She also bought four lemons. ☐

Conversation المحادثة

Leila has asked you to go back to the grocer and buy these items she forgot from her list:

- a large box of eggs
- a bottle of water
- a packet of biscuits

Look at the list on page 95 and the conversation opposite and prepare what you might say. Then follow the prompts on the recording.

زجاجة مياه zujājat miyāh *(a bottle of water)*

You say ṭamāṭim, I say ṭamāṭā

There are some variations in the vocabulary English-speakers use for everyday items such as foods. For example, the vegetable the British call 'aubergine' the Americans call 'eggplant'; 'chips' to the British means hot potato fries, but to the Americans it means salted potato crisps in a packet. These types of regional variations also exist in a more pronounced way in the Arabic-speaking world since the number of countries and influences involved are greater. Some vocabulary sets are more affected than others. Food and clothes are two topics that show significant regional differences.

The variations can be small: طماطم (ṭamāṭim, tomatoes) can also be طماطا (ṭamāṭā); بطاطس (baṭāṭis, potatoes) can be بطاطا (baṭāṭā), which in turn can sometimes be used to refer to sweet potatoes.

However, alternatives do not always sound similar: a third word for 'tomatoes' is بندورة (banadūra); yoghurt can be زبادي (zabādi) or لبن (laban), the latter also sometimes used to refer to milk.

In addition, the same word can have different meanings in different places: كرفس (karafs) can refer to celery in one area or parsley in another; خوخ (khawkh) can be peaches in some places or plums in others.

In general, the various nationalities of the Arab world will use the term most familiar to those they are addressing. Some foreign words adopted into Arabic don't have a 'standard' version and you may find variations even in more formal contexts such as newspaper articles. You should be aware that alternatives are possible and try to familiarise yourself with the most common.

Reserving the table حَجز المائدة

Exercise 7 تمرين ٧

Listen to three people telephoning the Nujoum restaurant and fill in the chart with the details of their reservations, as in the example.

الساعة *time*	اليوم *day*	عدد الأشخاص *number of people*	اسم الزبون *customer name*	
٨:١٥	الجمعة	٢	بركات	١
				٢
				٣

Tip: The plural of شخص (shakhṣ, person) is أشخاص (ash-khāṣ): مائدة لأربعة أشخاص (mā'ida li-arbaعat ash-khāṣ, a table for four people). Remember the dual ending for two people: مائدة لشخصين (mā'ida li-shakhṣayn, a table for two people).

Conversation المحادثة

You are going to telephone the Nujoum restaurant to make a booking. Follow the prompts on the recording. Here are your requirements:

- a table for five people
- Thursday
- 8.30pm

Now replay the conversation, this time changing the requirements. You can try this several times until you are confident.

In the restaurant في المطعم

It's Friday evening and Mr Barakat has arrived at the Nujoum restaurant with his wife.

Exercise 8 تمرين ٨

Mr and Mrs Barakat are welcomed by the *maitre d'* (المتر). Look at what they said below and think about in which the order the phrases might have come. Then listen to the conversation and mark the correct order in the boxes, as in the example.

☐ بركات.

١ مساء الخير!

☐ طبق اليوم كفتة مشوية مع سلاطة الزبادي.

☐ أنا سآخذ الكفتة. ونريد زجاجة مياه من فضلك.

☐ أهلا وسهلا يا سيّد بركات. تفضّلوا. مائدة رقم عشرة.

☐ طيّب... واحد سمك مقلي، واحد كفتة مشوية وزجاجة مياه.

☐ شكراً... من فضلك، ما هو طبق اليوم؟

☐ كفتة مشوية؟ أنا أفضل السمك. هل عندكم سمك؟

☐ الاسم من فضلك؟

☐ نعم يا سيّدتي. عندنا سمك مقلي ممتاز. وحضرتك يا سيّد بركات؟

☐ مساء النور. حجزنا مائدة لشخصين.

أنا أفضل السمك anā ufaḍḍil as-samak *(I prefer the fish)*

Methods of cooking أساليب الطبخ

مشوي (mashwī) grilled	محشي (maḥshī) stuffed
مقلي (maqlī) fried	مخلّل (mukhallal) pickled
محمّر (muḥammar) (pan-)fried	مهروس (mahrūs) creamed
مسلوق (maslūq) boiled	في الفرن (fil-furn) (oven) roasted

Exercise 9 تمرين ٩

Read the Arabic dishes and match them to the equivalent English. For example, ١ f.

a grilled chicken
b pickled cucumber
c potato chips (fries)
d fried fish
e stuffed tomatoes
f boiled eggs
g creamed carrot

١ بيض مسلوق
٢ سمك مقلي
٣ طماطم محشية
٤ جَزَر مهروس
٥ دجاج مشوي
٦ بطاطس محمّرة
٧ خيار مخلّل

Exercise 10 تمرين ١٠

Mr Barakat's bill has arrived, but there's a mistake (خطأ khaṭa').

Listen once without looking at your book and see if you can decide what mistake has been made.

Then listen again and fill in the missing words from the transcript below.

- يا متر! أعتقد أن هناك خطأ في ________ !

- ________ في الحساب؟ أنا ________ جداً يا سيدي!

- أنا طلبتُ كفتة ________ وفي الحساب كباب بالبطاطس ________ !

- آسف ________ يا سيدي! الكباب ________ .

- بسيطة يا متر! ________ وَجبة ممتازة! (an excellent meal!).

Forms of the verb الفعل المَزيد

We have seen how Arabic verbs have varied 'forms' which carry related meanings. We have also looked in detail at verbal nouns and participles for forms II, III and IV (see pages 62–3). The other five significant derived forms fall into two groups that share characteristics: forms V and VI; and forms VII, VIII and X (form IX being very rare).

Forms V and VI are characterised by being vowelled entirely with fatha in both present *and* past tenses:

تذكّرَت الكمّون والنعناع. (tadhakkarat al-kāmmūn wan-naɛnāɛ)	She remembered *(form V)* the cumin and the mint.
نتناول وجبة خفيفة في المساء. (natanāwal wajba khafīfa fīl-masā')	We eat *(form VI)* a light meal in the evening.
تعاونوا مع مفتّشي الأغذية. (taɛāwanū maɛa mufattishī l-aghdhiya)	They cooperated *(form VI)* with the food inspectors.

Forms VII and VIII and X are characterised by the intial alif (vowelled with kasra) in the past, and fatha/fatha/kasra vowelling in the present:

انكسر الطبق في الحوض. (inkasara aṭ-ṭabaq fīl-ḥawḍ)	The plate broke *(form VII)* in the sink.
أعتقد أن هناك خطأ في الحساب. (aɛtaqid anna hunāka khaṭa' fīl-ḥisāb)	I believe *(form VIII)* that there's a mistake in the bill.
استفسرنا عن الأسعار. (istafsarnā ɛan al-asɛār)	We enquired *(form X)* about the prices.

Remember that the subject prefixes and endings are the same whatever the form of the verb (see pages 48 and 82).

Verbal nouns from forms V–X follow predictable patterns as they do for other forms (see pages 62–3). Active and passive participles also follow the same principle, starting with مُـ (mu-) and having a final kasra for the active participle and a final fatḥa for the passive.

المستهلِك دائماً على حقّ. (al-mustahlik da'iman ɛalā ḥaqq)	The consumer is always right.
تناوُل الحلويات ضارّ بالأسنان. (tanāwul al-ḥalawiyāt ḍārr bil-asnān)	Eating sweet (things) is bad for the teeth.

Here is a summary of the patterns for all the forms of the verb:

	Present	*Past*	*Verbal noun*	*Active Part.*	*Passive Part.*
II	يُفَعِّل	فَعَّل	تَفعيل	مُفَعِّل	مُفَعَّل
III	يُفاعِل	فاعَل	مُفاعَلة/فِعال	مُفاعِل	مُفاعَل
IV	يُفعِل	أَفعَل	إِفعال	مُفعِل	مُفعَل
V	يَتَفَعَّل	تَفَعَّل	تَفَعُّل	مُتَفَعِّل	مُتَفَعَّل
VI	يَتَفاعَل	تَفاعَل	تَفاعُل	مُتَفاعِل	مُتَفاعَل
VII	يَنفَعِل	اِنفَعَل	اِنفِعال	مُنفَعِل	مُنفَعَل
VIII	يَفتَعِل	اِفتَعَل	اِفتِعال	مُفتَعِل	مُفتَعَل
X	يَستَفعِل	اِستَفعَل	اِستِفعال	مُستَفعِل	مُستَفعَل

Exercise 11 تمرين ١١

Copy out the table below and fill in the gaps in the patterns for the four verbs. Use a dictionary to check the meaning.

Present verb	يَختَلِف			
Past verb	اِختَلَف	تَناوَل		
Root letters			ل / ق / ط	
Form			VIII	
Meaning				
Verbal noun				اِستِهلاك
Active Part.				
Passive Part.				

The month of Ramadan شهر رمضان

Eating patterns change throughout the Islamic world during the month of Ramadan. Muslims perform the fast (الصوم aṣ-ṣawm) from the dawn call to prayer (آذان الفجر ādhān al-fajr) until the sunset call (آذان المغرب ādhān al-maghrib). At sunset, the main 'breakfast' meal (إفطار ifṭār) is served. There is also a lighter meal eaten just before the dawn call to prayer.

شهر رمضان

في شهر رمضان تجتمع العائلة حول مائدة الإفطار بعد صوم النهار من آذان الفَجر وحتى آذان المَغرِب.

يُفطر الصائمون تقليديّاً بِتناوُل التمر، ثمّ يُؤدّون الصلاة وبعد ذلك يجلسون حول المائدة لِتناوُل وجبة الإفطار الرئيسيّة.

وهناك وجبة أخرى خفيفة يتناولها المسلمون قبل صلاة الفجر اسمها «السُحور».

عادةً يزيد استهلاك الأغذِية والحلويات في رمضان رغم أنّه شهر الصوم!

صائم، ون/ين (ṣā'im, ūn/īn) person fasting

أفطر، يفطر (afṭara, yufṭir) to eat breakfast/to break the fast

تمر (tamr) dates

تقليديّاً (taqlīdīyan) traditionally

صلاة، صلوات (ṣalāh, ṣalawāt) prayer

زاد، يزيد (zāda, yazīd) to increase

أغذية (agh-dhiya) food(stuffs)

حلويات (ḥalawiyāt) sweets/desserts

Exercise 12 تمرين ١٢

Read the article about Ramadan opposite and decide if these statements are true (صحيح) or false (خطأ).

	صحيح	خطأ
١ الوجبة الرئيسية اسمها «الإفطار».	✔	☐
٢ يتناول الصائمون الإفطار في الصباح.	☐	☐
٣ تجتمع العائلة حول مائدة الإفطار بعد آذان الفجر.	☐	☐
٤ يتناول الصائمون تقليديّاً التَمر قبل الصلاة.	☐	☐
٥ «السُحور» وجبة قبل صلاة الفجر.	☐	☐
٦ عادةً يشتري الناس أغذِية أكثر في شهر الصوم.	☐	☐

التمر at-tamr (*dates*) - *traditionally eaten with milk to break the fast*

العالم العربي ... نظرة على لبنان

Arabic in Lebanon العربيّة في لبنان

Lebanon, part of the Levantine "fertile cresent", lies along the shores of the Eastern Mediterranean. Its position and varied history have left Lebanon with multiple religious and cultural communities. For much of its recent history it has been under the influence of France, and French is still the strongest outside influence on the local dialect. As in parts of North Africa, many Lebanese are equally comfortable speaking French or Arabic.

Lebanese Arabic dialect is part of the Levant group and shares many features with Syrian Arabic (see page 52), but with a greater French influence.

Listen to Fouad talking about himself in his Lebanese dialect. You will find a transcript and translation in the Answers section.

الكفتة المشوية مع سلاطة الزبادي

لثلاثة أشخاص

المقادير:

- **نصف كيلو ضأني مفروم**
- **بصلة مبشورة**
- **نعناع مقطّع**
- **ملعقة شاي كمون**
- **فص ثوم كبير مبشور**
- **كوب زبادي كبير**
- **ثلاث طماطم مقطّعة**
- **خيارة مبشورة**
- **ملح وفلفل**
- **ثلاث أرغفة خبز**

تحضير الكفتة

١ اخلطوا اللحم مع البصل والكمون.

٢ أضيفوا الملح والفلفل.

٣ قسموا الخليط إلى ستة حول الأسياخ.

٤ ضعوا أسياخ الكفتة تحت شواية لمدة عشر دقائق.

٥ اخلطوا الخيارة المبشورة مع الزبادي والطماطم والثوم والنعناع.

٦ أضيفوا الملح والفلفل.

٧ ضعوا الكفتة داخل الخبز مع السلاطة.

سيخ، أسياخ (sīkh, asyākh) skewer	ضأني (ḍa'nī) lamb/mutton
...اخلطوا (ikhliṭū) mix...	مفروم (mafrūm) minced
...أضيفوا (aḍīfū) add...	مبشور (mabshūr) grated
...قسّموا (qassimū) divide...	مقطّع (muqaṭṭaع) chopped
...ضعوا (ḍaعū) put...	فصّ ثوم (faṣṣ thūm) clove of garlic

Lebanese food is famous throughout the Middle East and beyond. Lebanese cooking has influenced the rest of the Mediterranean, and in turn has absorbed features from other countries such as Turkey and Greece. Minced meat is a key ingredient, as are cracked wheat (burghul), mint and parsley. Above is a recipe for the classic grilled 'Kofta' kebabs with yoghurt salad.

الأسئلة

١ الوجبة لكم شخصاً؟

٢ ما هي كمية الكمون؟

٣ وكمية الزبادي؟

٤ وكم رغيف خبز؟

٥ كم سيخ كفتة لكلّ شخص؟

Vocabulary in Unit 6

Nouns الأسماء

food	طَعام (أطعِمة)، غِذاء (أغذِية)
shop/store	مَحَلّ (ات)
bakery	مَخبَز (مَخابز)
grocery	بَقّالة (ات)
fishmonger	سَمّاك (ون/ين)
butcher shop	جَزّارة (ات)
greengrocer	خُضَرِيّ (ون/ين)
dairy/milkman	لَبّان (ون/ين)
measure/quantity	كَمّيّة (ات)
method	أُسلوب (أساليب)
preparation	تَحضير
glass/cup *(measuring)*	كوب (أكواب)
spoon	مِلعَقة (مَلاعِق)
skewer	سيخ، (أسياخ)
minced meat skewers	كُفتة
lamb/mutton	ضأني
salad	سَلاطة (ات)
cucumber	خيار
cumin	كَمّون
mint	نَعناع
garlic	ثوم
clove/segment	فَصّ (فُصوص)
dates	تَمر
sweets/desserts	حَلَوِيات
meal	وَجبة (ات)
person	شَخص (أشخاص)
consumer	مُستَهلِك (ون/ين)
bill/check	حِساب (ات)
price	سِعر (أسعار)
mistake/error	خَطأ (أخطاء)
tooth	سِنّ (أسنان)
fast(ing)	صَوم
person fasting	صائِم (ون/ين)
call to prayer	آذان
prayer	صَلاة (صَلَوات)

Adjectives الصفات

grilled	مَشوي
fried	مَقلي
fried/pan-fried	مُحَمَّر
boiled	مَسلوق
stuffed	مَحشي
pickled	مُخَلِّل
creamed/mashed	مَهروس
minced	مَفروم
grated	مَبشور
chopped	مُقَطَّع
harmful/bad (for)	ضارّ (بِـ)
correct	صَحيح

Verbs الأفعال

forget	نَسِيَ، يَنسَى
remember	تَذَكَّرَ، يَتَذَكَّر
eat/partake	تَنَاوَلَ، يَتَنَاوَل
eat breakfast	أفطَرَ، يُفطِر
consume	اِستَهلَكَ، يَستَهلِك
break/be broken	اِنكَسَرَ، يَنكَسِر
believe/think	اِعتَقَدَ، يَعتَقِد
differ	اِختَلَفَ، يَختَلِف
increase	زادَ، يزيد

Other phrases العبارات الأخرى

dish of the day	طَبَق اليَوم
bottle of water	زُجاجة مِياه
baked (in the oven)	في الفُرن
it's nothing ('easy')	بَسيطة
right/correct	على حَقّ
traditionally	تَقليديّاً
mix...	اِخلِطوا...
add...	أضيفوا...
divide...	قَسِّموا...
put...	ضَعوا...

unit 7

Review
المراجعة

Exercise 1 تمرين ١

Listen to Najiba introducing herself. Write down her details on the form below, as in the example.

الاسم ...نجيبة بدران.........................

تاريخ الميلاد ....

مكان الميلاد ....

العنوان ....

الجنسية ....

جنسية الأب ....

جنسية الأم ....

المهنة ....

الشركة ....

Now write a paragraph about Najiba, using the information on the form. Try to use some of the connecting expressions you have met. You could start like this:

وُلِدَت نجيبة بدران يوم ٦ فبراير عام ١٩٨٦ في مدينة حلَب...

Exercise 2 تمرين ٢

Write the plurals and meanings of the words in the table, as in the example.

Meaning المعَنى	Plural الجمَع	Word الكَلمة
stars	نُجوم	نَجم
______	______	كرسي
______	______	مَحطّة
______	______	حفيد
______	______	مُصمِّم
______	______	حمّام
______	______	مَركَز
______	______	غُرفة
______	______	كوب

Choose one of the plurals above to fill the gaps in the sentences below. (You may need to add الـ depending on the context.)

١ في هذه المدينة هناك أربعة مراكز التسوّق.

٢ كانت ______ لامعة في ليل الصحراء.

٣ لي سبعة ______ – خمس بنات وولدان.

٤ نحتاج إلي ثلاثة ______ أرزّ للعشاء.

٥ هل توجد ______ تطلّ على البحر؟

٦ استأجرنا فيللا بأربع غرف نوم وثلاثة ______.

٧ يعملون ______ في دار أزياء إيطاليّة.

٨ رأينا ______ بنزين كثيرة في الطريق.

٩ هل رأيتم ______ التقليديّة القديمة في بيت جدّي؟

Exercise 3 ٣ تَمرين

Join the verbs with the activities, as in the example.

قبل الساعة السابعة	يزور
التليفزيون	يلعب
العشاء للعائلة	يعمل
الملابس	يَركب
الأوراق على المكتب	يُعِدّ
متاحف	يكوي
الخضروات من السوق	يرتِّب
كرة القدم	يشتري
مساعداً للمدير العام	ينظِّف
الخيل	يستيقظ
المطبخ	يشاهد

Now decide how often you do the activities using one of the frequency words (see page 43). Make sentences that apply to you, for example:

أحياناً أزور متاحف.   I sometimes visit museums.

Exercise 4 ٤ تَمرين

How do you say these in Arabic?

1 Sometimes we play basketball in the club.

2 She rarely helps with the cooking.

3 The manager usually drives his car to the office.

4 We always eat breakfast before seven o'clock.

5 Every day I work until half past five.

6 They never tidy their rooms.

Exercise 5 تمرين ٥

Put this conversation in a restaurant in the correct order, as in the example:

☐ إذاً... واحد دجاج، وثلاثة سمك وأربعة ليمون...
☐ طبق اليوم سمك تونة مشوي مع أرزّ أحمر.
☐ أهلا وسهلا يا سيّد بدران. تفضلوا. مائدة رقم خمسة.
☐ شكراً.... من فضلك، ما هو طبق اليوم؟
١ مرحباً بكم في مطعم الصيّادين!
☐ سمك مشوي؟ أنا أفضل الدجاج. هل عندكم دجاج؟
☐ شكراً! كانت وَجبة ممتازة!
☐ ...يا متر! الحساب من فضلك!
☐ أنا والبنتان سنأخذ السمك. ونريد أربعة عصير ليمون.
☐ مساء الخير يا متر. حجزنا مائدة لأربعة أشخاص. الاسم بدران.
☐ الحساب؟ تفضلوا.
☐ نعم يا سيد بدران. عندنا دجاج مقلي ممتاز. وحضرتك يا مدام؟

Now listen to the recording and check your answer.

Conversation المحادثة

You have just entered a restaurant with two friends. You want to order the following. Prepare what you might say in Arabic.

- grilled kofta
- rice and salad
- pickled cucumber
- a mint tea
- a bottle of water

Now follow the prompts on the recording.

شاي بنعناع shāy bi-naعnāع *(mint tea)*

Exercise 6 تمرين ٦

Hisham is on a Meditteranean cruise, starting from the port of Alexandria. He has written a postcard from each port of call highlighting what he and the other passengers (الرُكّاب ar-rukkāb) did on the trip.

ميناء الأسكندريّة mīnā' al-iskandarīyya
(the port of Alexandria)

Look at the postcards opposite and answer these questions.

1 Who are all the postcards addressed to?

2 Which two ports does the ship call at before returning to Alexandria? (*Tip:* اليونان al-yūnān = Greece)

3 What did the passengers buy in the market in the first port of call?

4 What did they not have time to do on the first visit?

5 What famous landmark did they visit at the second port and how did they travel there?

6 Where did Hisham meet Adnan and what interest do they share?

7 What food reminds him of Egypt?

8 How did he pass the time during the journey to the third port?

9 Where and what did they eat in the third port?

10 How will Hisham travel home from Alexandria?

Exercise 7 تمرين ٧

Read the account below of the first leg of Hisham's cruise. Then continue the account using the information from the second and third postcards. You can use some additional sequencing words and expressions you know to link the events.

كانت رحلة هشام من ميناء الإسكندريّة إلى بيروت قصيرة ولكنها مثيرة لأنها أوّل رحلة له بالسفينة. أوّلاً نزل الركّاب صباحاً لزيارة بيروت وتوجّهوا نحو السوق. اشتروا هناك حلويات لذيذة وتفاحاً لبنانيّاً جميلاً. ولكن هشام لم يذهب إلى الجبل بسبب ضيق الوقت. غادرت السفينة بيروت متجهة إلى أثينا في نفس الليلة.

أبي العزيز وأمي الحبيبة،

كانت رحلتي من ميناء الإسكندريّة إلى بيروت قصيرة ولكنها مثيرة لأنها أوّل رحلة لي بالسفينة. نزلتُ مع الركّاب صباحاً لزيارة بيروت وتوجّهنا نحو السوق. اشترينا حلويات لذيذة وتفاحاً لبنانيّاً جميلاً. ولكنّني للأسف لم أذهب إلى الجبل بسبب ضيق الوقت. ستغادر السفينة بيروت الليلة مُتّجِهة إلى أثينا. سأكتب لكم من هناك.

ابنكما، هشام

عزيزي بابا وعزيزتي ماما،

تحيّاتي من اليونان. أخذنا الباص من الميناء لزيارة الأكروبوليس والحيّ القديم في أثينا. ذكّرَتني الكفتة هنا بمصر رغم أنّني الآن في أوروبا! قابلتُ طالباً سورياً على المركب اسمه عدنان. إنه يدرس الهندسة في دمشق وهوايته التصوير مثلي. سنغادر اليونان غداً في طريقنا إلى مرسيليا في جنوب فرنسا وسأرسل لكم بطاقة أخرى من هناك.

مع حبّي، هشام

والداي الحبيبان،

أمس جلستُ مع صديقي الجديد عدنان على سطح المركب بعد العشاء وتكلّمنا حتى الفجر ولم نشعر بالبرد إطلاقاً. بعد شروق الشمس وصلنا مرسيليا. زُرنا المدينة القديمة وأكلنا سمكاً مشوياً في مطعم شهير في وسط الميناء. كانت وجبة ممتازة! سنرجع إلى الإسكندريّة مساء اليوم وسأخذ القطار من المحطّة هناك.

إلى اللقاء... هشام

On this day... في مِثل هذا اليوم

في مثل هذا اليوم

● ١٨٨١: ميلاد وزير الخارجية البريطانية إرنست بيفن

● ١٩٤٥: الحلفاء يحتلون مدينة كولون الألمانية.

● ١٩٧٤: ألمانيا الغربية والشرقية تتبادلان الاعتراف بسيادتهما

● ١٩٧٩: الرئيس الأمريكي الأسبق جيمي كارتر يبدأ زيارته لمصر لأول مرة.

● ١٩٨٣: بدء مؤتمر قمة دول عدم الانحياز السابع في نيودلهي.

● ١٩٨٧: وفاة رجل أعمال المصري محمد أحمد فرغلي (فرغلي باشا ملك القطن).

● ٢٠٠٧: تحطم طائرة ركاب إندونيسية من طراز بوينج ٧٣٧

حليف، حلفاء (ḥalīf, ḥulafā’) ally, allies

احتلّ، يحتلّ (iḥtalla, yaḥtall) to occupy (land, etc.)

اعتراف (iɛtirāf) recognition

أسبق (asbaq) former

قمّة (qimma) summit

عدم الانحياز (ɛadam al-inḥiyāz) non-alignment

وفاة (wafāt) death

تحطّم (taḥaṭṭum) crash

(Adapted from *Al Ahram*, 7/3/08)

Exercise 8 تمرين ٨

Scan the article and the vocabulary above. Write the correct year next to the events below, as in the example. Try to say the date out loud in Arabic.

__١٩٧٩__ Visit of former president Jimmy Carter to Egypt
_______ Death of Egyptian businessman, Mohammed Ahmed Farghali
_______ Birth of British foreign minister, Ernest Bevan
_______ Crash of Indonesian Boeing 737
_______ Allied occupation of Cologne
_______ New Delhi summit of non-aligned states
_______ East and West Germany recognition of each other's sovereignty

Exercise 9 تمرين ٩

Now see if you can find these Arabic phrases in the article:

1 cotton king
2 passenger plane
3 for the first time
4 non-aligned states
5 of the make/type

Vocabulary in Unit 7

Nouns الأسماء

port *(f)*	ميناء (مَوانٍ)
passenger	راكب (رُكّاب)
Greece	اليونان
Athens	أثينا
ally	حَليف (حُلَفاء)
summit	قِمّة (قِمَم)
recognition	اِعتِراف
death/fatality	وَفاة (وَفَيات)
crash	تَحَطُّم (ات)

Adjectives الصفات

former	أسبَق

Verbs الأفعال

disembark, get off	نَزَلَ، يَنزِل
meet	قابَلَ، يُقابِل
occupy (land, etc.)	اِحتَلَّ، يَحتَلّ

Other phrases العبارات الأخرى

lack of time	ضِيق الوَقت
sunset	شُروق الشمس
at all	إطلاقاً
non-alignment	عَدَم الاِنحِياز

unit 8

Clothes and colours
الملابس والألوان

كُل ما يُعجِبك والبِس ما يُعجِب الناس.

Eat what pleases you and wear what pleases [other] people.

Talking about clothes التكلّم عن الملابس

Look at this list of clothing and listen to the recording:

قميص (qamīṣ) shirt	**حذاء** (ḥidhā') shoes
فستان (fustān) dress	**صندل** (ṣandal) sandals
بنطلون/سروال (banṭalūn/sirwāl) trousers	**جوارب** (jawārib) socks
	حزام (ḥizām) belt
جيبة/تنّورة (jība/tannūra) skirt	**سترة** (sutra) jacket
معطف (miعṭaf) coat	**حجاب** (ḥijāb) headscarf
قبّعة (qubbaعa) hat	**ربطة عنق** (rabṭat عunuq) tie
بدلة (badla) suit	**نظّارة** (naẓẓāra) glasses

Tip: Probably the most common general word meaning 'clothes' or 'clothing' is ملابس (malābis) the plural of ملبس (malbas), an item of clothing. You may also find ثياب (thiyāb) the plural of ثوب (thawb), a robe, and أزياء (azyā') the plural of زيّ (ziyy), an outfit or uniform.

Exercise 1 تمرين ١

Circle the items of clothing in the word square and write them next to the picture, as in the example. (Words can run right to left or top to bottom.)

ج	ف	ش	م	ا	ز	ح	ي	ع	م
ي	ص	غ	ط	ن	ر	ب	س	ك	د
ب	ق	ح	خ	ء	ا	ذ	ح	ش	ب
ة	ر	ت	س	ض	خ	ر	ث	ا	ن
ف	د	ء	ا	ذ	ه	ق	ا	ف	ط
ت	ع	ل	ف	ط	ع	م	س	د	ل
ي	ذ	ه	ص	غ	ة	ي	ش	ك	و
ط	س	م	ق	ء	ا	ص	م	غ	ن
ة	ع	ب	ق	ك	ض	ق	ة	ح	ث
ن	ف	ش	ر	ن	ا	ت	س	ف	ح

Traditional and Western clothing

The terms used for items of clothing show significant regional variations even within 'Standard' Arabic. Roughly speaking, there are three categories of words:

- words such as قميص qamīṣ (shirt) or حزام ḥizām (belt) that can be used to describe both traditional and Western items of clothing;

- words used for traditional Arabic items of clothing, such as ثوب thawb, عباية ʿabāya and جلابيّة jallābīyya (all meaning either robe or cloak); كوفية kūfīya and شماغ shimāgh (different kinds of men's headscarf). Exact use of these words will vary from region to region;
- words adopted from European languages and used to describe Western items of clothing, such as بنطلون banṭalūn (western-style trousers) and جيبة jība (skirt) from the French *pantalon* and *jupe*, or تي–شيرت tī-shīrt (T-shirt) and شورت shūrt (shorts) from the English. The terms used vary across the Arab world depending on the history of a particular region.

Traditional clothing for sale in Tunisia

Exercise 2 تمرين ٢

Here are some more familiar words for clothing. Can you work them out?

١ بلوزة ______	٥ بيجامة ______
٢ جينز ______	٦ بوت ______
٣ جاكيت ______	٧ سويتر ______
٤ بُلوفِر ______	٨ شال ______

Describing the outfit وَصف الزيّ

The most common way of describing what someone is wearing is to use the verb لبس، يلبس (labisa, yalbas) – from the same root as ملابس (malābis). لبس، يلبس is used with the meaning of *to wear* or *to put on*.

تلبس المرأة جلابية تقليديّة. (talbas al-mar'a jallābīyya taqlīdīyya)	The woman is wearing a traditional galabeyya.
هل يلبس نظّارة؟ (hal yalbas naẓẓāra)	Is he wearing glasses?/ Does he wear glasses?
لبستُ البيجاما ونمتُ. (labistu l-bijāmā wa-nimtu)	I put on [the] pyjamas and went to sleep.

In Modern Standard Arabic, you should add alif tanwīn (اً -an) to the object of the verb (in this case the item of clothing) if it is *indefinite* (i.e. the meaning is 'a/an' or 'some'). The main exceptions are if the object word ends in tā' marbūṭa (ة) or if it is a foreign loan word that sounds awkward with the alif tanwīn ending. Spoken dialects don't generally use the alif tanwīn in this way but you should try to include it when you are writing, or speaking in a more formal context.

ألبس قميصاً واسعاً وصُدَيرية. (albas qamīṣan wāsiعan wa-suḍayrīyya)	I'm wearing a loose shirt and a waistcoat.
هي تلبس فستاناً طويلاً. (hiya talbas fustānan ṭawīlan)	She's wearing a long dress.

Exercise 3 تمرين ٣

Listen to the four descriptions and write the correct number next to each picture.

Now describe what each person is wearing, for example:

١ تلبس المرأة تنّورة طويلة وبلوزة وحجاباً.

The woman is wearing a long skirt and blouse and a headscarf.

Describing colour وصف اللون

There are six basic colours that are made by putting the root letters into the pattern afعal. These six colours are amongst a handful of Arabic adjectives that *cannot* be made feminine by adding tā' marbūṭa. They have a special feminine form using the pattern faعlā':

colour	*masculine*	*feminine + plural (non-human)*
red	أحمَر aḥmar	حَمراء ḥamrā'
blue	أزرَق azraq	زَرقاء zarqā'
green	أخضَر akhḍar	خَضراء khaḍrā'
yellow	أصفَر aṣfar	صَفراء ṣafrā'
black	أسوَد aswad	سَوداء sawdā'
white	أبيَض abyaḍ	بَيضاء bayḍā'

Other colours are often made by forming *nisba* adjectives from natural items, in the same way as happens with nationalities (see page 5):

رماديّ (ramādīy) light grey ('ashen') ← رماد (ramād) ashes

ورديّ (wardīy) pink ('rosey') ← ورد (ward) roses

بنّي (bunnīy) brown ('beany') ← بنّ (bunn) coffee beans

Exercise 4 تمرين ٤

Make *nisba* colours from these natural items (see page 5 for rules):

١ ليمون lemons

٢ برتقال oranges

٣ مشمِش apricots

٤ ذهب gold

٥ بَنَفسَج violets

٦ عَسَل honey

٧ فضّة silver

٨ رَصاص lead

Exercise 5 تمرين ٥

Colour the picture of Amir and Amira with their daughter Fifi, using the key provided below.

١ أزرق ٢ أصفر ٣ مشمشي ٤ بنّي

٥ وردي ٦ أخضر ٧ رمادي ٨ رصاصي

Read this description of what Amir is wearing.

يلبس أمير بنطلون رصاصي مع قميص مشمشي وربطة عنق زرقاء.

أما حذاءه فهو بنّي مع جوارب بيضاء.

Now write a similar description for Amira and Fifi.

At the clothes shop في محلّ الملابس

Amir is in the clothes shop buying a new summer shirt and a sun hat.

– صباح الخير. هل عندكم قمصان صَيفيّة؟

– نعم. عندنا قمصان قطن خفيفة بِنصف كُمّ. كم مِقاسك؟ ١٦؟

– الياقة ١٦ ونصف.

– ما رأيك في هذا؟ الأخضر الفاتح مع الجيب البرتقاليّ؟

– لا، لا. الألوان زاهية جدّاً. أنا أفضّل الرماديّ مع الياقة الحمراء.

– تفضّل... القميص الرماديّ مقاس ١٦ ونصف.

– نعم... هذا القميص أنيق ومريح.

– شيء ثاني؟

– نعم. أحتاج إلى قبّعة عريضة للشمس.

– البنفسجيّة؟

– هذه القبّعة ضيّقة. ... ممكن أُجرِّب هذه... الزرقاء الداكنة؟

– تفضّل.... آه طَقم أنيق فِعلا!

(maqās) مقاس	size	(dākin) داكن	dark *(colour)*
(kumm) كمّ	sleeve	(zāhin) زاهٍ	bright *(colour)*
(yāqa) ياقة	collar	(ɛarīd) عريض	wide
(jayb) جيب	pocket	(dayyiq) ضيّق	narrow/tight
(ṭaqm) طقم	outfit/set	(anīq) أنيق	smart/elegant
(fātiḥ) فاتح	light *(colour)*	(ujarrib) أجرّب	I try (on)

Exercise 6 تمرين ٦

Fill in the information from Amir's visit to the shop, as in the example:

	First item	*Second item*
Type of clothing	*summer shirt*	
Size information:		
Colour offered:		
Colour preferred:		

Conversation المحادثة

You need some new jeans and a shirt. Prepare your part first by looking at the guide below and the conversation opposite. Then take part in the conversation on the recording. (Note: جينز (jeans) is *singular* in Arabic.)

Ask 'Do you have jeans?'.

- نعم. كم مقاسك؟

Give the shop assistant your waist size.

- ما رأيك في هذا الجينز؟ الأزرق الداكن؟

Say 'No. The colour is very dark. I prefer the light blue one(s).'

- هذا مقاسك.

Say 'Yes, these jeans are comfortable.'

- شيء ثاني؟

Say 'Yes, I need a short-sleeved shirt ['shirt with half sleeve'].'

- الليموني؟

Say 'This shirt is tight. Can I try the orange one with the green collar?'

- تفضّل. طقم أنيق فعلاً!

At the wedding party في حفلة الزَّفاف

Amira is showing a friend this picture taken at her brother's wedding party (حفلة الزفاف ḥaflat az-zifāf). She is pointing out who is who.

Exercise 7 تمرين ٧

Look at the names of the people who appear in the photo in the table below. Then listen once to the conversation and write the correct number in the box on the photo above next to each person, as in the example.

يلبس/تلبس *wearing*	قريب أميرة *relation to Amira*	الاسم *name*	
فستان أبيض	زوجة الأخ	هيلينا	١
		شكري	٢
		زينب	٣
		أشرف	٤
		فوزي	٥
		فضيلة	٦
		سامي	٧
		أمل	٨
		ميدو	٩

Now complete the table above, as in the example.

Identifying (relative pronouns)

English words such as 'who', 'which' or 'that' are used to identify people and things: 'the woman who is wearing the shawl', 'the red hats that are on the shelf', etc. These words are called *relative pronouns*.

Here are the most important Arabic relative pronouns:

الّذي (alladhī) *masc. sing.*	الّذين (alladhīna) *masc. plural (people)*
الّتي (allatī) *fem. sing. (+ non-human plural)*	اللاتي (allātī) *fem. plural (people)*

Arabic relative pronouns change according to the gender and number of the person(s) or thing(s) being identified:

المرأة التي تلبس الشال هي أختي. (al-mar'a allatī talbas ash-shaal hiya ukhtī)	The woman who is wearing the shawl is my sister.
الناس الذين في الصورة هم أقارب أميرة. (an-nās alladhīna fīṣ-ṣūra hum aqārib amīra)	The people who are in the photo are Amira's relatives.
الولد الذي يبتسم هو ابن أختي. (al-walad alladhī yabtasim huwa ibn ukhtī)	The boy who is smiling is my nephew (son of my sister).

Exercise 8 تمرين ٨

Pretend you are Amira describing the people in the wedding photo. Use your notes opposite, for example:

المرأة التي تلبس الفستان الأبيض هي زوجة أخي، هيلينا.

The woman who is wearing the white dress is my sister-in-law, Helena.

Tip: أب ab (father) and أخ akh (brother) change to أبو abū and أخو akhū when the first word of an iḍāfa, but to أبي abī and أخي akhī when the second word: أخو أميرة akhū amīra (Amira's brother) but زوجة أخي أميرة zawjat akhī amīra (Amira's brother's wife); أبو أميرة abū amīra (Amira's father) but صديق أبي أميرة ṣadīq abī amīra (Amira's father's friend).

If the person or thing being identified is not the subject of the rest of the sentence, as in 'the man whom we saw' ('we' is the subject, not the man), or 'the shirts that I bought' ('I' is the subject), then Arabic will phrase this as 'the man who we saw <u>him</u>', or 'the shirts that I bought <u>them</u>', using an attached pronoun:

الرجل الّذي رأيناه (ar-rajul alladhi ra'aynāhu)	the man whom we saw
القمصان الّتي اشتريتها (al-qumṣān allati ishtaraytuhā)	the shirts that I bought

The relative pronoun is not included if the subject is *indefinite* ('a man', 'some shirts', etc.):

رجل رأيناه (rajul ra'aynāhu)	a man whom we saw
قمصان اشتريتها (qumṣān ishtaraytuhā)	some shirts that I bought

Exercise 9 تمرين ٩

Join the two sentences or questions using a relative pronoun (if appropriate), as in the example.

أين القميص الأزرق؟ غَسلتُ القميص أمس. ←
أين القميص الأزرق الذي غَسلتُهُ أمس؟

١ أين القبّعة السوداء؟ كانت القبّعة في الخزانة.

٢ اشترَيتُ الفستان. تلبس ابنتي الفستان.

٣ هل خرج الأولاد؟ الأولاد كانوا في السينما.

٤ اجتمع الوزير مع البنات. البنات أرسلنَ خطاباً للجريدة.

٥ ذهبنا إلى مدينة. ليس في المدينة فندق.

٦ لم أتذكّر الأرقام. كتبتُ الأرقام على ورقة صغيرة.

Doubled verbs الفعل المُضاعَف

Doubled verbs have the same consonant as the second and third root.

Generally, doubled verbs follow the rule that the second and third root letters are written separately if the word pattern dictates that:

- the third root letter is followed directly by a consonant, *or*
- the second root letter is doubled, *or*
- the second root is followed by a long vowel.

Doubled verbs

	Present	*Past*	*Verbal noun*
I *(to block)*	يَسُدّ	سَدّ	*(varies)*
II *(to design)*	يُصَمِّم	صَمَّم	تَصميم
III	*(there are no common form III doubled verbs)*		
IV *(to be determined)*	يُصِرّ	أَصَرّ	إصرار
V *(to hesitate)*	يَتَرَدَّد	تَرَدَّد	تَرَدُّد
VI	*(there are no common form VI doubled verbs)*		
VII *(to join)*	يَنضَمّ	اِنضَمّ	اِنضِمام
VIII *(to occupy)*	يَحتَلّ	اِحتَلّ	اِحتلال
X *(to continue)*	يَستَمِرّ	اِستَمَرّ	اِستِمرار

Doubled verbs behave entirely regularly in Forms II and V, with the second and third roots written separately. For other verbal forms, whether or not the second and third roots are written together depends on the particular pattern and any ending added. For example, 'he liked' is أحبّ aḥabba but 'I liked' is أحببتُ aḥbabtu – the two roots separating as they are directly followed by the ending تُ -tu which starts with a consonant. You can see that the patterns for the verbal nouns from the derived forms largely dictate that the doubled root letters are written separately.

Other word patterns follow the same principles. For example, the passive participle from يسدّ yasudd is مسدود masdūd (blocked), with a long vowel between the second and third roots. However, the active participle has a short vowel in this position and so the doubled root is written together سادّ sādd (blocking).

The clothes show عرض الأزياء

An Iraqi fashion designer, Tariq Zakariya, is showcasing his latest designs. The show's commentator is introducing four girls modelling the outfits.

Exercise 10 تمرين ١٠

Firstly, listen once to the commentator and write the name of the model under the correct outfit. Don't try to understand every word, just the gist.

A

____

B

____

C

____

D

____

Exercise 11 تمرين ١١

Match the Arabic words and phrases to the English, for example ١c. (You can use the illustrations opposite to help you and listen again to the commentary for the context.)

a	embroidery	أزرار	١
b	those who wear the hijaab	مُحتَشِم	٢
c	buttons	سَيِّدات الأعمال	٣
d	neutral colours	طَبيعيّ	٤
e	handmade	مُحَجَّبات	٥
f	sapphire	تَطريز	٦
g	business women	حَرير	٧
h	modest	مَشغول باليَد	٨
i	natural	ألوان مُحايدة	٩
j	silk	الياقوت	١٠

Exercise 12 تمرين ١٢

Finally, write the outfit reference next to the descriptions used by the commentator, as in the example.

١ مناسب لسيّدات الأعمال A

٢ طقم رائع للصباح ____

٣ ألوان محايدة ومريحة للعين ____

٤ مع تطريز على الجيب والكمّ ____

٥ حذاء ذهبي اللون مع حقيبة يد ذهبية ____

٦ قلادة ذهبية كبيرة مع فصوص الياقوت الزرقاء ____

٧ محتشم وأنيق ____

٨ مناسب لحفلات الزفاف ____

٩ طقم تقليديّ ____

١٠ حقيبة أعمال من الجلد الطبيعيّ ____

العالم العربي ... نظرة على العراق

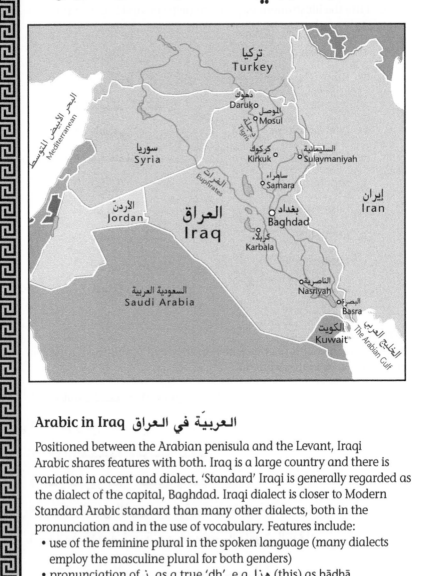

Arabic in Iraq العربيّة في العراق

Positioned between the Arabian penisula and the Levant, Iraqi Arabic shares features with both. Iraq is a large country and there is variation in accent and dialect. 'Standard' Iraqi is generally regarded as the dialect of the capital, Baghdad. Iraqi dialect is closer to Modern Standard Arabic standard than many other dialects, both in the pronunciation and in the use of vocabulary. Features include:

- use of the feminine plural in the spoken language (many dialects employ the masculine plural for both genders)
- pronunciation of ذ as a true 'dh', e.g. هذا (this) as hādhā
- use of particular expressions, e.g. زين zayn (fine/good); أكو akū (there is/are), thought to be derived from Aramaic

Listen to Ali talking about himself in his Iraqi dialect. You will find a transcript and translation in the Answers section.

الملابس التقليديّة في العراق هي مِثل الملابس التقليديّة في باقي دُوَل الجزيرة العربيّة والخليج.

الملابس مناسبة للطقس والبيئة، فهي بيضاء في شُهور الصيف الحارّة لِتعكس أَشِعّة الشمس، كما أنها واسعة وفِضفاضة ومصنوعة من القطن لِتَسمَح بحركة الهواء.

من المُهمّ تَغطِية الرأس للحِماية من الشمس أو الريح أو الرِمال.

إن الشتاء قصير ولكن جو الصحراء بارد جدّاً خاصّةً في الليل، ولذلك يلبس الناس ثِياباً مصنوعة من الصوف.

ملابس النساء أيضاً مُحتَشِمة وفضفاضة وتُغَطّي كلّ الجسم.

مثل (mithl) like/similar to

باقي... (bāqī) the rest of...

البيئة (al-bī'a) the environment

عكس، يعكس (ɛakasa, yaɛkis) to reflect

شعاع، أشعّة (shuɛāɛ, ashiɛɛa) ray

فضفاض (faḍfāḍ) flowing/loose

سمح، يسمح (لـ) (samaḥ, yasmaḥ (li)) to allow (for)

حماية (ḥimāya) protection

صوف (ṣūf) wool

جسم، أجسام (jism, ajsām) body

الأسئلة

١ ما لون الملابس التقليدية في الصيف؟

٢ لماذا تكون الملابس فضفاضة صيفاً؟

٣ كيف يكون الطقس في الشتاء؟

٤ هل ملابس الشتاء قطنية؟

٥ كيف وصفَت المقالة ملابس النساء؟

Iraq is a large multi-ethnic country, and the clothing reflects this diversity. In the cities, Paris fashions and the ubiquitous western jeans and T-shirts mix with traditional robes and headwear. Further north, Kurdish baggy trousers and colourful dresses and headscarves add local flavour.

Vocabulary in Unit 8

Nouns الأسماء

clothes	مَلابِس، ثِياب، أزياء
outfit	طَقم (طُقوم)
size	مَقاس (ات)
body	جِسم، (أجسام)
shirt	قَميص (قمصان)
dress	فُستان (فَساتين)
trousers	بَنطَلون (ات)، سِروال (سَراويل)
skirt	جيبة (ات)، تَنّورة (ات)
coat	مِعطَف (مَعاطِف)
suit	بَدلة (بِدَل)
shoes	حذاء (أحذية)
sandals	صَندَل (صَنادِل)
sock	جَورب (جَوارِب)
belt	حِزام (ات)
jacket	سُترة (سُتَر)، جاكيت (ات)
headscarf/hijab	حِجاب (ات)
tie	رَبطة (رِباط) عُنُق
waistcoat	صُدَيريّة (ات)
pyjamas	بيجامة (ات)
boots	بوت
sweater	سويتر (ات)
pullover	بُلوفِر (ات)
shawl	شال (شيلان)
blouse	بلوزة (ات)
jeans	جينز (ات)
glasses	نَظّارة (ات)
sleeve	كُمّ (أكمام)
collar	ياقة (ات)
pocket	جَيب (جُيوب)
button	زِرّ (أزرار)
embroidery	تَطريز
wool	صوف
sapphire	ياقوت
traditional robe/cloak	جَلابيّة (ات)، عَباية (ات)، ثَوب (ثِياب)
traditional men's headscarf	شِماغ، كوفيّة (ات)
people	ناس
woman	اِمرَأة (نِساء)
woman who wears the hijab	مُحَجَّبة (ات)
environment	بيئة (ات)
summer	صَيف
winter	شِتاء
ray	شُعاع، أشِعّة
protection	حِماية

Adjectives الصفات

grey	رَماديّ
pink	وَرديّ
orange *(adj)*	بُرتقاليّ
violet *(adj)*	بَنَفسَجيّ

lemon-coloured	لَيمونيّ
apricot-coloured	مِشمِشيّ
silver *(adj)*	فِضّيّ
gold *(adj)*	ذَهَبيّ
honey-coloured	عَسَليّ
(lead) dark grey	رَصاصيّ
light (colour)	فاتِح
dark (colour)	داكِن
loose	واسِع
wide	عريض
narrow/tight	ضَيِّق
bright (colour)	زاهٍ
smart/elegant	أنيق
summer *(adj)*	صَيفي
modest	مُحتَشِم
natural	طَبيعيّ
neutral	مُحايد
flowing	فَضفاض

Verbs الأفعال

wear/put on	لبِس، يلبَس
try (on)/test	جَرَّب، يُجَرِّب
design	صَمَّم، يُصَمِّم
reflect	عَكَس، يعكِس
allow (for)	سَمَح، يسمَح (لـ)
smile	اِبتَسَم، يبتَسِم
block	سَدَّ، يَسُدّ
be determined	أصَرَّ، يُصِرّ
hesitate	تَرَدَّد، يتَرَدَّد
join	اِنضَمَّ، يَنضَمّ

Other phrases العبارات الأخرى

like/similar to	مِثل
the rest of...	باقي...
really!	فِعلاً!
short-sleeved	بِنِصف كُمّ
handmade	مَشغول باليَد
clothes show	عَرض الأزياء

Additional note: Irregular words referring to people

Note these irregularities with some common words referring to people:

ناس (nās), people, has no singular

امرأة (imra'a), woman, changes slightly when written with al- becoming **المرأة** (al-mar'a)

the plural of **امرأة** (imra'a) is the unrelated word **نِساء** (nisā'), women

unit 9

Education and training
التعليم والتدريب

التعليم في الصِغَر مِثل النَقش على الحَجَر.

Education in youth is like carving in stone.

School and university المدرسة والجامعة

(lughāt) لغات
languages

(thānawīy) ثانويّ
secondary

(iعdādīy) إعداديّ
middle

(ibtidā'īy) ابتدائيّ
primary

(rawḍa) روضة
kindergarten

Tip: إعداديّ (iعdādīy) literally means 'preparatory', and caters roughly for ages 11–14. This stage is also referred to as متوسّط (mutawassiṭ).

Remember to add tā' marbūṭa if describing something feminine or plural:

(at-taعlīm al-ibtidā'īy) التعليم الابتدائي	[the] primary education
(al-marḥala ath-thānawīyya) المرحلة الثانوية	the secondary stage
(madāris iعdādīyya) مدارس إعدادية	middle schools
(ṣaff ibtidā'īy) صفّ ابتدائي	primary class/grade
(ṣufūf ibtidā'īyya) صفوف ابتدائية	primary classes/grades

School and university are divided into classes/grades or years:

(aṣ-ṣaff al-awwal) **الصفّ الأوّل**	the first class/grade
(as-sana ath-thāniya) **السنة الثانية**	the second year
(aṣ-ṣaff ath-thālith) **الصفّ الثالث**	the third class/grade

Note the feminine of awwal (first) is أُولى ūlā:

(as-sana al-ūlā) **السنة الأولى**	the first year

Exercise 1 تمرين ١

Mrs Mabrouk is talking about her five children. Fill in the chart below with their details as in the example.

السنة/الصفّ *class/year*	المدرسة/الجامعة *school/university*	العمر *age*	الاسم *name*	
السنة الأولى	الجامعة	١٩	سعيد	١
				٢
				٣
				٤
				٥

روضة المرح للأطفال rawḍat al-maraḥ lil-aṭfāl

(Al-Marah Kindergarten for children, Al Ain, United Arab Emirates)

Exercise 2 تمرين ٢

Read this description of Saeed Mabrouk.

سعيد عمره ١٩ سنة وهو في السنة الأولى من الجامعة.

Can you make four similar descriptions about the other children, using the information in the table on page 137?

Tip: Remember that a plural noun is only used after numbers 3 to 10: ١٠ سِنين ('10 years'), but ١٩ سَنَة ('19 year').

Exercise 3 تمرين ٣

How many of these school and university subjects do you recognise or can you work out? Write the equivalent English subject, as in the example.

Tip: علم (ɛilm) means 'science'.

التاريخ	history	(عِلم) الفيزياء	
الجغرافيا		(عِلم) الكيمياء	
الموسيقى		الطبّ	
الرسم والفنون		الحقوق	
الريّاضيات		الهندسة	
التربيّة الدينيّة		الفَلسَفة	
(اللغة) العربيّة		التِجارة	
الجَبر		الآداب	
التربية الرياضية		عِلم الإقتصاد	
(اللغة) الانجليزيّة		عِلم الاجتِماع	
(عِلم) الأحياء		عِلم النَفس	

Now listen to the answers on the recording. You can also use the recorded list to check yourself, pausing after the Arabic for each subject to see if you can remember what it means.

Talking about subjects التكلّم عن الموادّ

You can use the phrases you know for expressing likes and dislikes when talking about school or university subjects. You could also use one of the following phrases:

(anā ujīd ar-rasm) أنا أجيد الرسم.	I'm good at drawing.
هي موهوبة في الموسيقى. (hiya mawhūba fīl-mūsīqā)	She's talented at music.
إنّ أخي متفوّق في الرياضيّات. (inna akhī mutafawwiq fīr-riyāḍīyāt)	My brother excels at maths.
أنا ضعيف(ة) في الإنجليزية. (anā ḍaɛīf(a) fīl-ingilīzīyya)	I'm weak in English.
أظنّ أن اللغة الصينية صعبة التعلّم. (aẓunn an al-lugha aṣ-ṣīnīyya ṣaɛbat at-taɛallum)	I think that the Chinese language is difficult to learn.

Exercise 4 تمرين ٤

Listen to Munira and her friend, Akmal, talking about how they think they'll do in their final examinations (امتحانات imtiḥānāt). Copy the table below and note which they are feeling positive (إيجابي) or negative (سلبي) about, as in the example.

أكمل		منيرة	
سلبي	إيجابي	سلبي	إيجابي
		الإنجليزية	

Conversation المحادثة

You are going to take part in a conversation with Munira about which subjects you enjoy.

- choose two subjects from the list on page 138 that you are good at
- choose two subjects that you are not so good at
- prepare some statements about your subjects using the phrases above

Now join in the conversation on the recording. You can try this several times, changing the subjects you talk about.

ع/ل/م and د/ر/س

Two Arabic roots closely associated with education are د/ر/س (connected with studying) and ع/ل/م (connected with knowledge). From these two roots come a host of useful items of vocabulary:

د ر س

to study	دَرَس/يَدرُس
to teach	دَرَّس/يُدرِّس
lesson(s)	دَرس (دُروس)
studying	دِراسة
tuitional	دِراسيّ
teacher(s)	مُدرِّس (ـون/ين)
teaching	تَدريس
school(s)	مَدرَسة (مدارس)
scholastic	مَدرَسيّ
student(s)	دارس (ـون/ين)

ع ل م

to know	عَلِم/يَعلم
to instruct	عَلَّم/يعلِّم
to learn	تَعلَّم/يَتَعلَّم
knowledge/science(s)	عِلْم (عُلوم)
scientific	عِلميّ
instructor/teacher(s)	مُعَلِّم (ـون/ين)
education/instruction	تَعليم
educational	تَعليميّ
(process of) learning	تَعَلُّم
scientist(s)	عالِم (عُلَماء)

Exercise 5 تمرين ٥

Choose a word from one of the lists above to fill in the gaps below. (There may be more than one possible answer.)

١ أنا لا أجيد ______ الأحياء.

٢ ذهبَت أختي إلى الجامعة في باريس لِـ ______ الأدب الفرنسي.

٣ هل أنتم ______ اللغة العربية؟

٤ حضر اليوم وزير الـ ______ لزيارة مدرستنا.

٥ يبدأ اليوم الـ ______ الساعة الثامنة صباحاً.

٦ الطلبة يدرسون الكيمياء والفيزياء في قِسم الـ ______ .

٧ وكالة «ناسا» فيها مجموعة كبيرة من الـ ______ .

٨ أبي ______ ـني ركوب الدراجات في سن السابعة.

Munira asks for advice منيرة تطلب نصيحة

Exercise 6 تمرين ٦

Munira has written an email to her older brother Saeed asking for advice.

1 What final exam did she take yesterday?
2 Why is she enrolling in a summer English course?
3 What does she want to study at university next year?
4 What does her father think? What about her mother?
5 What is Munira's ambition after university?

أخي الحبيب سعيد،

اِنتهَيتُ أمس من آخر امتحاناتي وكان في مادة الكيمياء. غداً سوف أُسجِّل اسمي في دورة اللغة الانجليزية لهذا الصيف لأنني ضعيفة فيها.

أريد أن أدرس الهندسة المَدَنيّة في الجامعة العام المُقبِل. يقول بابا إنني متفوّقة في العلوم والرياضيّات، وأن الدراسة في كلية الهندسة ستناسبني. ولكن ماما قالت لي « يا منيرة الهندسة كلها تُراب ورمل ولا تناسب البنات! ينبغي عليك أن تدرسي المواد المناسبة مثل علم الاقتصاد أو التجارة لتعملي يوماً في مكتب.

وأنتَ يا سعيد؟ بماذا تنصحني؟ أريد إجابتك بسرعة! أُمنيتي هي أن أعمل مع شركة عالمية في مجال البناء لأُسافر وأبني بيوت كثيرة للفقراء.

أُكتب لي آخر أخبارك في شيكاغو.

مع تحياتي،

أختك منيرة

امتحان، ات (imtiḥān, āt) examination

سجّل، يسجّل (sajjala, yusajjil) to register, to enrol

دورة، ات (dawra, āt) course

الهَندَسة المدنيّة (al-handasa al-madanīyya) civil engineering

مقبل (muqbil) coming, next

تراب (turāb) dust

ينبغي على (yanbaghī ʿalā) should, ought to

نصح، ينصح (ب) (naṣaḥa, yanṣaḥ bi) to advise

أُمنية، ات (umniya, āt) wish

Weak verbs الفعل المُعتَلّ

Assimilated verbs

Assimilated verbs have one of the weak letters wāw or yā' as the first root consonant. In practice this is almost always wāw. Assimilated verbs generally behave as regular verbs, the main exceptions being:

- the initial wāw drops out in basic present verbs in almost all cases:

  وصل/يصل (waṣala, yaṣil) to arrive

  وضع/يضع (waḍaعa, yaḍaع) to put

- the wāw changes to a double tā' in Form VIII:

  اتّصل/يتّصل (ittaṣala, yataṣṣil) to contact

  اتّضع/يتّضع (ittaḍaعa, yattaḍiع) to humble oneself

Hollow verbs

Hollow verbs have a weak letter as the second root consonant and fall into two main categories depending on whether the middle root is wāw or yā'. The rules for how hollow verbs behave are somewhat complicated and you will need to consult a grammar reference for the details. However, here are some guidelines.

In the present tense, hollow verbs with middle root wāw are generally characterised by a long ū in place of the second root letter and those with middle root yā' by a long ī. There are a few hollow verbs that are characterised by a long ā in the present tense, for example yanām (sleep):

يقول أبي إنني ضعيف في الإنجليزية. (yaqūl abī innanī ḍaعīf fīl-ingilīzīyya)	My father says that I'm weak in English.
هل يبيعون الكتب هنا؟ (hal yabīعūn al-kutub hunā?)	Do they sell books here?
تنام قطّتي طوال النهار. (tanām qiṭṭatī ṭawāl an-nahār)	My cat sleeps all day.

In the past tense, hollow verbs display a long ā when the suffix starts with a vowel, but a short u or i when the suffix starts with a consonant:

قالت أمّي إنّني كُنتُ طفلاً نشيطاً. (qālat ummī innanī kuntu ṭiflan nashīṭan)	My mother said I was an energetic child.
بعنا البيت ولكنهم باعوا الأرض. (biعnā al-bayt walākinnahum bāعū al-arḍ)	We sold the house but they sold the land.

Defective verbs

Defective verbs have either wāw or yā' as the final root letter. As with hollow verbs, the rules associated with defective verbs are somewhat complicated but some general characteristics can be identified.

In the present tense, the final wāw or yā' is replaced by ū, ī or ā, and in the past tense by ā or iya. However, when suffixes are added the sound can change to aw, ay or ī, or drop out altogether.

مشَينا أمس إلى المقهى. (mashaynā ams ilā l-maqhā)	We walked yesterday to the café.
ينبغي أن تشكو للمدير. (yanbaghī an tashkū lil-mudīr)	You *(masc.)* should complain to the manager.
نسيَت أختي هاتفها المحمول. (nasiyat ukhtī hātif(a)hā al-maḥmūl)	My sister forgot her mobile phone.

Weak in the derived forms

Defective verbs are irregular in all the forms. Hollow verbs are irregular only in forms IV, VII, VIII and X. The irregularities follow a similar pattern to the basic verb form, with the weak root letter changing to a long or short vowel depending on the pattern associated with the particular form. Whether the weak root is wāw or yā', the irregular derived patterns will be the same.

أجاد/يجيد (ajāda/yujīd) to be good at; Form IV: root j/w/d جود

احتاج/يحتاج (iḥtāja/yaḥtāj) to need; Form VIII from root ḥ/w/j حوج

استفاد/يستفيد (istafāda/yastafīd) to benefit; Form X from root f/y/d فيد

اشترى/يشتري (ishtarā/yashtarī) to buy; Form VIII: root sh/r/y شري

أعطى/يعطي (aعṭā/yuعṭī) to give; Form IV from root ع/ṭ/y عطي .

Weak verbs in the jussive

In the short *jussive* form of the verb (see page 91), those parts of the present tense that do not have a suffix (ending) are written with sukūn. In hollow and defective verbs this sukūn shortens the long vowel:

لم أنسَ ولكن لم أقُلْ شيئاً. (lam ansa walākinn lam aqul shay'an)	I didn't forget but I didn't say anything.
لم تُجِبْ منيرة على كلّ الأسئلة. (lam tujib munīra عalā kulli l-as'ila.)	Munira didn't answer all the questions.

In the examination hall في صالة الامتحانات

Munira is taking her final school examinations in the exam hall. The invigilator is giving the students instructions before the start of the examination

أبنائي الطلبة، صباح الخير.

مدّة الِامتحان ساعتان ونصف. استَمِعوا إلى هذه التّعليمات المُهِمّة:

- ضعوا الهواتف المحمولة في حقائبكم لأنها ممنوعة.
- أُكتبوا التاريخ وأرقام الجلوس على ورقة الإجابة.
- لا تقلبوا ورقة الأسئلة قبل أن تسمعوا الجرس.
- لا تتكلّموا إطلاقاً أثناء الامتحان، ومن يريد شيئا يرفع يده.
- رَكِّزوا على أوراقكم فقط، ولا تنظروا إلى أوراق زملائكم.
- اِقرأوا الأسئلة كلها جَيِّداً ، ثم ابدأوا بالأسهل.

بالتوفيق إن شاء الله يا أبنائي.

تعليمات (taɛlīmāt) instructions

ممنوع (mamnūɛ) forbidden

رقم الجلوس (raqm al-julūs) candidate ('seating') number

ورقة الإجابة (waraqat al-ijāba) answer paper

ورقة الأسئلة (waraqat al-as'ila) question paper

قلب، يقلب (qalaba, yaqlib) to turn over

جرس، أجراس (jaras, ajrās) bell

أثناء (athnā') during

زميل، زملاء (zamīl, zumalā') colleague, fellow (student)

Giving instructions إصدار الأوامر

It is relatively straightforward to turn a verb into an instruction *(imperative)*. For the majority of verbs you can follow this simple process.

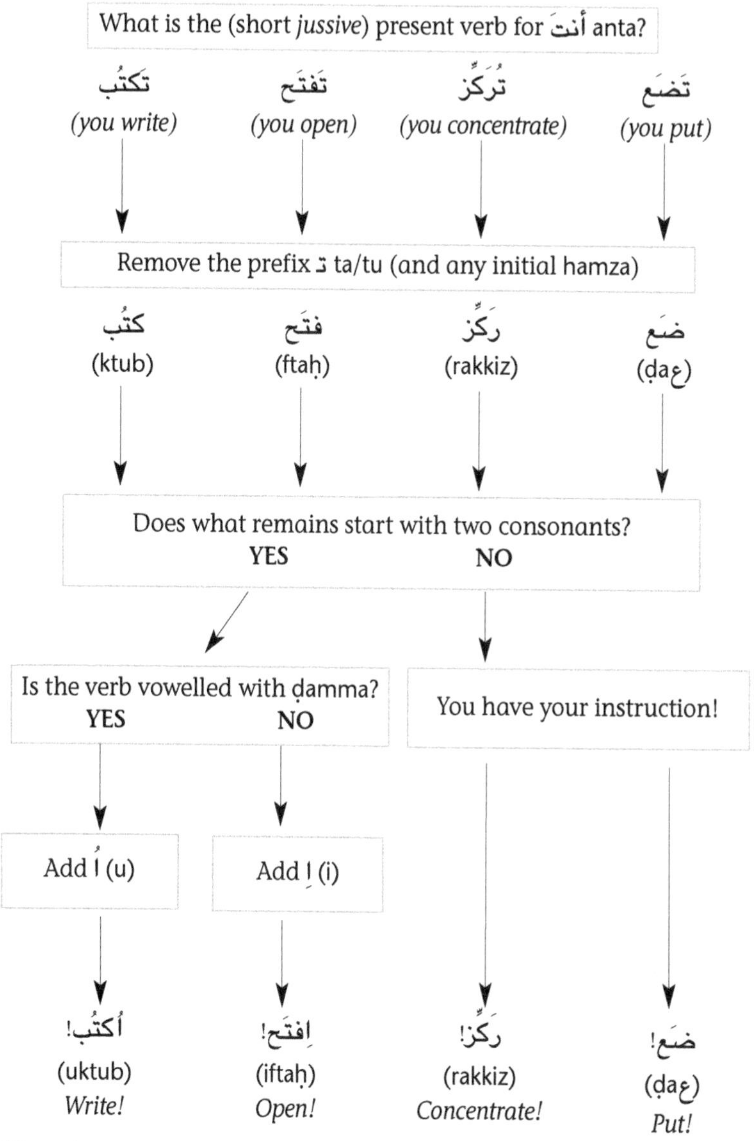

These instructions are masculine singular. To make feminine singular, add ي ī: افتحي iftaḥī; to make plural add وا ū: افتحوا iftaḥū.

Note that Form IV verbs start their imperative with a- rather than u- or i-:

Present	Imperative
تُرسل (tursil) you send	أرسِل! (arsil) send!

The verb that is fed into the top of the chart on page 145 should be the short (*jussive*) form of the verb – the same form that is used for a past negative after لم lam (see page 91). For regular verbs this distinction is not significant, but for hollow and defective verbs, the long vowel of the present tense may become short in the jussive, and so also be short in the imperative. Look at how these common verbs are made into instructions:

Present	Imperative (m/f/pl)
تقول (taqūl) you say/tell	قُل/قولي/قولوا! (qul/qūlī/qūlū) say/tell!
ترمي (tarmī) you throw	اِرمِ/اِرمي/اِرموا! (irmi/irmī/irmū) throw!
تجيب (tujīb) you answer	أجِب/أجيبي/أجيبوا! (ajib/ajībī/ajībū) answer!

Making a negative instruction

Negative instructions are made by using لا lā plus the (jussive) present verb – this time including the prefix تـ ta/tu:

(lā taktubī ismik) !لا تكتبي اسمك	Don't write *(f.)* your name!
(lā taqul lanā) !لا تقل لنا	Don't tell *(m.)* us!
(lā tatakallamū) !لا تتكلّموا	Don't talk *(pl.)*!

Exercise 7 تمرين ٧

Look back at page 144 and identify the following instructions the invigilator gave to the students. (All the instructions are in the plural.)

1 Read all the questions well.
2 Put your mobile phones in your bags.
3 Listen to these important instructions.
4 Don't talk at all during the exam.
5 Concentrate on your (own) papers.
6 Don't turn over the question paper.
7 Write the date.
8 Don't look at your fellow student's papers.
9 Begin with the easiest.

Exercise 8 تمرين ٨

Make instructions from the verbs below, as in the example. Use the chart on page 145, your dictionary and the notes opposite to help you.

	Past	Present	Instruction	Negative
draw	رسم	ترسِم	ارسِم!	لا تَرسِم!
mention	ذكر			
study	درس			
explain	شرح			
fill	ملأ			
use	استعمل			
complete	أكمل			
colour	لوّن			
describe	وصف			
close/switch off	أغلق			
stop	وقف			

Exercise 9 تمرين ٩

Some of the instructions from the exam question paper have been shredded by mistake. Can you join the two halves correctly as in the example? Use the extra vocabulary in the box to help you.

جملة، جمل (jumla, jumal) sentence	**حوار، ات** (ḥiwār, -āt) dialogue
سؤال، أسئلة (su'āl, as'ila) question	**معنى، معانٍ** (maɛnā, maɛānin) meaning
نص، نصوص (naṣṣ, nuṣūṣ) text	**فراغ، ات** (farāgh, -āt) blank/gap
علامة، ات (ɛalāma, -āt) mark/tick	**التالي** (at-tālī) the following

أمام الجملة الصحيحة.	استمع إلى
الحوار التالي.	اقرأ
الفراغات في الجمل.	اشرح
معنى الكلمات التالية.	اجب
النصّ التالي.	انظر
إلى الصُوَر.	املأ
على الأسئلة التالية.	صف
الصورة التي أمامك.	ضع علامة [✓]

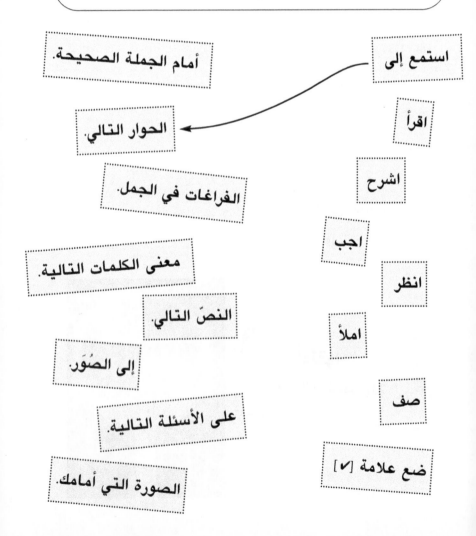

في صالة الامتحانات fī ṣālat il-imtiḥānāt *(in the examination hall)*

Exercise 10 تمرين ١٠

How would you give these instructions in Arabic?

1 Turn over the picture. *(to a male)*

2 Read these books. *(to a group)*

3 Switch off the television. *(to a female)*

4 Draw a picture of the room. *(to a group)*

5 Send me an email. *(to a female)*

6 Don't use mobile phones. *(to a group)*

7 Write a suitable word in the gap. *(to a male)*

8 Listen to the conversation. *(to a group)*

9 Tell me the meaning of the word. *(to a male)*

10 Don't answer these questions. *(to a female)*

العالم العربي ... نظرة على الجزائر

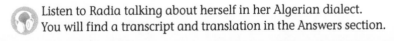

Arabic in Algeria العربيّة في الجزائر

Algeria was the last of the North African countries to gain independence in 1960. The fierce struggle was made more complicated by the fact that Algeria was considered a 'département' (an integral part of France) rather than a colony.

French has left its mark in the spoken dialect of Algeria, in a similar way to the other francophone North African countries. The Berber language is also an influence.

Some features of Algerian dialect are:

- use of verbal prefix نـ n- to refer to 'I': نـحب nḥibb (I like)
- specifically Algerian expressions such as بصح baṣṣeḥ (but) and ع على خاطر alakhaṭr (because)
- extensive use of French vocabulary (listen for the French words 'Août' (August) and 'famille' (family) in the extract)

Listen to Radia talking about herself in her Algerian dialect. You will find a transcript and translation in the Answers section.

BBC ARABIC.com

مساعدة | نصوص فقط

آخر تحديث: الأربعاء 31 أغسطس 2005 GMT 15:39

للمرة الأولى، تعليم الأمازيغية بالمدارس الجزائرية

أميمة احمد بي بي سي - الجزائر

تقارير مراسلينا

عودة الروح: عنوان القصة الفلسطينية، لكن بدون

قررت وزارة التربية الجزائرية لأول مرة تعليم اللغة الأمازيغية في العام الدراسي المقبل بدءا من السنة الرابعة ابتدائي.

وقال وزير التربية، بوبكر بن بوزيد، إن تعليم الأمازيغية سيطبق في بعض الولايات النموذجية، ومن ثم يتم تعميمه على جميع الولايات الجزائرية.

وقد رحب بعض الجزائريين الأمازيغ في تعليم الأمازيغية في المدارس، بدلا من تعلمها شفاهة من الوالدين.

ويقول كريمو (25 سنة) وهو من بني مزاب، في ولاية غرداية، ويعمل في مواد البناء: "شئ جيد أن يتم تعليم لغتنا، ويتعلمها الأطفال الصغار، وهي ليست صعبة التعلم".

تسليم "أبو قتادة"

تربية (tarbiya) education, upbringing *(sometimes used as an alternative to* تعليم*)*

بدءاً من (bad'an min) starting from

سيُطبَّق (sa-yuṭabbaq) will be applied

نموذجيّ (namūdhajīy) model *(adj)*

تعميم (taعmīm) general application

رحّب، يرحّب (raḥḥab, yuraḥḥib) to welcome

شفاهة (shifāhatan) orally ('by lip')

الأسئلة

١ متى سيبدأ تعليم الأمازيغية؟

٢ من أيّة مرحلة مدرسية؟

٣ ما هو اسم وزير التربية الجزائري؟

٤ هل سيُطبَّق في كلّ الولايات في البداية؟

٥ هل كريمو ضدّ تعليم الأمازيغية؟

'Berber' is a term used by outsiders from the Romans to the Arabs. The Berbers themselves prefer the indigenous word أمازيغ amāzīgh (Tamazight) to describe their ethnicity. The Tamazight language is still widely spoken and in some places is part of the curriculum. The article above concerns its introduction into Algerian schools.

Vocabulary in Unit 9

Nouns الأسماء

education	تَعليم
training	تَدريب
education/upbringing	تَربِية
teaching	تَدريس
studying	دِراسة
stage	مَرحَلة (ات)
class/grade	صَفّ (صُفوف)
kindergarten	رَوضة (رِياض)
course	دَورة (ات)
age	عُمر (أعمار)
subject	مادّة (مَوادّ)
science	عِلم (عُلوم)
biology	عِلم الأحياء
physics	عِلم الفيزياء
chemistry	عِلم الكيمياء
economics	عِلم الاِقتِصاد
sociology	عِلم الاِجتِماع
pyschology	عِلم النَفس
philosophy	الفَلسَفة
medicine	الطِبّ
law	الحُقوق
literature	الآداب
business studies	التِجارة
engineering	الهَندَسة
civil engineering	الهَندَسة المدنيّة
algebra	الجَبر
Chinese (language)	اللُغة الصينيّة
exam	اِمتِحان (ات)
student	دارِس (ون/ين)
instructor/teacher	مُعَلِّم (ون/ين)
instructions	تعليمات
scientist	عالِم (عُلَماء)
colleague, fellow (student)	زَميل (زُمَلاء)
sentence	جُملة (جُمَل)
question	سُؤال (أسئِلة)
text	نَصّ (نُصوص)
mark/tick	عَلامة (ات)
dialogue	حِوار (ات)
meaning	مَعنى (مَعانٍ)
blank/gap	فِراغ (ات)
wish	أُمنِية (ات)
bell	جَرَس (أجراس)
general application	تعميم
dust	تُراب

Adjectives الصفات

primary	اِبتِدائيّ
middle (school)	إعداديّ/مُتَوَسِّط
secondary	ثانويّ
talented (at)	مَوهوب (في)
excelling (in)	مُتَفَوِّق (في)
difficult to learn	صَعب التَعَلُّم
positive	إيجابيّ

negative	سَلبيّ
scholastic/school *(adj)*	مَدَرَسيّ
educational	تَعليميّ
scientific	عِلميّ
coming/next	مُقبِل
forbidden	مَمنوع
model *(adj)*	نَموذَجيّ

Verbs الأفعال

be good at	أجاد، يُجيد
think/believe	ظَنَّ، يَظُنّ
know	عَلِمَ، يَعلَم
instruct	عَلَّمَ، يُعَلِّم
learn	تَعَلَّمَ، يَتَعَلَّم
teach	دَرَّسَ، يُدَرِّس
enrol	سَجَّلَ، يُسَجِّل
advise	نَصَحَ، يَنصَح (بِ)
put, place	وَضَعَ، يَضَع
give	أعطَى، يَعطي
turn over	قَلَبَ، يَقلِب
concentrate	رَكَّزَ، يُرَكِّز
contact	اِتَّصَلَ، يَتَّصِل
complain	شَكا، يَشكو
benefit (from)	اِستَفاد، يَستَفيد (من)
mention	ذَكَرَ، يَذكر
explain	شَرَحَ، يَشرَح
fill	مَلأَ، يَملأ
use/employ	اِستَعمَلَ، يَستَعمِل
complete	أكمَلَ، يُكمِل
colour	لَوَّنَ، يُلَوِّن
close/switch off	أغلَقَ، يُغلِق
stop	وَقَفَ، يَقِف
apply	طَبَّقَ، يُطَبِّق
welcome	رَحَّبَ، يُرَحِّب

***Other phrases* العبارات الأخرى**

should/ought to	يَنبَغي على
examination hall	صالة الاِمتِحانات
candidate number	رَقم الجُلوس
question paper	وَرَقة الإجابة
answer paper	وَرَقة الأسئِلة
starting with	بَدءاً من
orally	شِفاهةً

Additional note: Exercise instructions

For the final units of *Mastering Arabic 2* most of the exercise instructions will be in Arabic. This will help you to understand written instructions in material for native speakers and when Arabic is used as part of examinations for learners of Arabic.

If necessary, clarification or additional details will be included in English in the instructions.

unit 10

News and media
الأخبار ووسائِل الإعلام

يا خَبَر اليوم بِفلُوس... بُكرة ببلاش.
News that costs money today... tomorrow will be free.
(Egyptian proverb)

Talking about the news التكلُّم عن الأخبار

الأخبار الدُوَليّة
(al-akhbār ad-duwalīyya)
international news

المجتمع
(al-mujtamaع)
society

الأخبار المحليّة
(al-akhbār al-maḥallīyya)
local news

الثقافة والفنّ
(ath-thaqāfa wal-fann)
culture and art

السياسة
(as-siyāsa)
politics

الطبّ والصحّة
(aṭ-ṭibb waṣ-ṣiḥḥa)
medicine and health

الاقتصاد والمال
(al-iqtiṣāḍ wal-māl)
economics and finance

العلوم والتكنولوجيا
(al-ع ulūm wal-taknūlūjiyā)
science and technology

الرياضة
(ar-riyāḍa)
sport

الطقس والمناخ
(aṭ-ṭaqs wal-munākh)
weather and climate

Exercise 1 تمرين ١

اقرأ هذه العناوين *(headlines)* **واكتب نوع الخبر، كما هو موضح في المثال.**

Don't worry about understanding every word. Try to categorise the headlines according to the topics on page 154, using the extra vocabulary below to help you.

١ الخسارة الثانية لميلان في الكأس الايطالي ______ الرياضة

٢ نجاح كبير لمعرض الفنّون اللبنانية في لندن ______

٣ عمره ١٠٨ سنوات ولم يرَ طبيباً في حياته ______

٤ ارتفاع نسبة الطلاق في السنة الماضية ______

٥ خمس فوائد رائعة للنوم المبكر ______

٦ نسبة الرطوبة تزيد كلّ سنة! ______

٧ مؤتمر دولي للتعرّف على احتياجات المرأة ______

٨ علماء الفيزياء يشرحون تجربة الانفجار العظيم ______

٩ البنك المركزي يرفع أسعار الفائدة مرة أخرى ______

١٠ البرلمان يصوّت على قانون المرور الجديد ______

١١ وفاة أشهر نجمات السينما الصامتة ______

١٢ زيت الزيتون يحدّ من الكولسترول الضارّ ______

١٣ زيادة التوتُّر في العلاقات بين دول إفريقيا ______

خسارة (khasāra) defeat, loss

نجاح (najāḥ) success

ارتفاع (irtifāع) increase

نسبة (nisba) proportion, percentage

طلاق (ṭalāq) divorce

فائدة، فوائد (fā'ida, fawā'id) interest, benefit

انفجار (infijār) explosion

صوّت، يصوّت (ṣawwata, yaṣawwit) to vote

قانون، قوانين (qānūn, qawānīn) law, statute

حدّ، يحدّ (ḥadda, yaḥidd) to limit, to restrict

توتُّر (tawattur) strain, stress

Exercise 2 تمرين ٢

اكتب العبارة *(phrase)* **العربيّة بجانب الانجليزيّة، كما هو موضح في المثال.**

You'll find all the phrases in the headlines on page 155.

1 harmful cholesterol ______ الكولسترول الضارّ

2 sleeping early ______

3 silent movies ______

4 traffic law ______

5 the needs of women ______

6 the Big Bang ______

7 the Italian cup ______

8 level of humidity ______

9 last year ______

10 strain in relations ______

11 a great success ______

12 interest rates ______

Broadcasting الإذاعة

Arabic uses the word محطّة maḥaṭṭa (pl. محطّات maḥaṭṭāt) to refer to a radio station but قناة qanāt (pl. قنوات qanawāt) to refer to a television station. In addition, television channels can either be أرضيّة arḍīyya ('earthly', *terrestrial*) or فضائيّة faḍā'īyya ('spacey', *satellite*). The transmission (البثّ al-baththth) can be حيّ ḥayy (*live*) and مباشر mubāshir (*direct*), or مسجّل musajjal (*recorded*).

مكة	غرينتش	نوع البث	مادة البث
17:55	14:55	إعادة	القرى الفلسطينية 1948- بيار عدس
18:00	15:00	حي	موجز الأخبار
18:07	15:07	مسجل	عين على العالم
18:15	15:15	حي	النشرة الرياضية
18:30	15:30	حي	الاقتصاد اليوم
19:00	16:00	حي	الجزيرة هذا المساء
19:57	16:57	مسجل	صور حالة الطقس
20:00	17:00	حي	موجز الأخبار
20:05	17:05	مسجل	برنامج وثائقي- سبتمبر الأخرى ج2
21:00	18:00	حي	نشرة الأخبار
21:30	18:30	حي	ما وراء الخبر
22:00	19:00	حي	موجز الأخبار
22:05	19:05	حي	بلا حدود- محمد العدلوني
23:00	20:00	حي	حصاد اليوم

(www.aljazeera.net)

Exercise 3 تمرين ٣

انظر إلى الجدول *(schedule)* في صفحة ١٥٧ وأجب على الأسئلة التالية:

1 What is the significance of the two columns of numbers on the left of the schedule on page 157?

2 How many programmes are live this evening?

3 What Arabic word is used meaning 'repeat'?

4 When is the only repeat showing? What is it about?

5 How many news programmes are shown in the schedule?

6 What do you think the word موجز mūjaz means in the phrase موجز الأخبار?

7 What time is the programme *Behind the News*?

8 Is the programme *Eye on the World* live or recorded? What about *Without Limits*?

9 What is the name of the programme concerned with the economy?

10 When can you see the latest sports news?

11 What time is the weather forecast?

12 The programme أكثر من رأي is advertised at the top of the schedule for later in the week. What kind of programme do you think this is and when is it showing?

الدوحة، قطر *Doha, Qatar*

Qatar is one of the Gulf countries home to pan-Arab satellite TV companies.

REVIEW: **Formal Arabic** الفصحى

It is common to think of Arabic as having a clear division between the formal Modern Standard Arabic (MSA) of the press and official communication and the informal colloquial dialects of everyday speech. In reality this is over-simplistic. The distinction has always been blurred and is becoming more so in the age of instant information and live broadcasting.

There are broadcast programmes both in colloquial (films and soap operas) and MSA (news and current affairs). Standard Arabic itself works on several different levels. At the top end is the 'high' Arabic used in formal scripted speeches and by scholars and media professionals. In the middle is a version used for educated live debate and spontaneous discussion. Finally at the lower level there is a utilitarian version – often a mixture of MSA and colloquial – used by many Arabic-speakers for pan-Arab communication. Within one programme – a live debate and listener phone-in, for example – it is possible to hear all these different levels from the various participants.

Mastering Arabic concentrates on teaching the less formal version of Standard Arabic, the 'middle way', since you are unlikely to need to produce 'high' Arabic unless you are planning a career as a news announcer or an academic scholar! However, it is important to be able to listen to and understand the more formal version.

Although there are some phrases restricted mainly to formal MSA, understanding 'high' Arabic is largely a question of recognising familiar vocabulary with fully pronounced endings. These endings represent:

1. Grammatical cases on nouns and adjectives
Most words take the case endings shown below. (More details of how the cases are formed and used are in the Structure Note sections of *Mastering Arabic 1*.)

	indefinite	definite
nominative	ولدٌ walad<u>un</u>	الولدُ al-walad<u>u</u>
accusative	ولداً walad<u>an</u>	الولدَ al-walad<u>a</u>
genitive	ولدٍ walad<u>in</u>	الولدِ al-walad<u>i</u>

(*Tip:* If the case ending is added to a word ending with tā' marbūṭa the final t is pronounced: madrasa<u>tun</u>, al-madras<u>tu</u>, etc.)

2. Final vowels on present tense verbs
Present verbs with no suffix end with ḍamma (-u) when fully pronounced: يشربُ (yashrab<u>u</u>, he drinks). This becomes fatḥa (-a) in the subjunctive يشربَ (yashrab<u>a</u>) and sukūn in the jussive يشربْ (yashrab). See pages 73 and 91 for more details of the subjunctive and jussive.

Listen to these news headlines from earlier in the unit delivered firstly in formal Standard Arabic by a radio announcer, and then less formally, as if read out loud by someone to a friend.

نجاحٌ كبيرٌ لمعرضِ الفنونِ اللبنانيةِ في لندن

A great success for the exhibition of Lebanese arts in London

نسبةُ الرطوبةِ تزيدُ كلَّ سنةٍ!

The level of humidity rises every year!

البرلمانُ يصوّتُ على قانونِ المرورِ الجديد

Parliament votes on the new traffic law

البنكُ المركزيُّ يرفعُ أسعارَ الفائدةِ مرّةً أخرى

The central bank raises interest rates once more

Exercise 4 تمرين ٤

استمع إلى موجز الأخبار وضع علامة ✔، كما هو موضح في المثال.

Just try to get the gist of each headline the first time you listen.

					✔		عنوان ١
							عنوان ٢
							عنوان ٣
							عنوان ٤
							عنوان ٥

Exercise 5 تمرين ٥

استمع مرة أخرى إلى الموجز واملأ الفراغات، كما هو موضح في المثال.

Tip: أيها السادة المستمعون ayyuhā s-sādatu l-mustamiعūn ('dear listeners') is a common way of addressing radio listeners. The television equivalent is أيها السادة المشاهدون ayyuhā s-sādatu l-mushāhidūn ('dear viewers').

أيها السادة المستمعون مرحباً بكم في __موجز__ أخبار الساعة السادسة.

البرلمان يوافق بالإجماع على ______ الهجرة *(immigration)* **الجديد، ورئيس الوزراء يصف التصويت بأنه نَصر** *(victory)* **______ للديموقراطية.**

سفينة ______ الروسية تبعث بأوّل صور للكوكب ______ ، والعلماء حول العالم يحتفلون *(celebrate)* **بهذا الاكتشاف** *(discovery)* **الرائع.**

قمة المجموعة ______ تطلب من البنوك المركزيّة التعاون معها في مكافحة التضخُّم *(curbing inflation)* **في ______ وآسيا.**

يوم ______ للعرب في الدورة الأوليمبيّة: ذهبيّة لمصر في الجودو وللإمارات في الرماية *(shooting)* **وللمغرب في العدو ولتونس في ______ .**

طبيب يمنيّ يكتشف علاجاً *(a cure)* **لسقوط الشعر باستخدام زيت ______ وأوراق شجر التين.**

والآن، إليكم الاخبار بالتفصيل....

Arabic on the Worldwide Web العربيّة على الشَبَكة العالميّة

Like many other languages, Arabic has had to adapt quickly to the terminology of the computer and internet age. Words have been adopted from English, for example the words إنترنت (Internet), كمبيوتر (computer) and إيمايل (email) have come straight into Arabic. Some of the loan words used have pure Arabic equivalents, for example 'computer' is also حاسوب ḥāsūb from the root ḥ/s/b (to calculate). The more extreme Anglicisms might not be acceptable in a more formal context, for example أونلاين ('online') or كيبورد ('keyboard').

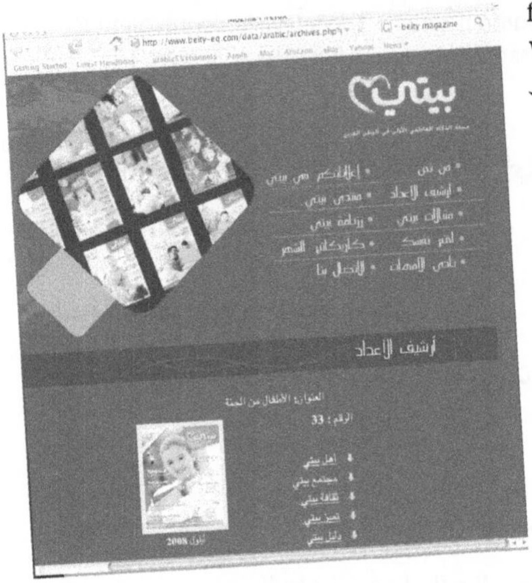

Existing Arabic words are being applied to new concepts. For example, مدوّنة mudawanna, traditionally used to refer to a diary or journal, is now also used to mean 'blog'; منتدى muntadan (assembly room) to mean 'forum'; افتراضي iftirāḍīy (imaginary) to mean 'virtual'; and تفاعلي tafāعulīy (reactive) to mean 'interactive'. In addition, new Arabic words are being coined on the hoof to suit the circumstances – for example مكلمة maklama ('place of talking') for 'chatroom'.

Comparing media مقارنة وسائل الإعلام

To compare the different news media, we first need to review the two ways of making adjectives comparative in Arabic.

afعal *pattern*

For short, basic adjectives the root letters can be put into the afعal pattern to produce a comparative:

أكثر (akthar) more ← كثير (kathīr) many

أصغر (aṣghar) smaller ← صغير (ṣaghīr) small

أشهر (ash-har) more famous ← شهير (shahīr) famous

Doubled roots are written together in the comparative pattern, and adjectives with a final weak root are written with alif maqṣūra:

أخفّ (akhaff) lighter ← خفيف (khafīf) light (weight)

أقوى (aqwā) stronger ← قوي (qawī) strong

أحلى (aḥlā) sweeter ← حلو (ḥilw) sweet

akthar + *noun*

For longer adjectives, in particular those derived from forms of the verb, the comparative is formed by using akthar (more). In these comparative constructions, the adjective needs to be transformed into a noun.

أكثر إثارةً (akthar ithāratan) more exciting ← مثير (muthīr) exciting

أكثر تفاعلاً (akthar tafāعulan) more interactive ← تفاعليّ (tafāعulīy) interactive

The structure in Arabic is 'more as to excitement', 'more as to interactivity'. The 'as to' is reflected in the accusative ending -an, carried by alif tanwin if the noun does not end in ta marbūṭa.

Exercise 6 **تمرين ٦**

كوّن مقارنات، كما هو موضح في المثال.

١ عميق (عamīq) deep ← أعمق ________

٢ غنيّ (ghanī) rich ← ________

٣ محدّد (muḥaddad) limited ← ________

٤ تضخُّمي (taḍakhkhumīy) inflationary ← ________

٥ مبدع (mubdiع) creative ← ________

٦ تحليليّ (taḥlīlīy) analytical ← ________

٧ حديث (ḥadīth) modern ← ________

٨ محتشم (muḥtashim) modest ← ________

٩ مسلٍّ (musallin) entertaining ← ________

The King's speech خطاب الملك

Students of communications have been asked to compare the coverage (تغطية taghṭiya) across different media of a speech given by the king to parliament. One of their reports is shown below.

خِطاب الملك أمام البرلمان

مُقارنة تغطية وسائل الإعلام

في البداية اختَرتُ صَحيفة يوميّة ومجلّة أسبوعيّة ورأيتُ أن المجلة الأسبوعيّة ركّزت على التحليل العميق في عامود رئيس التَحرير، بَينَما الصحيفة اليوميّة غطَّت الموضوع دون تحليل بسبب ضيق الوقت.

وبعد ذلك قارنتُ التغطية في قنوات التليفزيون الأرضيّة بالتغطية في الفضائيّات. وبدا لي أن تغطية الفضائيات للخطاب عن طريق البثّ المباشر والحوارات بين المذيعين والضيوف كانت أكثر إثارةً من القنوات الأرضيّة التي أذاعته مسجلاً في المساء. وأخيراً، رأيتُ أن المُساهمات الشعبية التي وجدتُها على الانترنت كانت أكثر تفاعُلاً وتسليةً من التليفزيون، وذلك بفضل فُرَص التصويت والآراء الكثيرة المكتوبة في المدوّنات والمنتديات.

Exercise 7 تمرين ٧

ضع علامة ✓، كما هو موضح في المثال.

Which media are included in the report?

Daily newspapers	✔	Radio	☐
Weekly newspapers	☐	Terrestrial TV	☐
Weekly magazines	☐	Satellite TV	☐
Mobile phones	☐	Internet	☐

Exercise 8 تمرين ٨

اكتب مقارنة.

Find a prominent news story in the Arabic- or English-language press and compare the coverage of the story in three or or more media. Use the report opposite and the table below to help you present your findings.

في الصحيفة (fīṣ-ṣaḥīfa) in the newspaper	أكثر إثارةً (akthar ithāratan) more exciting	تغطية ... كانت (taghṭiyat ... kānat) the coverage of ... was	وجدتُ أنّ... (wajadtu anna) I found that
في المجلّة (fīl-majalla) in the magazine	أكثر تحليليةً (akthar taḥlīlīyyatan) more analytical		رأيتُ أنّ... (ra'aytu anna) I saw that
في التليفزيون (fīt-tilīfizyūn) on the television	أكثر تفاعلاً (akthar tafāع ulan) more interactive		بدا لي أنّ... (badā lī anna) It appeared to me that
على الانترنت (عalā l-intarnat) on the internet	أكثر تسليةً (akthar tasliyatan) more entertaining		
etc.	etc.		

Try to link your opinions together using expressions such as بينما baynamā (whereas) and بفضل bifaḍl (thanks to). For example:

وجدتُ أن تغطية زيارة الرئيس كانت أكثر تحليليةً في الصحيفة بينما كانت أكثر إثارةً في التليفزيون بفضل المناقشة الحيّة.

I found that the coverage of the president's visit was more analytical in the newspaper whereas it was more exciting on the television thanks to the live discussion.

العالم العربي ... نظرة على الخليج واليمن

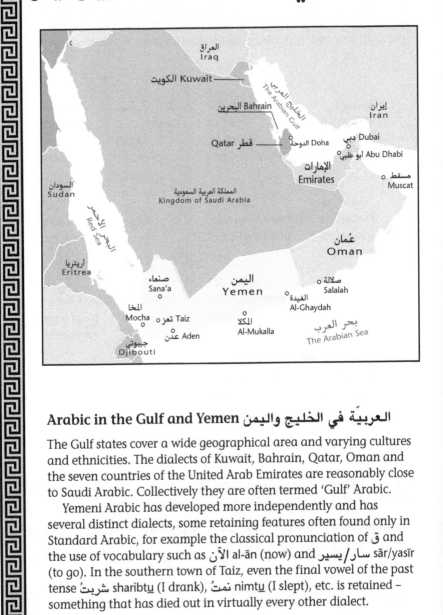

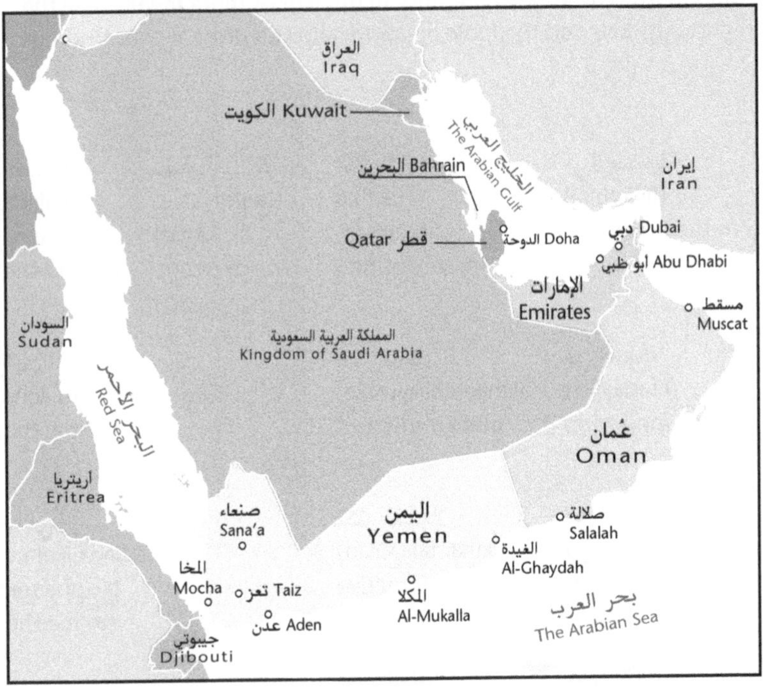

Arabic in the Gulf and Yemen العربيّة في الخليج واليمن

The Gulf states cover a wide geographical area and varying cultures and ethnicities. The dialects of Kuwait, Bahrain, Qatar, Oman and the seven countries of the United Arab Emirates are reasonably close to Saudi Arabic. Collectively they are often termed 'Gulf' Arabic.

Yemeni Arabic has developed more independently and has several distinct dialects, some retaining features often found only in Standard Arabic, for example the classical pronunciation of ق and the use of vocabulary such as الآن al-ān (now) and سار/يسير sār/yasīr (to go). In the southern town of Taiz, even the final vowel of the past tense شربتُ sharibtu̲ (I drank), نمتُ nimtu̲ (I slept), etc. is retained – something that has died out in virtually every other dialect.

Listen to Mohammed talking about himself in his Yemeni dialect. You will find a transcript and translation in the Answers section.

في التسعينات شعرت دول الخليج بالفراغ الإعلامي العربي خاصة أثناء حرب الخليج الثانية حيث كان مصدر الأخبار الوحيد هو قناة سي إن إن (CNN) الإخبارية الأمريكية. ومن هنا، مالت دول الخليج نحو البث الفضائي، فبدأت باستئجار قنوات فضائية خاصة بها على الأقمار الصناعية المتاحة في ذلك الوقت.

وفي فترة قصيرة، ساهم البث الفضائي في تسويق الدول الخليجية حول العالم، وشجّع على تطوير أنشطة كثيرة بدأت جميعها خلال التسعينات من القرن الماضي، مثل المهرجانات الثقافية والفنية والمعارض التجارية والصناعية والكثير من الأنشطة الأخرى التي أدت إلى زيادة كبيرة في زوّار دول الخليج.

حرب الخليج (ḥarb al-khalīj) the Gulf war
مصدر، مصادر (maṣdar, maṣādir) source
مال، يميل نحو (māla, yamīl naḥwa) to incline toward
استئجار (isti'jār) renting
متاح (mutāḥ) available
تسويق (taswīq) marketing
شجّع، يشجّع (shajjaεa, yushajjiε) to encourage
مهرجان، ات (mahrajān, āt) festival
زائر، زوّار (zā'ir, zuwwār) visitor

الأسئلة

١ ما كان مصدر الأخبار الوحيد أثناء حرب الخليج؟

٢ كيف بدأت الدول الخليجيّة البثّ الفضائيّ؟

٣ ما هي فوائد القنوات الفضائية للدُوَل الخليجيّة؟

The Gulf is home to many of the Arab world's satellite TV companies. Smaller states such as the UAE and Qatar are keen to provide backing for this kind of broadcasting as such ventures can enhance their profile, influence and image in the region and beyond. The article above outlines the rise of satellite stations in the Gulf countries.

Vocabulary in Unit 10

Nouns الأسماء

news item (*pl* = news)	خَبَر (أخبار)
media	وَسائِل الإعلام
broadcasting	إذاعة
transmission	بَثّ
coverage	تَغطِية
analysis	تَحليل
channel	قَناة (قَنَوات)
headline	عُنوان (عَناوين)
column	عامود (عَواميد)
topic	مَوضوع (مَواضيع)
source	مَصدَر (مَصادِر)
repeat	إعادة (ات)
broadcaster	مُذيع (ون/ين)
editor	رَئيس (رُؤَساء) التَحرير
listener	مُستَمِع (ون/ين)
viewer	مُشاهِد (ون/ين)
politics	السِياسة
finance	المال
society	المُجتَمَع
technology	التكنولوجيا
proportion/percentage	نِسبة
climate	مُناخ (ات)
defeat	خَسارة (ات)
success	نَجاح (ات)
increase	اِرتِفاع (ات)

interest/benefit	فائِدة (فَوائِد)
law/statute	قانون (قَوانين)
divorce	طَلاق (ات)
stress/tension	تَوَتُّر
need/requirement	اِحتِياج (ات)
explosion	اِنفِجار (ات)
experiment/test	تَجرِبة (تَجارِب)
cholesterol	الكولَسترول
traffic	المُرور
immigration	هِجرة
inflation	تَضَخُّم
curbing	مُكافَحة
victory	نَصر
shooting	رِماية
discovery	اِكتِشاف (ات)
cure	عِلاج (ات)
computer	حاسوب (ات)
blog/journal	مُدَوَّنة (ات)
forum	مُنتَدىً (مُنتَدَيات)
participation	مُساهَمة (ات)
rental/renting	اِستِئجار
marketing	تَسويق
festival/carnival	مَهرَجان (ات)
visitor	زائِر (زُوّار)
the Gulf	الخَليج

Adjectives الصفات

international	دُولِيّ
local	مَحَلّيّ
terrestrial	أرضيّ
satellite *(adj)*	فَضائيّ
daily	يَوميّ
weekly	أُسبوعيّ
live	حَيّ
direct	مُباشِر
recorded	مُسَجَّل
interactive	تَفاعُليّ
popular/public	شَعبيّ
early	مُبكِّر
silent	صامِت
deep/profound	عَميق
available	مُتاح

Verbs الأفعال

cover	غطّى، يُغَطّي
compare	قارَنَ، يُقارِن
vote	صَوَّتَ، يُصَوِّت
limit	حَدَّ، يَحِدّ
explore/study	تَعرَّفَ، يَتَعَرَّف على
incline (towards)	مالَ، يَميل (نحو)
celebrate	احتَفَلَ، يَحتَفِل
encourage	شَجَّعَ، يُشَجِّع

Other phrases العبارات الأخرى

the Big Bang	الانفِجار العَظيم
the Gulf War	حَرب الخَليج
again ('another time')	مَرَّة أُخرَى
news summary	موجَز الأخبار
Worldwide Web	الشَبَكة العالميّة
dear…	أيُّها السادة…
…listeners	…المُستَمِعون
…viewers	…المُشاهِدون
it seemed that	بَدا أن
thanks to	بِفَضل

unit 11

Climate and the environment
المُناخ والبيئة

الشاطِرة تَغزل بِرِجل حمار.

The clever woman spins with a donkey's leg.

Talking about weather and climate التكلُّم عن الطقس والمناخ

شمس/ مشمس
(shams/mushmis)
sun/sunny

عاصفة، عواصف
(ɛāṣifa, ɛawāṣif)
storm

مطر/ ممطر
(maṭar/mumṭir)
rain/rainy

ضباب
(ḍabāb)
fog

ثلج/ مثلج
(thalj/muthlij)
snow/snowy

صحو
(ṣaḥw)
fine, clear

سحابة، سحب
(saḥāba, suḥub)
cloud

جافّ
(jāff)
dry

ريح، رياح
(rīḥ, rīyāḥ)
wind

غائم
(ghā'im)
overcast, cloudy

اتّجاه الريح (ittijāh ar-rīḥ) wind direction

سرعة الريح (surɛat ar-rīḥ) wind speed

كثيف (kathīf) thick (fog, etc.)

سحب منخفضة (ṣuḥub munkhafiḍa) low clouds

تراوح، يتراوح (tarāwaḥa, yatarāwaḥ) to vary

مضطرب (muḍṭarib) unsettled

Tip: 'the weather' in Arabic is either الطقس aṭ-ṭaqs or الجوّ al-jaww, the latter also meaning 'the atmosphere'. The more general word for 'climate' is المناخ al-munākh. 'Climate change' is تغيير المناخ taghyīr al-munākh.

Exercise 1 تمرين ١

استمع إلى النشرة الجويّة وضع علامة ✔، كما في المثال.

إن السحب كثيفة ومنخفضة. inna s-suḥub kathīfa wa-munkhafiḍa

(The clouds are thick and low.)

Exercise 2 تمرين ٢

انظر إلى تَنَبُّؤات الطقس في تونس وأجب على الأسئلة التالية:

ما هي...

١ درجة الحرارة في تونس يوم الأحد؟

٢ درجة الحرارة في المنستير يوم السبت؟

٣ سرعة الريح يوم الأحد؟

٤ اتجاه الريح يوم السبت؟

٥ درجة الحرارة في جربة يوم الاثنين؟

٦ نسبة الرطوبة يوم الاثنين؟

٧ درجة الحرارة في قفصة السبت؟

٨ نسبة الرطوبة يوم الأحد؟

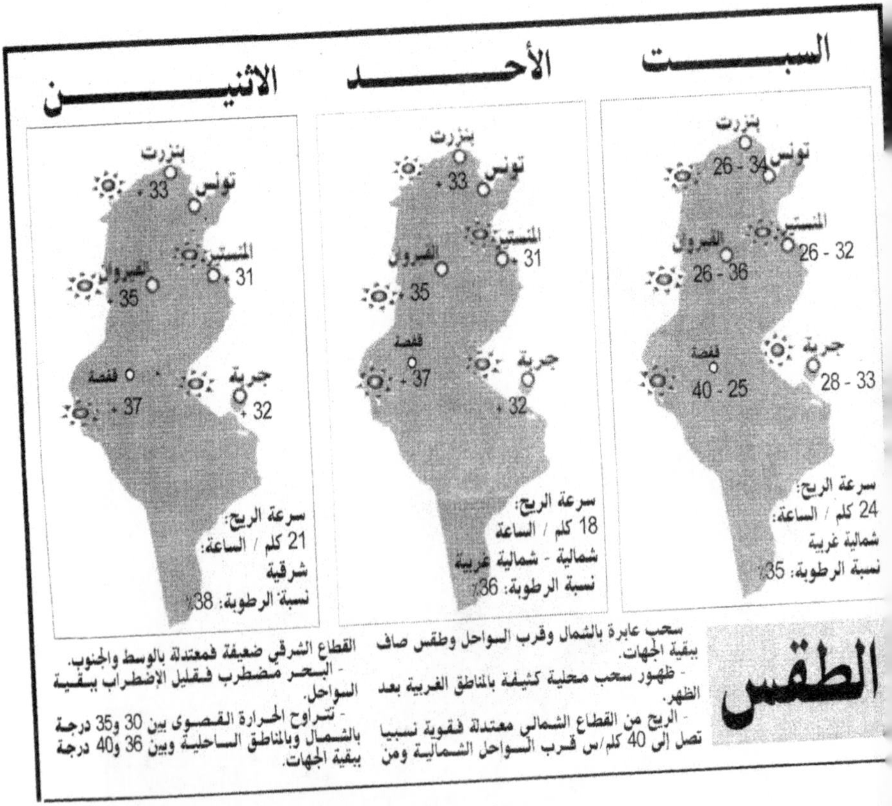

Tip: Adjectives can be formed from the compass directions, for example: جنوب janūb (south), جنوبيّ janūbīy (southerly, or southern); غرب gharb (west), غربيّ gharbīy (westerly, or western).

The seasons الفُصول

الربيع (ar-rabīع)

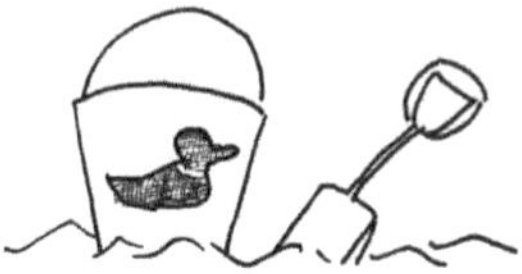

الصيف (aṣ-ṣayf)

الخريف (al-kharīf)

الشتاء (ash-shitā')

Exercise 3 تمرين ٣

Zeinah is talking about the climate in Lebanon.

استمع إلى زينة واختر الإجابة الصحيحة.

١ المناخ في لبنان عُموماً...

معتدل ☑ ممطر ☐ جافّ ☐

٢ نسبة الرطوبة في لبنان...

عالية ☐ عالية جدّاً ☐ منخفضة ☐

٣ في الصيف الجوّ...

بارد ومثلج ☐ حارّ وممطر ☐ جافّ ومشمس ☐

٤ في الشتاء يوجد ثلج...

على الشاطئ ☐ على الجبال ☐ في المُدُن ☐

٥ أحياناً في الربيع هناك رياح شديدة و...

عواصف ☐ ضباب ☐ رطوبة ☐

٦ درجة الحرارة في الخريف بين...

١٥ و٢٠ ☐ ٢٠ و٢٥ ☐ ٢٥ و٣٠ ☐

Exercise 4 تمرين ٤

صف المناخ في بلدك مقارنةً بمناخ لبنان.

Compare the climates in general and say something specific about the weather in each season. You could start something like this:

إنّ المناخ في لبنان عُموما معتدل والجوّ في الصيف جافّ وحارّ. أما في بلدي، فالمناخ أيضاً معتدل ولكنه ممطر جدّاً حتّى في الصيف.

The climate in Lebanon is generally moderate and the weather in summer is hot and dry. As for my country, the climate is also moderate but it's very rainy, even in summer.

Holiday plans خِطَط العُطلة

Maha and her husband are discussing whether to go on holiday to the coast (الساحل as-sāḥil) or to the desert (الصحراء aṣ-ṣaḥrā') .

Exercise 5 تمرين ٥

استمع إلى المناقشة واكتب ملاحظات (notes)، كما في المثال.

Copy the table below and make notes on the advantages and disadvantages of each type of holiday as you hear about them in the discussion.

Advantages		Disadvantages	
coast الساحل	desert الصحراء	coast الساحل	desert الصحراء
short journey	*peaceful*	*crowded*	*long journey*

REVIEW: The future المستقبل

There is no separate future tense in Arabic. Verbs can be given a future meaning by putting سـ sa- or سوف sawfa in front of the present tense.

سنصل قبل الظهر. (sa-naṣil qabla ẓ-ẓuhr)	We will arrive before noon.
سيجدون لنا شقّة. (sa-yajidūna lanā shaqqa)	They will find an apartment for us.
ستكون درجة الحرارة منخفضة بالليل. (sa-takūn darajat al-ḥarāra munkhafiḍa bil-layl)	The temperature will be low at night.
سوف تستغرق الرحلة ساعتين فقط. (sawfa tastaghriq ar-riḥla sāعatayn faqaṭ)	The journey will take two hours only.

Negative

You can make a future negative by putting لن lan in front of a present verb. Lan is emphatically negative, and carries the implication of 'definitely not' or 'not ever'. The verb following lan is the subjunctive (see page 73), and so any final nūn will disappear:

لن أنام في الخيمة. (lan anām fīl-khayma)	I won't sleep in the tent.
ألن تأكلي السمك؟ (a-lan ta'klī as-samak)	Won't you *(fem.)* eat the fish?
لن يجدوا لنا غرفة في الفندق. (lan yajidū lanā ghurfa fīl-funduq)	They won't find a room for us in the hotel.

Exercise 6 تمرين ٦

How do you say these in Arabic?

1 The weather will be hot tomorrow.

2 It will be rainy on Saturday.

3 I will find a room in a hotel for us.

4 We will go to the coast.

5 The journey will take six hours.

6 He won't sleep before nine o'clock.

7 My sister won't arrive before us.

8 Won't they eat the meat?

Talking about possibilities التكلّم عن الاحتمالات

إذا/إن ذهبنا ... فسَنزور ...

future + (so) فَـ ... past + (if) إذا/إن

You can talk about future possibilities using إذا idhā or إن in, both meaning 'if' (إن being a little more formal). Notice that the first verb is in the past tense – literally 'if we *went*...', 'if you *drove*' – although the meaning is 'if we *go*...', 'if you *drive*...'. It is usual to introduce the second half of the sentence using فـ fa- ('then' or 'so'):

إذا ذهبنا إلى الصحراء، فسنرى واحات كثيرة. (idhā dhahabnā ilā ṣ-ṣaḥrā, fa-sa-narā wāḥāt kathīra)	If we go to the desert, (then) we'll see lots of oases.
إذا قُدتَ السيّارة، فستكون تعبان جداً. (idhā qudta s-sayyāra, fa-satakūn taعbān jiddan)	If you *(masc.)* drive, (then) you'll be very tired.
إن لم نقتصد في الطاقة، فلن نوقف تغيير المناخ. (in lam naqtaṣid fī ṭ-ṭāqa, fa-lan nūqif taghyīr al-munākh)	If we don't save energy, (then) we won't stop climate change.

Exercise 7 تمرين ٧

املا الفراغات في الجمل، كما في المثال.

Choose a verb from below and use the correct tense and subject (in brackets after the sentence). You can use a verb more than once.

go ذهب/يذهَب	eat أكل/يأكُل	drink شرِب/يشرَب
visit زار/يزور	drive قاد/يقود	reserve حجز/يحجِز
arrive وصل/يصِل	buy اِشترَى/يَشترَي	see رأى/يرى

١ إذا ذهبنا إلى الساحل، فسنأكل سمكاً كلّ يوم. (نحن)

٢ إذا ______ إلى الصحراء، فـ______ الماء من البئر. (أنتِ)

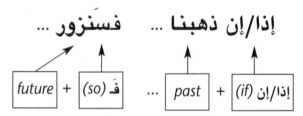

٣ إذا .... المتحف، فـ .... التِمثال (statue) الشهير. (هي)

٤ إذا .... قبلنا، فـ .... غرفة لنا. (هم)

٥ إذا .... السيارة، فلن .... قبل الساعة التاسعة. (أنا)

٦ إن لم .... التذكرة اليوم فلن .... المسرحية. (أنتَ)

The second half of an 'if' sentence can be an instruction (see page 145):

إذا وصلتِ قبلنا، فاحجزي لنا غرفة. (idhā waṣalti qablanā, fa-ḥjizī lanā ghurfa)	If you *(fem.)* arrive before us, (then) reserve a room for us.
إذا لم تكن مشغولاً، فساعدني. (idhā lam takun mashghūlan, fa-sāعidnī)	If you *(masc.)* are not busy, (then) help me.

إذا لَم تَكُن مَطَرًا يا حَبيبي... فَكُن شَجَرًا

If you're not [the] rain, my love, then be [the] trees

مُشبِعاً بالخُصوبةِ...كُن شَجَرًا.

Full of fertility... be [the] trees.

وإن لَم تَكُن شَجَرًا يا حَبيبي... فَكُن حَجَرًا

And if you're not [the] trees, my love, then be [the] stones

مُشبِعاً بالرُطوبةِ...كُن حَجَرًا.

Full of moisture... be [the] stones.

وإن لَم تَكُن حَجَرًا يا حَبيبي ... فَكُن قَمَرًا

And if you're not [the] stones, my love... then be a moon

في مَنام الحَبيبةِ ...كُن قَمَرًا

In the dreams of a loved one... be a moon.

From حالة حصار *(State of Seige)* by Mahmoud Darwish (Palestinian poet, 1941–2008)

Al-Mustaqbal Beverages Company شركة مشروبات المستقبل

Listen to the guide taking a group on a tour of a drinks factory.

بدأ نشاط الشركة قبل عشرين سنة.

الآلات في المصنع تُدار بالطاقة الشمسية لأنّها طاقة طبيعية وصديقة للبيئة.

تُستَخرَج المِياه المَعدِنيّة من الآبار في أعماق الصحراء.

أما العصير فيُستخلَص من الليمون العُضوي...

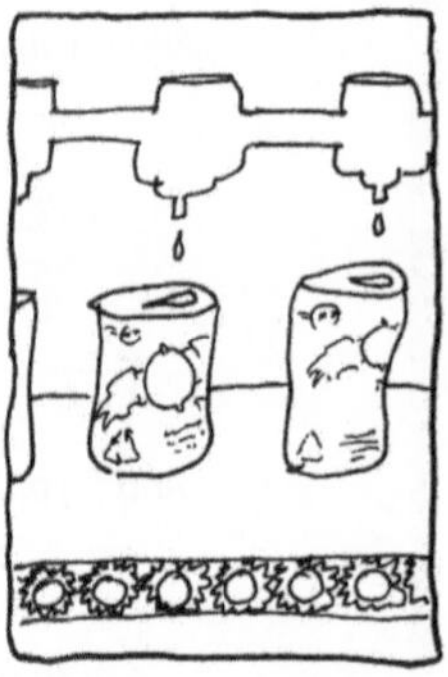

ويُضاف إلى بعض مشروباتنا.

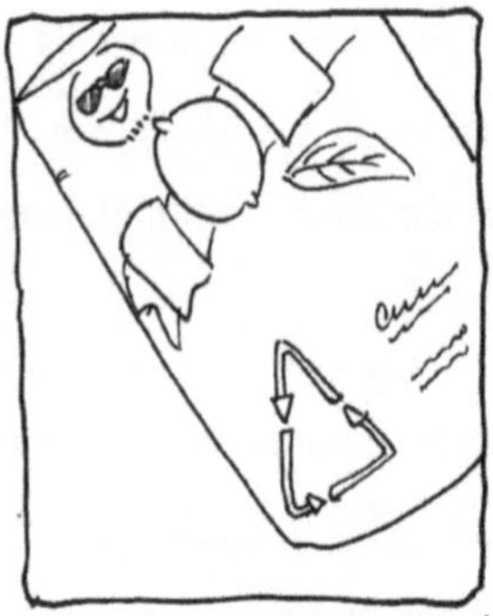

تُعبّأ المشروبات في عُلَب يمكن إعادة تدويرها مَنعاً للتلوُّث.

وأخيراً تُنقَل مشروباتنا إلى السوق لتُباع للناس.

Exercise 8 تمرين ٨

اقرأ النصّ واكتب العبارة الصحيحة، كما في المثال.

Don't try and understand every word yet, just pick out the phrases below.

1 mineral water(s) المياه المعدنيّة

2 solar energy ....

3 organic lemons ....

4 can be recycled ....

5 environmentally friendly ....

6 preventing pollution ....

Talking about processes التكلّم عن الاجراءات

Sometimes a process is more important than who or what carries out that process. In this case, we often use a *passive* verb. Examples of the passive in English would be 'the juice *is extracted*', 'the machines *are operated* by solar energy' (rather than the *active* 'we *extract* the juice', 'solar energy *operates* the machines').

In Arabic the passive is made by changing the vowelling of a verb. In the present tense, the first vowel is changed to a ḍamma and the final vowel to fatḥa. This is true for *all* forms of the verb. Basic verbs in the present tense only have ḍamma/fatḥa in the passive; derived verbs retain any additional vowelling in the middle:

يَنقُل (yanqul) transports → يُنقَل (yunqal) is transported
يَستَخرِج (yastakhrij) extracts → يُستَخرَج (yustakhraj) is extracted
يُعَبِّئ (yuɛabbi') packages → يُعَبَّأ (yuɛabba') is packaged

The final fatḥa vowel of the passive turns any long vowel in present tense hollow and defective verbs into a long ā:

يَبيع (yabīɛ) sells → يُباع (yubāɛ) is sold
يُدير (yudīr) operates → يُدار (yudār) is operated
يُضيف (yuḍīf) adds → يُضاف (yuḍāf) is added

Assimilated verbs drop the first root letter wāw in the active present, but the wāw reappears as a long ū in the passive:

يَجِد (yajid) finds → يُوجَد (yūjad) is found
يَضَع (yaḍaɛ) puts → يُوضَع (yūḍaɛ) is put

Exercise 9 تمرين ٩

اكمل الترجمة.

Look at the Arabic text on page 178 and complete the English below.

- The company's activities ______________ 20 years ago.
- The machines in the factory are ______________ by solar energy because it is ______________ energy and environmentally friendly ('a friend to the environment').
- The mineral water is ______________ from wells in the far reaches of the ______________ .
- As for the ______________ , it is squeezed from organic ______________ ...
- ... and ______________ to some of our drinks.
- The drinks are ______________ in cartons that can be ______________ preventing pollution.
- Finally our drinks are ______________ to the market and ______________ to the public (' people').

Conversation المحادثة

Imagine you work for the Drinks of the Future Company and you are the tour guide talking about the factory and the processes.

- review the guided tour on page 178. Replay the audio, pausing and repeating each step out loud;
- try to memorise as much of the Arabic as you can.

Now deliver the tour speech yourself. You can use the pictures on page 178 as prompts, but try not to look at the Arabic.

Keep repeating this until you are fluent. Memorising and delivering a speech will help with your vocabulary and oral confidence.

There's no additional recording for this conversation, but you can replay the tour guide on page 178 to check your version.

Talking about processes in the past

The principle of changing the vowelling of a verb to create the present passive extends to the past passive. As for the present, the first vowel in the past passive is a ḍamma, but the final vowel in the past passive is kasra. You may also see an additional ḍamma as the middle vowel in derived forms:

نَقَلَ (naqala) transported → نُقِلَ (nuqila) was transported

وَجَدَ (wajada) found → وُجِدَ (wujida) was found

اِستَخرَجَ (istakhraja) extracted → اُستُخرِجَ (ustukhrija) was extracted

The final kasra vowel of the past passive creates a long ī in the derived forms of hollow verbs. However, the past passive of basic hollow verbs has no initial ḍamma, leaving *only* the long ī:

أدارَ (adāra) operated → أُديرَ (udīra) was operated

باعَ (bāɛa) sold → بيعَ (bīɛa) was sold

Exercise 10 تمرين ١٠

Convert these past verbs into the passive, as in the example.

1 صَنَعَ (ṣanaɛa) manfactured → صُنِعَ (ṣuniɛa)

2 اِستَخدَمَ (istakhdama) used/employed→ ……

3 قالَ (qāla) said → ……

4 اِستَخلَصَ (istakhlaṣa) squeezed/extracted → ……

5 أَضافَ (aḍāfa) added → ……

6 عبّأَ (ɛabba'a) packaged → ……

Exercise 11 تمرين ١١

Imagine that the Al-Mustaqbal Beverages factory was forced to close down and that you are now describing the former company. Re-write the description of the processes, this time using *past* verbs. Begin like this:

- الآلات في المصنع أُديرَت بالطاقة الشمسية لأنّها طاقة طبيعية وصديقة للبيئة.

العالم العربي ... نظرة على ليبيا

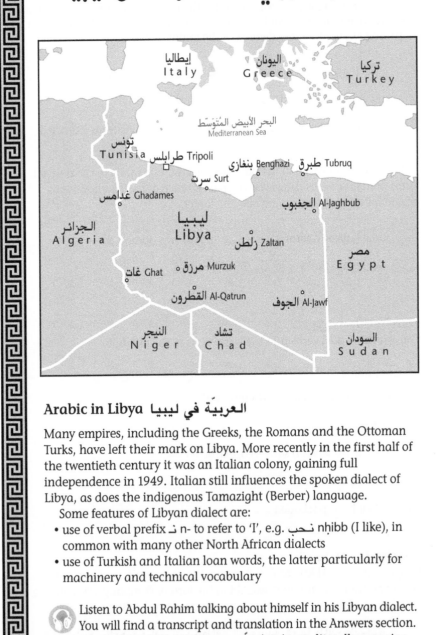

Arabic in Libya العربيّة في ليبيا

Many empires, including the Greeks, the Romans and the Ottoman Turks, have left their mark on Libya. More recently in the first half of the twentieth century it was an Italian colony, gaining full independence in 1949. Italian still influences the spoken dialect of Libya, as does the indigenous Tamazight (Berber) language.

Some features of Libyan dialect are:

- use of verbal prefix نـ n- to refer to 'I', e.g. نـحب nḥibb (I like), in common with many other North African dialects
- use of Turkish and Italian loan words, the latter particularly for machinery and technical vocabulary

Listen to Abdul Rahim talking about himself in his Libyan dialect. You will find a transcript and translation in the Answers section. (Notice how Abdul Rahim uses طبعاً ṭabعan, literally meaning 'of course' or 'naturally', as a general filler word.)

مشروع، ات (mashrūع, āt) project
صناعي (sināعīy) manmade/manufactured
حفر، يحفر (ḥafara, yaḥfir) to dig
أنبوبة، أنابيب (anbūba, anābīb) pipe
ضخم (ḍakhm) huge
قطر (quṭr) diameter
طول (ṭūl) height/length
متر، أمتار (mitr, āmtār) metre
كيلومتر (kilūmitr) kilometre
مياه عذبة (miyāh عadhba) fresh water
بحيرة، ات (buḥayra, āt) lake

بدأ مشروع النهر الصناعي العظيم عام ١٩٨٤.

حُفِرَت آبار كثيرة في الصحراء الجنوبيّة ووُضِعَت أنابيب ضخمة في الأرض يبلغ قُطر كلّ منها أربعة أمتار وطولها سبعة أمتار.

إن طول النهر الصناعي أربعة آلاف كيلومترا تمتدّ من آبار واحات الكفرة في الجنوب الشرقي وآبار جبل الحساونة في الجنوب الغربي.

تُنقَل المياه العَذبة عَبر الأنابيب حتّي تصل إلى الساحل في الشمال في رحلة تستغرق تسعة أيام. تُجمَع المياه عند وصولها إلى الشمال في خمس بحيرات صناعية.

الأسئلة

١ متى بدأ المشروع؟
٢ أين حُفرت الآبار؟
٣ ما هو قُطر الأنابيب وطولها؟
٤ ما هو طول النهر الصناعيّ؟
٥ كم يوماً تستغرق رحلة المياه؟
٦ أين تُجمع المياه عند وصولها؟

The 'Great Manmade River' is an ongoing ambitious project to carry water stored in vast quantities in rock under the southern Libyan Sahara desert to the coastal towns and agricultural areas in the North. The Libyans call it 'the eighth wonder of the world'. Libya has no major natural rivers and the project has reduced its reliance on expensive desalination plants.

Vocabulary in Unit 11

Nouns الأسماء

climate	مُناخ (ات)
rain	مَطَر (أمطار)
snow	ثَلج (ثُلوج)
cloud	سَحابة (سُحُب)
wind *(f)*	ريح (رِياح)
storm	عاصِفة (عَواصِف)
fog	ضَباب
direction	اتِّجاه (ات)
speed	سُرعة (ات)
atmosphere/weather	جوّ (أجواء)
forecast	تَنَبُّؤات
spring	الرَبيع
summer	الصَيف
autumn/fall	الخَريف
winter	الشِتاء
coast	ساحِل (سَواحِل)
beach	شاطِئ (شَواطِئ)
desert *(f)*	صَحراء (صَحارَى)
oasis	واحة (ات)
lake	بُحَيرة (ات)
statue	تِمثال (تَماثيل)
machine/instrument	آلة (ات)
power/energy	طاقة (ات)
pollution	تَلَوُّث
project/scheme	مَشروع (ات)
pipe/tube	أنبوبة (أنابيب)
diameter/section	قُطر (أقطار)
height/length	طول (أطوال)
metre	مِتر (أمتار)
kilometre(s)	كيلومِتر

Adjectives الصفات

sunny	مُشمِس
rainy	مُمطِر
snowy	مُثلِج
dry	جافّ
thick	كَثيف
passing/transient	عابِر
unsettled/disturbed	مُضطَرِب
organic	عُضَويّ
manmade/manufactured	صِناعيّ
huge	ضَخم
tired	تَعبان

Verbs الأفعال

see	رَأَى، يَرَى
vary	تَراوَحَ، يَتَراوَح
conserve/save	اِقتَصَدَ، يَقتَصِد في
stop/prevent	أوقَفَ، يُوقِف
operate/manage	أدارَ، يُدير
extract	اِستَخرَجَ، يَستَخرِج

extract essence of/squeeze (juice)
اِستَخلَصَ، يَستَخلِص

package عَبَّأ، يُعَبِّئ

transport نَقَلَ، يَنقُل

dig حَفَرَ، يَحفِر

Other phrases العبارات الأخرى

climate change تَغيير المُناخ

weather forecast النَشرة الجَويّة

recycling إعادة تَدوير

environmentally friendly
صَديق للبيئة

mineral water مِياه مَعدِنيّة

fresh water مِياه عَذبة

in the depths of في أعماق

preventing/avoiding مَنعاً لـ...

unit 12

Health and happiness
الصحّة والسعادة

الصِحّة تاج على رُؤوس الأصِحاء لا يَراهُ إلا المَرضى.

Health is a crown on the heads of the healthy that only the sick can see.

Talking about the body التكلّم عن الجسم

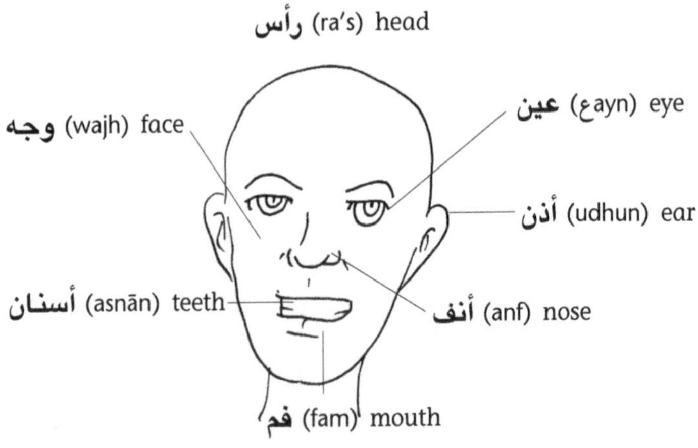

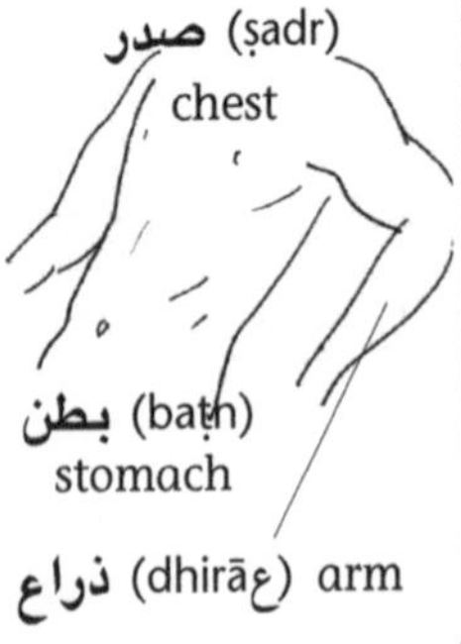

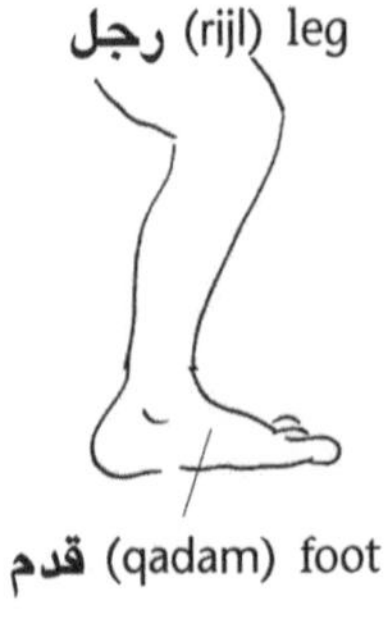

Tip: There are alternative words for some of the parts of the body, two of the most common being ساق sāq for 'leg' and معدة miعda for 'stomach'.

Exercise 1 تمرين ١

اكتب العربية والإنجليزية، كما في المثال.

ط ن ب

١ بطن (stomach)

ر ص د

٢ ________

أ ر س

٣ ________

ج ل ر

٤ ________

ر ع ذ ا

٥ ________

ف ن أ

٦ ________

ب إ ص ع

٧ ________

ن ي ع

٨ ________

س ن ن أ ا

٩ ________

ن ذ أ

١٠ ________

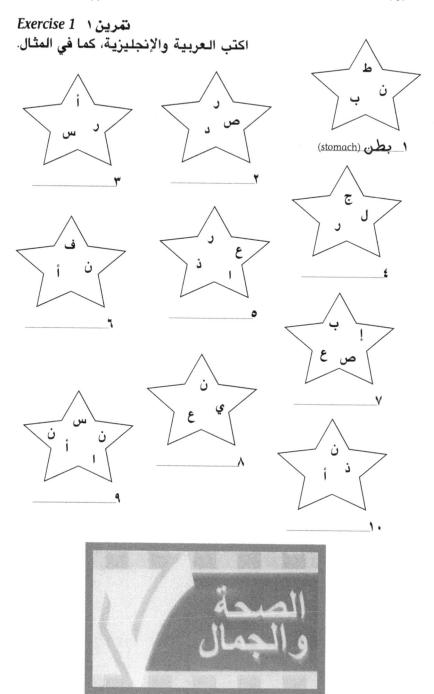

Supermarket aisle sign: aṣ-ṣiḥḥa wal-jamāl *(Health and Beauty)*

Talking about illness التكلّم عن المرض

The equivalent of 'what's the matter' is ما بك؟ mādhā bika/ki?, literally 'what with you?'. Here are expressions you could use to describe your ailments:

أشعر بالمرض. (ashʿur bil-maraḍ)	I feel ill.
عندي صداع. (ʿindī ṣudāʿ)	I have a headache.
عندي برد/حمّى. (ʿindī bard/ḥummā)	I have a cold/a fever.
عندي ألم (شديد) في... (ʿindī alam (shadīd) fī...)	I have a (bad) pain in...
أنا مصاب(ة) بـ... (anā muṣāb(a) bi...)	I'm suffering from...
عندي حساسيّة من... (ʿindī ḥassāsīyya min...)	I have an allergy to...

Exercise 2 تمرين ٢

استمع واكتب الرقم الصحيح.

Match the ailments with the patients on the recording. for example, **١c**.

a

b

c
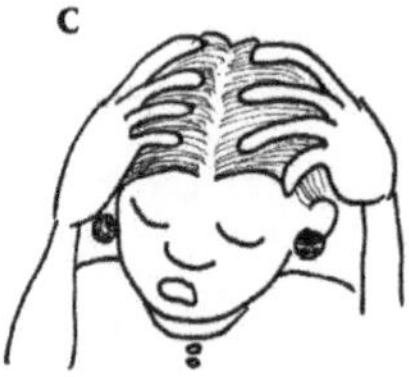

d

e

f

g

h

At the pharmacy في الصَيدَليّة

A customer is asking for advice at the pharmacy.

ـ صباح الخير. ممكن أُساعِدَك؟

ـ أنا أشعر بالمرض.

ـ ماذا بك بالضَبط؟ هل عندك صُداع؟

ـ نعم، وأيضاً عندي آلام في رجليَّ وذراعيَّ.

ـ همم... هل تشعر بأعراض أخرى؟

ـ نعم، عندي ألم شديد في بطني. لا أستطيع أن آكل.

ـ الطقس حارّ جدّاً. هل كُنت في الشمس؟

ـ طبعاً، أنا شرطيّ مرور!

ـ أشُكّ أنك مصاب بِضَربة شمس. جَرِّب هذا الدَواء، اشرب ماءً كثيراً ولا تقف في الشمس.

ـ أنا عندي حساسية من البراسيتمول. هل هناك براسيتمول في الدواء؟

ـ نعم، نعم. لا تأخذ هذا الدواء إذاً. أنصَحك باستشارة الطبيب في أسرع وقت.

Tip: Parts of the body that come in pairs (legs, eyes, etc.) are usually feminine: رجل مكسورة rijl maksūra (a broken leg). If referring to both parts, you will need to use the dual: رجلان طويلتان rijlān ṭawīlatān ([two] long legs), آلام في قدميَّ ālām fī qadamayya (pains in my [two] feet).

بالضبط (biḍ-ḍabṭ) exactly

أعراض (aƐrāḍ) symptoms

شرطيّ مرور (shurṭīy murūr) traffic policeman

دواء (dawā') medicine

استشارة (istishāra) consultation

Exercise 3 تمرين ٣

استمع إلى المحادثة في الصيدلية وأجب على الأسئلة بالإنجليزية.

1 What are the first questions the pharmacist asks the customer?

2 What symptoms other than a headache does the customer have?

3 Why does the customer have to work in the sun?

4 What does the pharmacist think he is suffering from? Can you find the Arabic expression for the ailment?

5 Why can the customer not take the medicine suggested?

6 What does the pharmacist advise he does?

Exercise 4 تمرين ٤

استمع مرّة ثانية واملأ الفراغات، كما في المثال.

Try to complete the exercise *without* looking at the transcript on page 189.

ـ صباح _____ . ممكن أُساعِدَك؟

ـ أنا _____ بالمرض.

ـ ماذا بك بالضَبط؟ هل عندك _____ ؟

ـ نعم، وأيضاً عندي آلام في _____ وذراعيَّ.

ـ همم... هل تشعر بأعراض أخرى؟

ـ نعم، عندي ألم _____ في بطني. لا أستطيع أن آكل.

ـ الطقس _____ جدّاً. هل كُنت في الشمس؟

ـ طبعاً، أنا _____ مرور!

ـ أشُكّ أنك _____ بضربة شمس. جَرِّب هذا _____ ، اشرب ماءً كثيراً ولا تقف في _____ .

ـ أنا عندي _____ من البراسيتمول. هل هناك براسيتمول في الدواء؟

ـ نعم، نعم، لا تأخذ هذا الدواء _____ . أنصَحك باستشارة الطبيب في _____ وقت.

ṣaydalīyat suhā al-jadīda; khidma arbaع‎a wa-ع‎ishrīn sāع‎a
(The new Soha Pharmacy; 24 hour service)

Exercise 5 تمرين ٥

Write out the dialogue on page 189 again, but change the customer to a female.

Conversation المحادثة

You don't feel well and you're going to the pharmacy to take some advice. These are your symptoms:

- a headache
- pains in your stomach
- a fever
- a bad pain in your ear

You also have an allergy to penicillin (البنيسيلين).

Prepare what you will need to say and then join in the conversation on the recording, following the prompts.

Talking about health التكلّم عن الصحّة

Here are some of the factors that can influence health. Notice how general concepts usually include الـ al- (التدخين at-tadkhīn, [the] smoking).

(at-tadkhīn) التدخين	smoking
(akl al-khuḍrawāt) أكل الخضروات	eating vegetables
(at-tamrīnāt ar-riyāḍīyya) التمرينات الرياضيّة	physical exercise
(talawwuth al-hawa') تلوّث الهواء	air pollution
(as-saعāda) السعادة	happiness
(at-tawattur) التوتّر	stress
(al-badāna) البدانة	obesity
(taqlīl al-milḥ) تقليل الملح	reducing salt
(al-hawā' aṭ-ṭalq) الهواء الطلق	fresh air

Exercise 6 تمرين ٦

اكتب العبارات في العامود *(column)* الصحيح، كما في المثال.

ضارّ بالصحّة **harmful to health**	مُفيد للصحّة **beneficial to health**
التدخين	أكل الخضروات

Now make statements about two contrasting factors, as in this example:

التدخين ضارّ جدّاً بالصحّة <u>في حين أن</u> أكل الخضروات مُفيد.

Smoking is very harmful to health <u>whereas</u> eating vegetables is beneficial.

Giving advice

You have already met ينبغي على yanbaghī ع alā (to be incumbent on) and ينصح yanṣaḥ (to advise).

Another useful and very flexible structure is من الـ... أن min al-... an. Literally this means 'from the ... that ...'. It can be used with a number of different possibilities to produce the equivalents of the English 'should', 'must', 'might', etc.

MUST = 'it is imperative that'	من اللازِم أن
NEED TO = 'it is necessary that'	من الضَروريّ أن
SHOULD = 'it is incumbent that'	من المَفروض أن
LIKELY TO = 'it is probable that'	من المُرَجَّح أن
MIGHT = 'it is possible that'	من المُحتَمَل أن

من اللازم أن أُقلع عن التدخين. (min al-lāzim an uqliع ع an at-tadkhīn)	I must give up smoking.
من الضروريّ أن ترى طبيباً. (min aḍ-ḍarūrīy an tarā ṭabīban)	You *(masc.)* need to see a doctor.
من المفروض أن تقلّلي من الملح. (min al-mafrūḍ an taqillilī min al-milḥ)	You *(fem.)* should reduce salt.
من المرجّح أنه سَيضرّ بصحّتك. (min al-murajjaḥ annahu sa-yaḍurr bi-ṣiḥḥatak)	It is likely that it will damage your health.
من المحتمل أن يسبّب ارتفاع الضغط. (min al-muḥtamal an yusabbib irtifāع aḍ-ḍaghṭ)	It might cause a rise in [blood] pressure.

The combination of أن an and لا lā becomes ألا allā (that not).

من اللازم ألا تأكل الطعام الدهنيّ. (min al-lāzim allā ta'kul aṭ-ṭaعām ad-duhnīy)	You *(masc.)* must not eat fatty food.
من المفروض ألا تعملي كلّ يوم. (min al-mafrūḍ allā taعmalī kull yawm)	You *(fem.)* should not work every day.

Exercise 7 تمرين ٧

كيف تقول هذه الجمل بالعربية؟

1 He should give up smoking.

2 We need to eat vegetables every day.

3 You *(masc.)* must do physical exercise every day.

4 You *(fem.)* should not eat fatty food. It might damage your health.

5 Air pollution is likely to damage our health.

6 You *(pl.)* mustn't put a lot of salt on your food.

Exercise 8 تمرين ٨

إنصح هؤلاء الأشخاص.

Try to give them as much advice as possible using the language that you know. There's no single correct answer, but you'll find some suggestions in the answer section.

Tip: In colloquial Arabic, the construction 'min al-… an' is often reduced to just the key word. So min al-lāzim an would become simply lāzim; min aḍ-ḍarūrī an would become ḍarūrī: lāzim tākul al-khuḍrawāt (you must eat vegetables); ḍarūrī aktub eemayl (I need to write an email).

Abdul Aziz asks for advice عبد العزيز يطلب نصيحة

Abdul Aziz is waiting for the result of a blood test (تحليل الدم taḥlīl ad-dam). While he's waiting he writes a note to his friend, Safwan.

عزيزي صفوان،

أكتب لك هذا الخطاب وأنا أنتظر نَتيجة تحليل الدم.

قال لي الطبيب إن ضغط دمي عالٍ جداً ومن الضروري أن أتناول حبوباً لعلاج هذا الخَلَل.
وذكر أيضاً أنه ينبغي عليّ أن أُقلع عن التدخين لأنه ضارّ بالصحّة عموماً كما أنه من أسباب ارتفاع الضغط عندي.

في الحقيقة يا صفوان أنا لا أشعر بأي مرض ولا أريد الإقلاع عن التدخين أو تناوُل الدواء كلّ يوم. أنا صغير في السنّ وأريد أن أستمتع بحياتي.

ما رأيك؟ هل أنا على حقّ؟ أم أنّي عنيد وغبيّ كما وَصَفَني صديقنا حمدي؟

المخلص عبد العزيز

نتيجة، نتائج (natīja, natā'ij) result

تناول، يتناول (tanāwala, yatanāwal) to take (pills)/to eat

حبّة، حبوب (ḥabba, ḥubūb) pill

خلل، خلال (khalal, khilāl) condition/disorder

ارتفاع (irtifāع) increase/rise

استمتع، يستمتع بـ (istamtaعa, yastamtiع bi-) to enjoy

على حق (عala ḥaqq) right/correct

عنيد (عanīd) stubborn

غبي (ghabī) stupid

Exercise 9 تمرين ٩

اقرأ الخطاب في صفحة ١٩٥ وأجب على الأسئلة التالية:

1 What health problem has the doctor told Abdul Aziz he suffers from?

2 What two things is the doctor suggesting that Adbul Aziz does to tackle the problem?

3 How is Adbul Aziz feeling at the moment?

4 What is his attitude to the doctor's advice?

5 Why does he feel this way?

6 What does he tell Safwan about their friend Hamdy's reaction?

Safwan's reply رَدّ صفوان

The next day Safwan emailed this reply to Adbul Aziz.

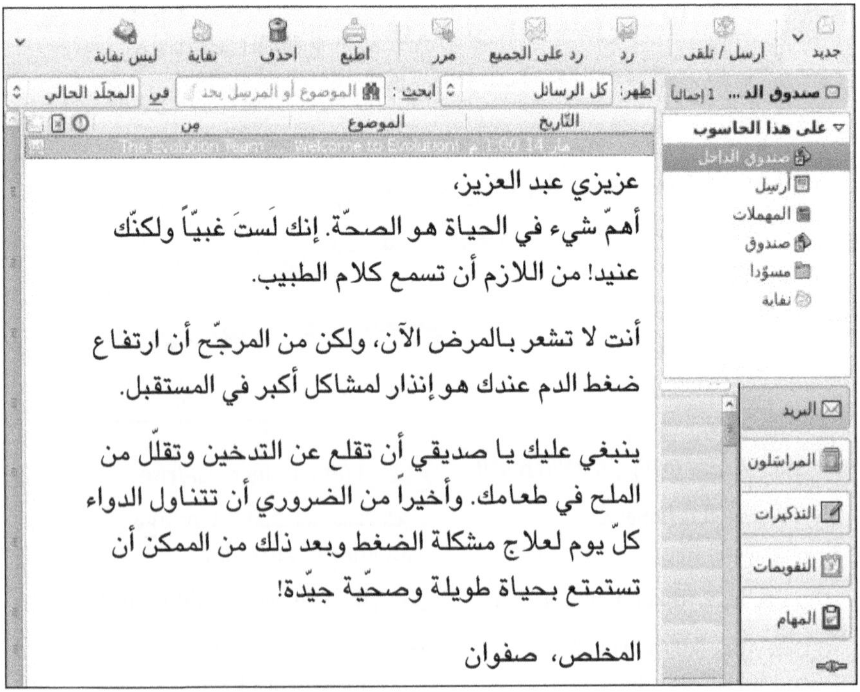

عزيزي عبد العزيز،

أهمّ شيء في الحياة هو الصحّة. إنك لَستَ غبيّاً ولكنّك عنيد! من اللازم أن تسمع كلام الطبيب.

أنت لا تشعر بالمرض الآن، ولكن من المرجّح أن ارتفاع ضغط الدم عندك هو إنذار لمشاكل أكبر في المستقبل.

ينبغي عليك يا صديقي أن تقلع عن التدخين وتقلّل من الملح في طعامك. وأخيراً من الضروري أن تتناول الدواء كلّ يوم لعلاج مشكلة الضغط وبعد ذلك من الممكن أن تستمتع بحياة طويلة وصحّية جيّدة!

المخلص، صفوان

Exercise 10 تمرين ١٠

اقرأ ايمايل صفوان وصِل بين العربية والإنجليزية، كما في المثال.

a in the future	١ أخيراً
b the doctor's words	٢ علاج مشكلة الضغط عندك
c finally	٣ في المستقبل
d warning of bigger problems	٤ أهمّ شيء
e to cure your [blood] pressure problem	٥ ارتفاع ضغط الدم
f the most important thing	٦ كلام الطبيب
g blood pressure increase	٧ إنذار لمشاكل أكبر

Exercise 11 تمرين ١١

اقرأ الخطاب التالي من نادية.

Tip: وزن زائد (wazn zā'id) = excessive weight
مرض السكّر (maraḍ as-sukkar) = diabetes ('sugar illness')

أكتب لك هذا الخطاب وأنا أنتظر الطبيبة.

قالت لي الطبيبة إن وزني زائد جدّاً ومن الضروري أن أمارس التمرينات الرياضيّة كل يوم وأيضاً ذكرَت أنه ينبغي علي ألا آكل الطعام الدهني لأن البدانة ضارّة بالصحّة كما أنها تسبّب مرض السكّر.

في الحقيقة أنا لا أشعر بأي مرض ولا أريد الإقلاع عن أكلاتي المفضّلة مِثل البيتزا والبطاطس المحمّرة. أنا صغيرة في السنّ وأريد أن أستمتع بحياتي.

ما رأيك؟ هل أنا على حقّ؟ أم أنّي عنيدة وغبيّة كما وَصَفَتني صديقتنا سارة؟

المخلصة، نادية

Use Safwan's email opposite and the expressions on pages 192–5 to compose a reply to Nadia. Take care to use the feminine to address her.

العالم العربي ... نظرة على السودان

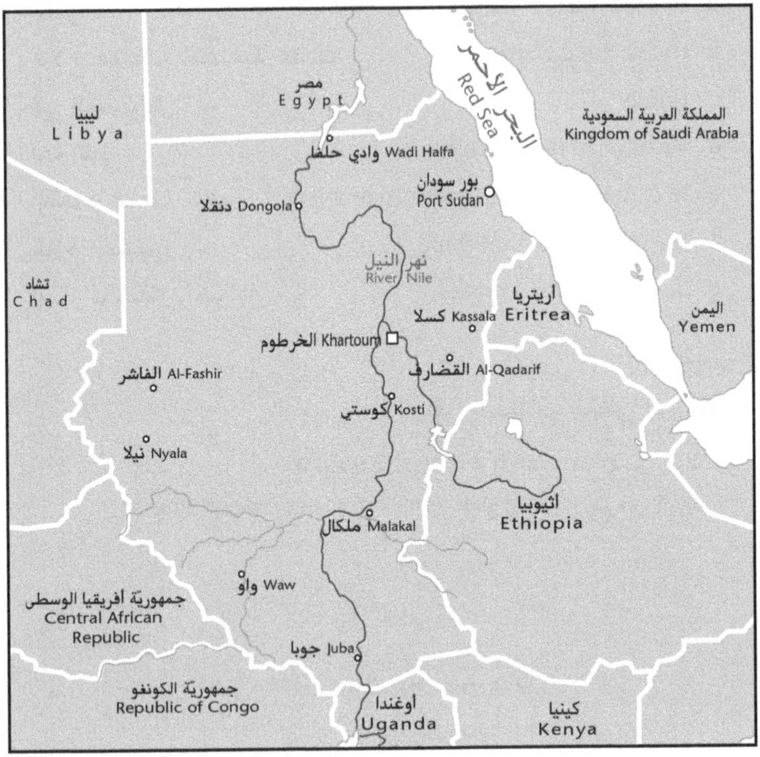

Arabic in Sudan العربيّة في السودان

'Sudanese' Arabic usually refers to the spoken language of Khartoum and the north of Sudan. In addition to Arabic, there are over a hundred indigenous languages, three of the most widely spoken being Nubian in the north and Dinka and Nuer in the south.

Features of Sudanese Arabic include:

- pronunciation of ق as a hard 'g', e.g. وقت (time) as wagt
- use of b- in front of present verbs describing habitual actions, in common with many other dialects, e.g. باحبّ baḥibb (I like)
- use of specifically Sudanese expressions, e.g. حسع ḥassaع (now) and الليلة al-layla with the meaning of 'today'.

Listen to Ashraf talking about himself in his Sudanese dilaect. You will find a transcript and translation in the Answers section.

شهدت وفيات الحصبة في أفريقيا انخفاضا بنسبة ٩١ في المئة في الفترة بين الأعوام ٢٠٠٠ و٢٠٠٧.

تحت شعار «لَقّحوا الأطفال ضد الحصبة» سُجِّلَت أسماء أغلبية تلاميذ المدارس خلال حملة التلقيح في السودان.

وبالرَغم من بعض مشاكل الأمن والتحدّيات اللوجيستية، عمل السودان على تلقيح حوالي ٤,٥ مليون طفل تتراوح أعمارهم بين ستة أشهر و١٥ سنة حتى نهاية عام ٢٠٠٧.

شهد، يشهد (shahida, yash-had)
to witness

لقّح، يلقّح (laqqaḥa, yulaqqiḥ)
to innoculate

الحصبة (al-ḥaṣba) measles

حملة (ḥamla) campaign

انخفاض (inkhifāḍ) decrease

بالرغم من (bir-raghm min) despite

شعار (shiعār) slogan

أمن (amn) security

أغلبيّة (aghlabīyya) majority

تحدّيات (taḥaddiyāt) challenges

A successful campaign against measles in Africa was conducted in the early years of the 21st century. Sudan innoculated millions of children, despite security and logistical challenges. Fatalities due to the disease were reduced by 91 percent.

الأسئلة

١ متى كانت الحملة ضد الحصبة؟

٢ ماذا كان شعار الحملة؟

٣ كم عدد الأطفال الذين لُقِّحوا في السودان؟

٤ ما هو عمر أصغرهم؟

٥ وأكبرهم؟

Vocabulary in Unit 12

***Nouns* الأسماء**

happiness	سَعادة
beauty	جَمال
body	جِسم (أجسام)
head	رَأس (رُؤوس)
face	وَجه (وُجوه)
mouth	فَم (أفواه)
teeth	سِنّ (أسنان)
nose	أنف (أُنوف)
eye	عَين (عيون)
ear	أُذُن (آذان)
chest	صَدر (صُدور)
arm	ذِراع (أذرُع)
hand	يَد (أيادٍ)
finger	إصبَع (أصابِع)
stomach	بَطن (بُطون)/مِعدة (مِعَد)
leg	رِجل (أرجُل)/ساق (سيقان)
foot	قَدَم (أقدام)
blood	دَم
illness	مَرَض (أمراض)
pain	ألَم (آلام)
symptom	عَرَض (أعراض)
condition/disorder	خَلَل (خِلال)
headache	صُداع
cold/chill	بَرد
fever	حُمّى
allergy	حَسّاسيّة (ات)
diabetes	مَرَض السُكَّر
measles	الحَصبة
weight	وَزن (أوزان)
obesity/corpulence	بَدانة
pressure	ضَغط
test/analysis	تَحليل (ات)
result	نَتيجة (نَتائِج)
medicine	دَواء (أدوِية)
pharmacy/chemist	صَيدَليّة (ات)
pill	حَبّة (حُبوب)
penicillin	البنيسيلين
smoking	تَدخين
air	هَواء
salt	مِلح
increase/rise	اِرتِفاع (ات)
decrease	اِنخِفاض (ات)
reduction/reducing	تَقليل
warning	إنذار (ات)
slogan	شِعار (ات)
campaign	حملة (ات)
challenge	تَحَدٍّ (تَحَدِّيات)
policeman	شُرطيّ (ون/ين)
security	أمن
majority	أغلَبيّة

Adjectives الصفات

suffering (from)	مُصاب (بـ)
fatty	دُهنيّ
excessive	زائِد
stubborn	عَنيد
stupid	غَبيّ

Verbs الأفعال

give up	أقلَعَ، يُقلِع عَن
damage	ضَرَّ، يَضُرّ بـ
cause	سَبَّبَ، يُسَبِّب
take (pills)	تَناوَلَ، يَتَناوَل
innoculate	لَقَّحَ، يُلَقِّح
enjoy	اِستَمتَع، يَستَمتِع بـ
witness	شَهِدَ، يَشهَد

Other phrases العبارات الأخرى

exactly	بِالضَبط
fresh air	الهَوا الطَلق
blood pressure	ضَغط الدَم
exercise(s)	تَمرينات رِياضيّة
must	من اللازِم أن
need to	من الضَروريّ أن
should	من المَفروض أن
likely to	من المُرَجَّح أن
might	من المُحتَمَل أن
right/correct	على حَقّ
despite	بالرَغم من

unit 13

Arts and cinema
الفُنون والسينما

وخَير جلَيس في الأنام كتاب.

The best companion of all [mankind] is a book.

Talking about culture التكلّم عن الثقافة

Look at these forms of art and artists and listen to the recording:

رواية، ات (riwāya, -āt) novel

مسرحيّة، ات (masraḥīyya, -āt) play

شعر، أشعار (shiɛr, ashɛār) poetry

قصّة، قصص (qiṣṣa, qiṣaṣ) story

فيلم، أفلام (film, aflām) film

أغنية، أغانٍ (ughniya, aghānin) song

أوبرا (obarā) opera

رقص (raqṣ) dance

مؤلّف، ون/ين (mu'allif, -ūn/īn) writer/composer

مخرج، ون/ين (mukhrij, -ūn/īn) director

ممثّل، ون/ين (mumaththil, -ūn/īn) actor

شاعر، شعراء (shāɛir, shuɛarā') poet

مغنٍّ، ون/ين (mughanin, -ūn/īn) singer

موسيقيّ، ون/ين (mūsīqīy, -ūn/īn) musician

راقص، ون/ين (rāqiṣ, -ūn/īn) dancer

Tip: when talking about the author of a work, Arabic uses the expression من تأليف min ta'līf ('written by'): رواية من تأليف نجيب محفوظ riwāya min ta'līf nagīb maḥfūẓ (a novel [written] by Naguib Mahfouz). The equivalent of 'starring' is من بطولة min buṭūlat: فيلم من بطولة شكري سرحان film min buṭūlat shukrī sarḥān (a film starring Shukri Sarhan).

مسرح الزمالك: عفروتو masraḥ az-zamālik: ɛafrūtū

(Zamalik Theatre: "Afrotto" (Little Devil))

Exercise 1 تمرين ١

ضع علامة ✔ أو (✔)، كما في المثال.

✔ = *necessary* to the activity (✔) = a *possible/secondary* participant

	رواية	فيلم	أغنية	قصّة	مسرحية	رقص	أوبرا	شعر
مغنٍّ		(✔)	✔		(✔)		✔	
مؤلّف								
راقص								
ممثّل								
مخرج								
شاعر								
موسيقي								

Exercise 2 تمرين٢

كوّن جملا، كما هو موضح في المثال.

Make a list of your favourite works in the categories first and then talk about them, using the example as a model.

١ رواية	٣ فيلم	٥ شعر
٢ مسرحية	٤ قصة قصيرة	٦ أغنية

روايتي المفضّلة هي «Great Expectations» من تأليف المؤلّف الإنجليزي الشهير تشارلز ديكنز.

(My favourite novel is *Great Expectations* by the famous English author, Charles Dickens.)

Talking about cultural activities التكلّم عن الأنشطة الثقافية

Look back at the phrases on pages 58–9 for talking about preferences. You can also use the verb يستمتع بـ yastamtiع bi- (to enjoy) that you met in the last unit.

أستمتع بقراءة الروايات ولكني لا أهتم بالمسرحيات. (astamtiع bi-qirā'at ar-riwāyāt wa-lākinnī lā ahtamm bil-masraḥīyyāt)	I enjoy reading novels, but I'm not interested in plays.
نحبّ مشاهدة التليفزيون ولكنّنا لا نذهب إلى السينما كثيراً. (nuḥibb mushaahadat at-tilīfizyūn wa-lākinnanā lā nadh-hab ilā s-sīnimā kathīran)	We like watching TV, but we don't go to the cinema often.
تستمتع بنتي بأغاني الشباب ولكني أفضّل الأوبرا. (tastamtiع bintī bi-aghānī ash-shabāb wa-lākinnī ufaḍḍil al-obarā)	My daughter enjoys pop songs, but I prefer the opera.

يستمتع زوجي بقراءة الأدب العربيّ.

yastamtiع zawjī bi-qirā'at al-adab al-عarabīy

(My husband enjoys reading Arabic literature.)

Conversation المحادثة

You're going to talk to an Arabic friend about:

- what type of literature you enjoy and don't enjoy
- who your favourite author is
- cultural activities you enjoy and something you don't do very often
- something a member of your family enjoys which you don't

Prepare what you might need to say and then join in the conversation on the recording, following the prompts.

Film genres أنواع الأفلام

غراميّ (gharāmīy) romantic

تاريخيّ (tārīkhīy) historical

هزليّ (hazalīy) comic

تسجيليّ (tasjīlīy) documentary

رعب (ruعb) horror

حرب (ḥarb) war

خيال علميّ (khayāl عilmīy) science fiction

(shabaḥ, ashbāḥ)	شبح، أشباح	ghost(s)
(maعraka, maعārik)	معركة، معارك	battle(s)
(nār, nīrān)	نار، نيران	fire(s)
(kawkab, kawākib)	كوكب، كواكب	planet(s)
(asad, usūd)	أسد، أسود	lion(s)

Exercise 3 تمرين٢

اكتب نوع الفيلم بجانب العنوان، كما في المثال.

١ ليلة في قَصر الأشباح .... فيلم رعب

٢ مَعرِكة فوق بحر النار ....

٣ رِسالة من الكَوكب الأزرق ....

٤ نابلِيون بونابَرت ....

٥ قُلوب في العاصفة ....

٦ الحياة مع الرِمال ....

٧ مِشمِش في وادي الأُسود ....

Exercise 4 تمرين٤

استمع إلى الصديقَين نديم وعثمان واكتب أوقات الأفلام، كما في المثال.

	يوم الجمعة	يوم السبت
ليلة في قَصر الأشباح	٧،٣٠	
مَعرِكة فوق بحر النار		
نابليون بونابرت		
مشمش في وادي الأسود		

Exercise 5 تمرين ٥

Nadim and his friend Othman have decided to read the descriptions of the films on the internet to help them make up their minds which one to see.

اقرأ العبارات التالية واكتب عنوان الفيلم، كما في المثال.

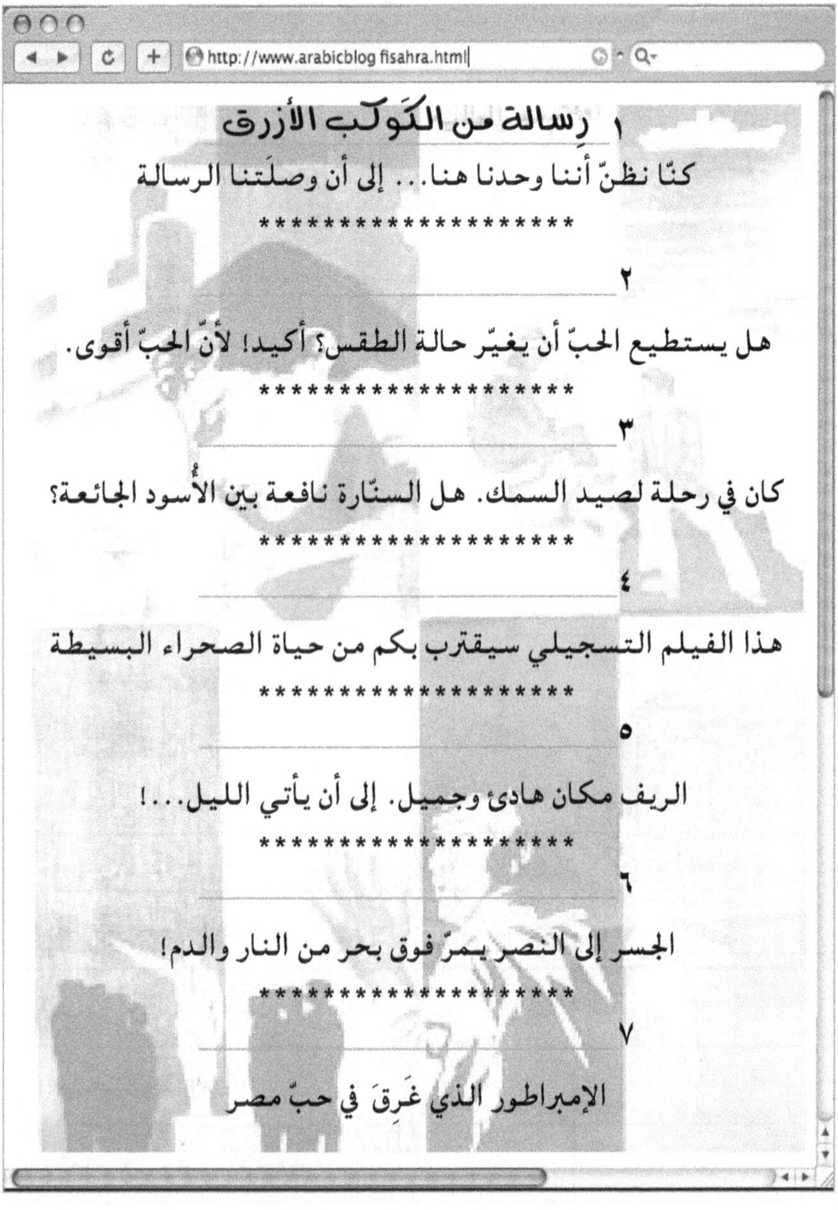
http://www.arabicblog fisahra.html
١ رِسالة من الكَوكب الأزرق
كنّا نظنّ أننا وحدنا هنا... إلى أن وصلَتنا الرسالة
****
٢
هل يستطيع الحبّ أن يغيّر حالة الطقس؟ أكيد! لأنّ الحبّ أقوى.
****
٣
كان في رحلة لصيد السمك. هل السنّارة نافعة بين الأُسود الجائعة؟
****
٤
هذا الفيلم التسجيلي سيقترب بكم من حياة الصحراء البسيطة
****
٥
الريف مكان هادئ وجميل. إلى أن يأتي الليل...!
****
٦
الجسر إلى النصر يمرّ فوق بحر من النار والدم!
****
٧
الإمبراطور الذي غَرِقَ في حبّ مصر

Talking about past habits التكلم عن عادات الماضي

Look at these phrases from the conversation between the two friends:

كنتَ تحبّ أفلام الرعب. (kunta tuḥibb aflām ar-ruعb)	You (m.) used to like horror films.
كنتُ أستمتع بها لما كان عمري ١٤ سنة! (kuntu astamtiع bihā lamma kāna عumrī arbaعat عashar sana)	I used to enjoy them when I was 14 years old!
كنّا نذهب إلى السينما كلّ يوم جمعة. (kunnā nadh-hab ilā s-sīnimā kull yawm jumعa)	We used to go to the cinema every Friday.

Although Arabic only has two basic tenses, the verb كان kaan (was/were) can be combined with a second verb to modify the meaning:

كان + *present verb* = 'used to do' or 'was doing'

كنتُ أقرأ الروايات كثيراً. I used to read novels a lot.

كان + *past verb* = 'had done' (often combined with قد qad)

كانت قد خرجَت قبل وصولي. She had gone out before my arrival.

كان + *future verb* = 'would have done'

كانوا سيستمتعون بالفيلم. They would have enjoyed the film.

Exercise 6 تمرين ٦

اكتب الفعل الصحيح كما هو موضح في المثال.

1 I used to go to the cinema a lot. كنتُ أذهب إلى السينما كثيراً.

2 He used to enjoy sci-fi films. ______ ______ بالأفلام خيال علمي.

3 She had read the novel. ______ قد ______ الرواية.

4 They had seen the film. ______ قد ______ الفيلم.

5 We would have gone to the theatre. ______ ______ إلى المسرح.

6 You *(f)* would have enjoyed the poetry. ______ ______ بالشعر.

Reviewing النقد

Your Arabic is now at a level where you can talk or write in a more sophisticated way about books you have read, or films, plays and shows you have seen. You can use the following guide to give you some ideas of what you could include in a review.

When?

yesterday	أمس
the day before yesterday	أوّل أمس
on Saturday	يوم السبت
last week	الاسبوع الماضي
last month	الشهر الماضي

What?

I read...	قرأتُ...
a novel/a short story	رواية/قصّة قصيرة
I saw...	شاهَدت
a film/a play	فيلما/مسرحيّة
an opera/a show	أوبرا/عرضاً

Who?

written by/ starring...	من تأليف/من بطولة
an unknown writer	مؤلّف مَجهول
a talented dancer	راقصة موهوبة
the famous star...	النَجم الشهير...

Characters?

the hero/heroine is...	إنّ البَطَل/البطلة...
a man/a boy who...	رجل/ولد...
a woman/a girl who...	اِمرَأة/بنت...
the main characters are...	إنّ الشخصيّات الرئيسيّة هي...
members of a large family	أعضاء عائلة كبيرة
a group of friends	مَجموعة أصدقاء

Story?

the story is about...	تَدور القصّة حول...
his life	حياته
her childhood	طفولتها
the events of...	أحداث...
during...	أثناء...
the war	الحَرب
the ... century	القَرن الـ...

Impression?

I found that ...	وجدتُ أنّه /أنّها...
I felt that ...	شعرتُ أنّه/أنّها...
it was moving, etc.	كان مؤثّراً/كانت مؤثّرة
I would have enjoyed it but...	كنتُ سأستمتع به/بها ولكنّ...
it was longer than necessary	كان/كانت أطول من اللازم
difficult to understand	صعب/صعبة الفهم

Now read this review of a new play, *The Lost Years*:

السنوات الضائعة

الأسبوع الماضي شاهدت هذه المسرحيّة الجديدة من تأليف فادية نور — المؤلّفة الفلسطينية المجهولة حتى الآن. المسرحية من بطولة النجم الشهير نبيل راضي.

إن بطل المسرحيّة هو إبراهيم حُسني، رجل رجع إلى عائلته بعد غياب خمس سنين. وتدور القصّة حول أحداث حياته كَجُنديّ أثناء الحرب العالمية الثانية وعمله مع الجيش الإنجليزي في صحراء ليبيا قبل رجوعه لحياته كَربّ الأسرة بعد نهاية الحرب.

الشخصيات الرئيسية هي العائلة: هو وزوجته مريم وأبناءه الثلاث. المؤلّفة تنظر إلى التحديات التي واجَهَتهُم أثناء الغياب وتأثير الحرب عليهم.

وجدتُ أن المسرحيّة كانت مؤثِّرة. كنت سأستمتع بها أكثر ولكن إيقاع الأحداث كان بطيئاً وشعرتُ أن المسرحية كانت أطول من اللازم.

(ghiyāb) غياب	absence
(jundīy) جنديّ	soldier
(jaysh) جيش	army
(rabb al-usra) ربّ الأسرة	head of the family
(ta'thīr) تأثير	effect
(mu'aththir) مؤثّر	moving/affecting
(īqāع) إيقاع	pace

Exercise 7 تمرين ٧

اكتب نقداً لكتاب أو عمل فنّي.

Use the guide on pages 210–11 and the review on page 212 to help you. You can write about a book, a film, a play or a show. Try to plan your review first and then write using only your notes as much as possible.

الرقص التونسيّ التقليديّ ar-rāqṣ at-tūnisīy at-taqlīdīy

(Traditional Tunisian dancing)

العالم العربي ... نظرة على الأردن وفلسطين

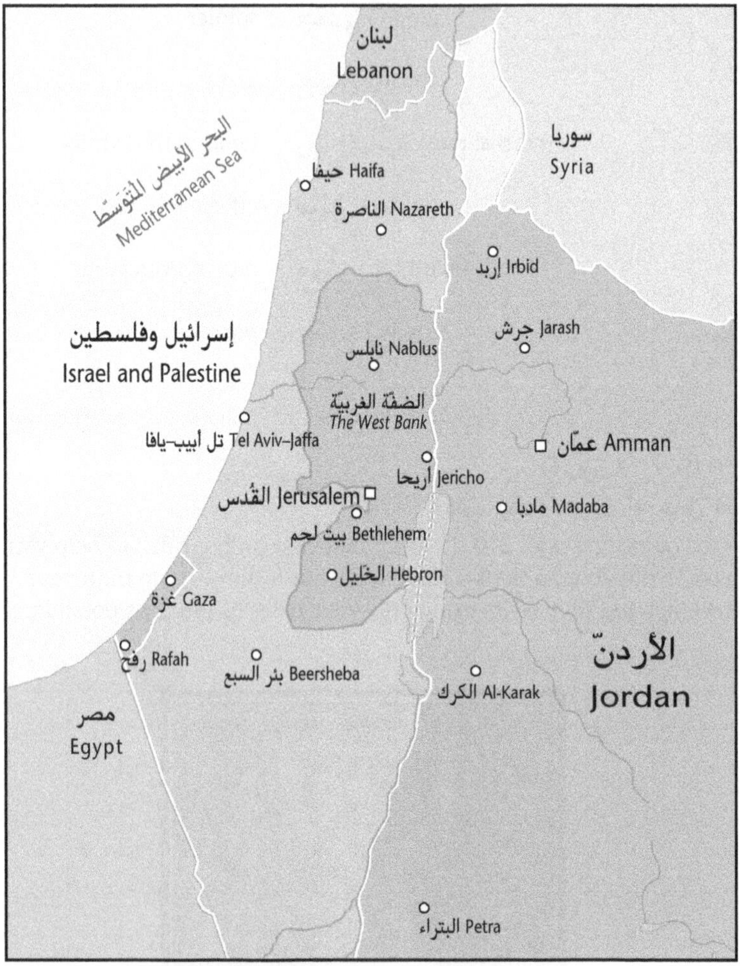

Arabic in Jordan and Palestine العربيّة في الأردنّ وفلسطين

A large proportion of the population of Jordan were originally from Palestine and the two dialects are very similar. They also share many features with Syrian colloquial (see page 52), particularly the softer lilt and the pronunciation of ة as 'eh' or 'ee'.

Listen to Youssef talking about himself in his Palestinian dialect. You will find a transcript and translation in the Answers section.

She had reached her seventy-fifth year... and if she were asked about the meaning of this word, "the homeland", then the matter would have confused her... Is it the house? The washing tub and the pestle for 'kibba' [minced meat] which she inherited from her mother?... Or is it the call of the milkmaid in the morning... Or the chesty cough of the husband, and the wedding nights of her children, who departed this threshold for the marital home one after the other, leaving her by herself?

لقد بَلَغَت الخامسة والسبعين من
عُمرها... ولَو سُئِلَت عن مَعنَى هذه
الكلمة، «الوَطن»، لاِختَلَطَ الأمر
علَيها... أهو البيت؟ إناء الغَسيل
وجُرن الكُبّة الذي وَرِثَتها عن أمّها؟...
أو هو نِداء بائِعة اللّبَن في الصباح...
أو سُعال الزوج المَصدور، ولَيالي
زفاف أولادها، الذين خَرَجوا من هذه
العَتَبة إلى بيت الزَوجيّة واحِداً وراء
الآخر وتَرَكوها لِوَحدها؟

Palestine has produced some of the most powerful poets and storytellers of the 20th and 21st centuries – the poets Mahmoud Darwish (1941–2008, see page 177) and Samih al-Qasim (1939–) and the writer Emile Habibi (1922–1996) to name but three. Poetry readings can still attract mass audiences and there is a strong Arabic tradition of storytelling. Not surprisingly, exile, loss and confused identity are common themes in Palestinian literature.

The above extract is taken from a short story by Emile Habibi, بوّابة مندلباوم "The Mandelbaum Gate" (a checkpoint between the Israeli and the Jordanian sectors of Jerusalem until 1967). In this passage, the author is exploring the experiences and memories of an old Palestinian woman and her attitude to the 'homeland' (الوطن al-waṭan).

Emile Habibi (1922–1996), writer and politician, lived all his life in Haifa.

Vocabulary in Unit 13

Nouns الأسماء

novel	رِواية (ات)
play	مَسرَحِيّة (ات)
poetry	شِعر (أشعار)
song	أُغنية (أغانٍ)
opera	أُوبرا
dance	رَقص
writer/composer	مُؤَلِّف (ون/ين)
director	مُخرِج (ون/ين)
poet	شاعِر (شُعَراء)
musician	موسيقيّ (ون/ين)
dancer	راقِص (ون/ين)
hero	بَطَل (أبطال)
member (of family/club, etc.)	عُضو (أعضاء)
group	مَجموعة (ات)
horror	رُعب
ghost	شَبَح (أشباح)
war	حَرب (حُروب)
battle	مَعرَكة (مَعارِك)
army	جَيش (جُيوش)
soldier	جُنديّ (جُنود)
fire	نار (نيران)
event	حَدَث (أحداث)
effect	تأثير (ات)
absence	غِياب
pace/rhythm	إيقاع
criticism/review	نقد
century	قَرن (قُرون)
planet	كَوكَب (كَواكِب)
lion	أَسَد (أُسود)
fishing rod	سَنّارة (ات)

Adjectives الصفات

romantic	غَراميّ
historical	تاريخيّ
comic	هَزليّ
documentary	تَسجيليّ
moving/affecting	مُؤَثِّر
unknown	مَجهول
difficult to understand	صَعب الفَهم
useful	نافِع
hungry	جائِع
lost	ضائِع

Verbs الأفعال

concern/be about	دارَ، يَدور حَول
come	أتَى، يأتي
pass (over)	مَرَّ، يمُرّ (فَوق)
drown	غَرِقَ، يَغرَق
face/confront	واجَهَ، يُواجِه

Other phrases العبارات الأخرى

written by من تَأليف

starring من بُطولة

pop songs أغاني الشَباب

science fiction الخَيال العِلميّ

head of the family رَبّ الأُسرة

Second World War

الحَرب العَالميّة الثانية

until *(+ verb)* إلى أن

unit 14 Review
المراجعة

Exercise 1 **تمرين ١**

اكتب معاني هذه الكلمات المستخدمة في وسائل الإعلام، كما في المثال.

الكلَمة	المعَنى		
أخبار	*news*	إعادة	______
صحيفة	______	مستمعون/ين	______
إذاعة	______	مشاهدون/ين	______
مصدر	______	جدَول	______
قناة	______	مدوَّنة	______
بثّ	______	تغطية	______
		فضائية	______

والآن املأ الفراغات بكلمة من هذه الكلمات، كما في المثال.

١ أحبّ أن أشتري صحيفة «الأهرام» كلّ يوم.

٢ أفضّل أن أستمع إلى موجز الـ ______ في الراديو.

٣ كلّ أسبوع يكتب أخي الـ ______ على الأنترنت.

٤ أيها السادة الـ ______ مرحباً بكم في راديو الشمس.

٥ نرحّبكم في هذا الـ ______ الحيّ من البرلمان.

٦ إن «الجزيرة» ______ شهيرة في قطر.

٧ الـ ______ من الرجال يفضّلون القنوات الرياضيّة.

Exercise 2 تمرين ٢

كيف تقول هذا بالعربيّة؟

1 She's wearing a red skirt.

2 I always wear a blue suit for the office.

3 He's wearing a grey coat and a black hat.

4 My daughter put on the pink shoes for the party.

5 I put on my brown coat before I went out.

6 My grandfather always wears glasses.

7 My brother wore a silk tie for the wedding party.

8 The woman who is wearing the green hat is my (maternal) aunt.

Exercise 3 تمرين ٣

Farida is at 'Lost and Found' reporting the contents of her small suitcase which has been lost by the airline.

استمع إلى المحادثة واكتب تفاصيل المفقودات، كما في المثال.

المادة *material*	اللون *colour*	المفقودات *lost items*	
حرير	أحمر	فستان	١
			٢
			٣
			٤
			٥
			٦

صف الملابس التي في حقيبة فريدة، مثلاً:

الحقيبة فيها فستان أحمر حريري.

In the suitcase [there] is a red silk dress.

Exercise 5 تمرين ٥

صف الطقس، كما في المثال.

الطقس صحو ومشمس.

____

____

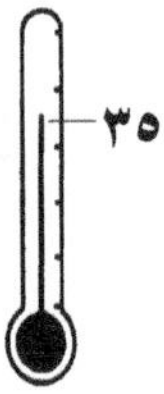

____

____

____

Conversation المحادثة

You want to buy a leather school bag for your son. You will need the following information:

- your son is ten years old
- he's in the fourth grade of primary school
- he needs a spacious, sturdy (مَتين) black bag with pockets for his pens

Note that your budget is 50 dinars.

Prepare what you might say in Arabic. Then follow the prompts on the recording.

تاجر جلود tājir julūd
(leather merchant)

Exercise 6 تمرين ٦

اكمل الجمل العربية، كما في المثال.

١ هو ضعيف .... في التاريخ و ....

He's weak in history and languages.

٢ إن أختي .... في ....

My sister excels in the sciences.

٣ ابني في السنة .... من ....

My son is in the first year of kindergarten.

٤ قال .... إنّك .... في الموسيقى.

The teacher said that you *(masc.)* are talented in music.

٥ أغلق .... الهواتف المحمولة قبل ....

The students turned off their mobile phones before the exam.

Exercise 7 تمرين ٧

You are instructing a friend how to insert a new sim card into his phone.

اقرأ التعليمات وضع الرقم الصحيح، كما في المثال.

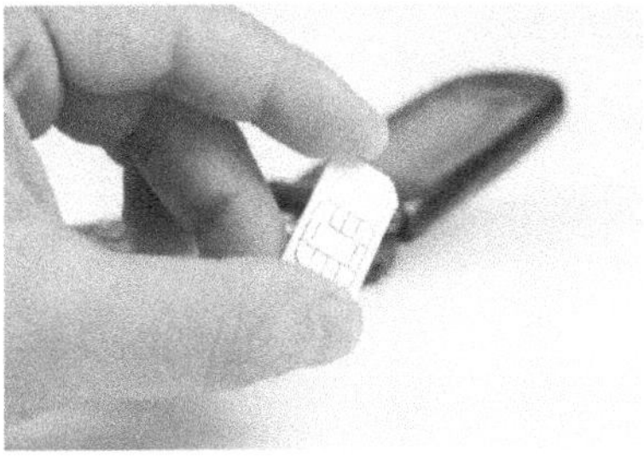

امسك السيمكارت بأطراف الأصابع
imsik as-simkārt bi-aṭrāf il-aṣābiع
(Hold the sim card with the fingertips)

☐ **أخرِج البطاريّة.**

☐١ **أغلق الهاتف المحمول.**

☐ **أعِد البطاريّة.**

☐ **افتح الغِطاء في ظهر الهاتف.**

☐ **امسك السيمكارت بأطراف الأصابع.**

☐ **ضع السيمكارت في مكانه.**

☐ **أعِد الغطاء.**

Now describe the process for inserting the sim card. Use the passive (see page 179) and join the stages of the process using sequencing words, e.g.:

First the mobile phone is switched off. **أوّلاً يُغلَق الهاتف المحمول.**

Exercise 8 تمرين ٨

You have seen the review opposite of a new film, حيـاتـي بين يديـك! (hayātī bayna yadayk) *My life in your hands*!

اقرأ النصّ وأجب على الأسئلة التالية.

1 When did the reviewer see the new film?

2 Who is the director and where is he from?

3 Who is the starring actress and where is she from?

4 What happens to the character Dina in the film?

5 What do the other main characters want from Dina?

6 Who does she fall in love with?

7 Which scenes does the reviewer like particularly?

8 What were the titles of the starring actress's last two films?

9 What were the audience doing in the second half of the film?

Exercise 9 تمرين ٩

جد العبارات التالية في النصّ واكتب العربيّة بجانب الإنكليزيّة.

1 a young doctor طبيب شابّ

2 she falls in love

3 millionairess

4 just as we saw

5 car chase scenes

6 the theft of her millions

7 river of blood

8 in her two last films

9 finishes with a surprise

10 until she meets

11 an unknown disease

12 'love storm'

حياتي بين يديك!

شاهدت أمس الفيلم الجديد للمخرج الكويتي الكبير أيمن لطفي ومن بطولة الممثّلة السورية الموهوبة أمل حلبي.

تدور أحداث القصّة حول دينا، المليونيرة المصابة بمرض مجهول، والمعركة التي تدور بين الشخصيات الرئيسية لسرقة ملايينها، إلى أن تلتقي بطبيب شاب ينقذها من المرض المجهول

ومن اللصوص الذين يريدون ملايينها، فتقع في غرام الطبيب ولكن الفيلم ينتهي بمفاجأة، وطبعاً لن أقول لكم عنها.

أنا دائماً أشعر أن أيمن لطفي مخرج بارع في ضبط إيقاع الأحداث، وخاصّةً مشاهد المطاردة بالسيارات، كما أن أمل حلبي كانت مؤثرة جدا كما رأينا في فيلميها الأخيرين «نهر الدم» و«عاصفة الحبّ».

استمتعت بالفيلم رغم أنّ المشاهدين كانوا يبكون بصوت عال طوال النصف الثاني من الفيلم.

īn, malāyīn) **مليون، ملايين**	million
(shābb) **شابّ**	young, youthful
(anqadha, yunqidh) **أنقذ، ينقذ**	to save
(mufāja'a, -āt) **مفاجأة، ات**	surprise
(bāriʿ) **بارع**	masterful, skilful
(muṭārada, -āt) **مطاردة، ات**	chase
(bakā, yabkī) **بكا، يبكي**	to cry, to weep

Vocabulary in Unit 14

Nouns الأسماء

million	مِليون (مَلايين)
surprise	مُفاجَأة (ات)
chase	مُطارَدة (ات)

Verbs الأفعال

hold	مَسَكَ، يَمسِك
save	أنقَذَ، يُنقِذ
cry/weep	بَكا، يَبكي

Adjectives الصفات

sturdy	مَتين
young/youthful	شابّ
masterful/skilful	بارِع

صنعاء، اليمن ṣanā', al-yaman

(Sanaa, the capital of Yemen, is classified as a World Heritage Site.)

Suggestions for further study

You have now come to the end of this second level course. You have acquired a solid foundation in Modern Standard Arabic and can tailor any further study to your particular needs and interests.

The expansion of the internet means that at the click of a mouse you will have access to a wealth of material, from more formal Arabic newspapers, radio and television to popular songs and chatrooms.

Courses

Some colleges and universities will run higher-level Arabic courses which you can join if you have the time and opportunity. You may also be able to find a course offering a particular dialect.

If you wish to continue studying by yourself with the help of a textbook, there are a number of programmes which will take you beyond the scope of *Mastering Arabic 2.* Make sure you choose one that matches your needs. Some, for example, are designed for use in a classroom and can be difficult to follow if you're working by yourself.

There are also a number of organisations offering online tuition, some better organised than others. Try to sign up for a sample lesson before you commit.

Material online

Most Arabic newspapers, magazines and satellite stations have their own internet sites, some also offering recorded material and live streaming.

In addition, video-sharing sites carry large amounts of professionally and home-recorded material in Arabic. Try searching in Arabic script for a subject, song or author that interests you and see what is available. Watch out in particular for clips with English subtitles or translations.

Literature

We have included some samples of Arabic poetry and literature in *Mastering Arabic 2.* If you are interested in reading more, try to start with bi-lingual or student editions that have the English and Arabic alongside each other. This will help you to develop a feel for the style and enable you to tackle Arabic-only editions subsequently. Some authors and publishers also have their own websites. Again, search in Arabic script to find what is available.

Visiting

There is never any substitute when learning a language for actually visiting or staying in the area. You can take a langauge course in one of the major Arabic-speaking countries, or simply use your Arabic while travelling and meeting local people. Most Arabs love an outsider willing to give it a go. Fortune favours the brave!

part 2

Reference material

Answers to exercises

UNIT 1

Exercise 1

الجنسيّة (*nationality*)	المهنة (*profession*)	مكان الإقامة (*place of residence*)	العنوان (*address*)	الاسم (*name*)
٣	٢	١	٩	٥
٦	٧	٤		٨
	١٠			

Exercise 2

١ ما
٢ مَن
٣ كَيف
٤ ما
٥ أيّة
٦ أين
٧ هل/أ
٨ ماذا
٩ كيف
١٠ لماذا

Exercise 3

١ أنا بَحرَينيّ/بحرينيّة.
٢ هل أنتِ من فلسطين؟
٣ أنا من الكُويت.
٤ هي إيطاليّة.
٥ هو من اليَمَن.
٦ هل أنتَ سوريّ؟
٧ هو انجليزيّ.
٨ هل هي من مصر؟

Exercise 4

الاسم ...... خالد نور ....
مكان الإقامة .... قطر ....
العنوان ١٠٥ شارع الخليفة، الدوحة ...
الجنسية .. مصري ....
المهنة .. مراسل ....

الاسم ... سامية بن حمد ....
مكان الإقامة .... المغرب ....
العنوان ٧٥ شارع السوق، الدار البيضاء
الجنسية .. تونسيّة ....
المهنة ... مهندسة ....

Exercise 5

أنا اسمي خالد نور وأنا أصلا من مصر. أقيم الآن في قطر وأنا مُراسِل هُناك. عنواني ١٠٥ شارع الخليفة، الدوحة.

أنا اسمي سامية بن حمد وأنا أصلا من تونس. أقيم الآن في المغرب وأنا مهندسة هناك. عنواني ٧٥ شارع السوق ، الدار البيضاء.

Exercise 6

The answer to this exercise depends on your personal circumstances. Try to check your answer with an Arabic-speaker.

Exercise 7

١ اِبنة أخي (my niece)
٢ أخي (my brother)
٣ زوجة أخي (my sister-in-law)
٤ اِبني (my son)
٥ زوجي (my husband)
٦ أخو زوجي (my brother-in-law)
٧ أمّي (my mother)
٨ أبي (my father)
٩ عَمّي (my paternal uncle)
١٠ حَماتي (my mother-in-law)
١١ حَمي (my father-in-law)
١٢ جَدّي (my grandfather)
١٣ جَدّتي (my grandmother)
١٤ جَدّ زوجي (my husband's grandfather)
١٥ جَدّة زوجي (my husband's grandmother)

Exercise 8

١ أمّي من لبنان.
٢ زوجي فَرَنسيّ.
٣ جدّتي أصلا من مصر.
٤ زوجة أخي إنجليزيّة.
٥ حماتي مدرّسة.
٦ ابن أختي مراسل في قطر.

Exercise 9

١ هي أصلا من كندا.

٢ هم في المكتب.

٣ هذا هو مكتبهم.

٤ أين وجدتَ حقيبتها؟

٥ هنّ في المستشفى.

٦ سيّارته جديدة.

٧ نحن في البنك.

٨ هل هما في البيت؟

Exercise 10

1 My mother is very graceful.
2 Her father is tall and active.
3 Our uncle is intelligent and generous.
4 Your mother-in-law is generous.
5 My brother is lazy and stubborn.
6 Their grandfather is very wise.
7 Your cousin is cunning.

Exercise 11

١ إنّ خالي ذكي ولكنّه عنيد.

٢ إنّ أختي محبوبة ولكنّها مكّارة.

٣ إنّ ابن عمّي كسول ولكنّه موهوب.

٤ إنّ جدّتي فقيرة ولكنّها كريمة.

٥ إنّ حفيدي قَصير ولكنّه نشيط.

٦ إنّ ابنة خالتي طويلة ولكنّها رشيقة.

Exercise 12

١٤ فبراير عام ١٩٧٥

٧ مارس عام ١٩٨٢

٢٢ يونيو عام ١٩٩١

٧ أبريل عام ١٩٦٧

٣٠ ديسمبر عام ٢٠٠٣

٧ أبريل عام ٢٠٠٩

Exercise 13

The answer to this exercise depends on your personal circumstances. Try to check your answer with an Arabic-speaker.

Exercise 14

The answer to this exercise depends on your choice of singer. Try to check your article with an Arabic-speaker.

نظرة على مصر *(A look at Egypt)*

Arabic in Egypt: transcript and translation, page 16

صباح الخير. أنا عماد. أنا مصري، اتولدت في القاهرة. أنا عايش دلوقتِ في الجيزة جنب الأهرامات. أنا عندي حوالي ثلاثين سنة. باشتغل في مكتبة – أنا مدير الفرع بتاع الزمالك. باشتغل حوالي ستة أيّام في الأسبوع – كلّ يوم من تسعة لستّة ما عدا يوم الجمعة.

متجوّز من حوالي ثمان سنين، سنة ألفين وواحد (٢٠٠١) وعندي بنتين. ماريا عندها خمس سنين بتروح المدرسة. أنا باوصّلها كلّ يوم الصبح بالعربيّة. وكلير عندها سنتين بنسيبها في البيت مع جدّتها عشان مامتها بتشتغل.

يوم الإجازة، يوم الجمعة، باحبّ أروح النادي ألعب تنس مع الكابتن رمضان وكمان باحب أعمل أكل في البيت، يعني ده من الحاجات اللي أنا باحبّها قوي... مع السلامة.

Good morning. I'm Emad. I'm Egyptian. I was born in Cairo. I currently live in Giza near the pyramids. I am about 30 years old. I work in a bookshop – I'm the manager of the Zamalik branch. I work about six days a week – every day from nine to six except Friday.

I've been married for about eight years, [since] 2001, and I have two girls. Maria is five years old and goes to school. I take her every day in the car. Claire is two years old and we leave her in the house with her grandmother because her mum works.

On the day off, Friday, I like to go to the club and play tennis with the coach, Captain Ramadan. And I also like to cook ['make'] food at home, I mean that is one of the things I like doing a lot... goodbye.

Questions on passage, page 17

١ وُلد نجيب محفوظ في ١١ ديسمبر عام ١٩١١.

٢ بدأ الكتابة عام ١٩٣٦.

٣ نشر الثُلاثيّة الشهيرة عام ١٩٥٦.

٤ مات في مستشفى بالقاهرة.

UNIT 2

Exercise 1

صالة ١ — غرفة جلوس ٤

حمّام ٨ — مطبخ ٢

غرفة نوم ٧ — شرفة ٥

سفرة ٣ — حديقة ٦

Exercise 2

a٩; b١٠; c١١; d٨; e١; f٥; g٧; h٤; i٦; j١٢; k٢; l٣

Exercise 3

(Model answer. Yours may vary slightly.)

غرفة النوم/ مكتب	السفرة/ غرفة الجلوس	الحمّام	المطبخ	الحديقة/ الجراج
سرير	خزانة	خزانة	خزانة	شَجَر
خزانة	مائدة	مرآة	مائدة	سيّارة
كمبيوتر	تليفزيون	غسّالة	ساعة	درّاجة
مكتب	صورة	حوض	كرسيّ	عشب
صورة	كرسيّ	دش	غسّالة	ورد
مائدة	ستائر		حوض	
كرسيّ	سجّاد		ثلاّجة	
ستائر	كنبة/أريكة		فرن	
سجّاد				
مرآة				

Exercise 4

١ ✗ ٢ ✗ ٣ ✓ ٤ ✓ ٥ ✓ ٦ ✗ ٧ ✓ ٨ ✓ ٩ ✓ ١٠ ✗

Exercise 5

١ أما الشقّة فهي في الطابق الرابع.

٢ أما السجاد فهو تقليديّ.

٣ أما العِمارة فهي حديثة.

٤ أما الشرفة فهي تطِلّ على حديقة.

٥ أما المطبخ فهو صغير.

Exercise 6

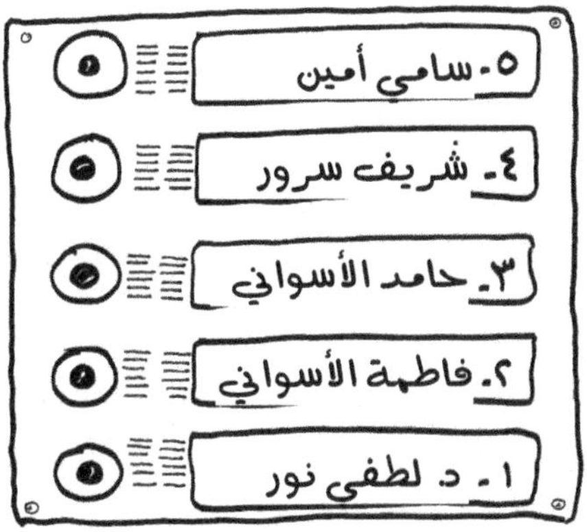

Exercise 7

الكلمة Word	الجمع Plural	المعنى Meaning
صورة	صُوَر	pictures
ثَلاجة	ثَلاجات	fridge
مَطبَخ	مَطابِخ	kitchen
حَوض	أحواض	sink
شُرفة	شُرفات	balcony
كمبيوتر	كمبيوترات	computer
خَزانة	خَزانات	cupboard
طابق	طَوابِق	storey/floor
سرير	أسرّة	bed

Exercise 8

apartment	small house	villa ✔
garden ✔	garage	view of sea
hall ✔	dining room	two bathrooms ✔
flowers	trees ✔	grass
old couch ✔	mirrors	desk ✔

Exercise 9

أقيم في فيلاّ في مدينة جديدة قريبة من العاصمة.

الفيلاّ تطلّ على الجبال وتتكوّن من صالة، غرفة جلوس، ثلاث غرف نوم، مطبخ واسع وحمّامين. الفيلا لها حديقة خاصّة فيها شجر ليمون ولكن ليس هناك ورد أو عشب.

غرفة الجلوس فيها كراسي مريحة وأريكة قديمة... هَدِية من أمّي ... ووراء الأريكة يوجد مكتب عليه كمبيوتر لابني. أما الصالة فهي بطراز تقليديّ.

Exercise 10

The answer to this exercise depends on your personal circumstances. Try to check your answer with an Arabic-speaker.

Exercise 11

١ الأولاد نشيطون.

٢ هناك شرفات واسعة.

٣ الكراسي مريحة.

٤ البيوت لها حدائق خاصّة.

٥ الشوارع مُزدَحِمة.

٦ إنّهنّ بنات موهوبات.

٧ إنّ أحفادي طوال.

٨ هناك سجاد تقليديّ في الغُرَف.

Exercise 12

1 Traditional house in the countryside *(bottom right)*

2 Modern apartment *(top right)*

3 Villa in a quiet area *(top left)*

4 Large apartment *(bottom left)*

Exercise 13

	شقة حديثة	فيلا هادئة	منزل تقليدي	شقة كبيرة
مصعد	✔	✘	✘	✘
حديقة	✘	✔	✔	✘
جراج	✘	✔	✘	✔
منظر	✔	✘	✔	✘
شرفة/سطح	✔	✔	✘	✘
حمّامان أو أكثر	✘	✔	✔	✔
سجاد	✘	✘	✔	✘
سفرة	✘	✔	✘	✘
تكييف هواء	✘	✔	✘	✔
رخام	✘	✔	✘	✘
حمام سباحة	✔	✘	✘	✘
ملعب تنس	✔	✘	✘	✘

Exercise 14

(Model answer. Yours may vary.)

شقّة كبيرة مفروشة للإيجار

الطابق الثالث (مصعدان).

تتكوّن من ٤ غرف نوم و٣ حمّامات فاخرة.

شرفة كبيرة تطلّ على الريف.

تكييف هواء وسجاد إيرانيّ تقليديّ.

هاتف محمول: ٤٥٦٧٦ ٠٩٦٧٨

نظرة على السعودية *(A look at Saudi)*

Arabic in Saudi Arabia: transcript and translation, page 34

سلام يا حبايب. أوّل شيء أحب أعرفكم بنفسي، أنا اسمي أحمد بن محمد صالح بن أحمد المليباري. أنا من أهل مكة المكرّمة في المملكة العربية السعودية.

متزوّج واحدة زيّي كمان من مكة واسمها نادية بنت أحمد الحويش. عندنا الله يحفظ لنا ولكم خمسة أولاد وبنتين، الأولاد هم هتّان وعبد الرحمن ومحمد ومعن وزياد والبنات هم لجين ومروج، الله يحفظ لنا ولكم.

أنا الولد البكر وعشان كده أبويا سماني باسم جدي الله يرحمه، جدي كان اسمه أحمد ويعني عندنا إحنا عادة في مكة إنه الأب يسمّي باسم أبوه ويسمي ولده زي اسم أبوه.

بالنسبة لهواياتي عندي هوايات كثيرة بس أكثر شيء أحبّه، أحبّ أركب أحصنة، وأحبّ أسبح وأحبّ أسافر كمان كثير أحبّ أسافر وأحبّ أتعرف على البلدان وأتعرف على الناس.

Salaam [hello], loved ones. First of all, I'd like to introduce myself to you. My name is Ahmed bin Mohammad Salih bin Ahmed Al-Meliebary. I'm from the holy city of Mecca in the Kingdom of Saudi Arabia.

I'm married to one who, like me, is also from Mecca; her name is Nadia bint Ahmed Al-Huwaish. We have (may God protect ours and yours) five sons and two daughters. The sons are [called] Hattan, Abdulrahman, Mohammad, Ma'an and Ziyad; and the daughters are [called] Lujain and Morouj (may God protect ours and yours).

I'm the eldest son of my parents and so my father named me after my grandfather (may he rest in peace). My grandfather's name was Ahmed and, well, we in Makkah have this tradition of fathers naming their children after their grandfathers.

As for my hobbies, I have many but most of all I like horse riding, swimming, and travelling. I love travelling a lot. I like getting to know countries and people.

Questions on passage, page 35

١ قلب البيت هو الباحة.

٢ يوجد حوض أو نافورة في وسط الباحة.

٣ بيوت الريف لها طابق واحد.

٤ البيت القديم الشهير في جدّة هو بيت نصيم.

٥ يجلسون في الباحة في النهار.

UNIT 3

Exercise 1

الكَلمة Word	الجَمع Plural	المَعنى Meaning
مدرّس	مدرّسون/ين	teacher
محاسب	محاسبون/ين	accountant
طالب	طَلَبَة/طُلاّب	student
مراسل	مراسلون/ين	correspondent
ممرّضة	ممرّضات	nurse
مهندس	مهندسون/ين	engineer
خَبّاز	خَبّازون/ين	baker
مُغَنٍّ	مغنّون/مغنّين	singer
تِلميذ	تَلامِذة	pupil
طَبّاخ	طَبّاخون/ين	cook/chef
نجّار	نجّارون/ين	carpenter

Exercise 2

١ هو فنّان.
٢ هو سائق.
٣ هي سائقة.
٤ هم مراسلون.
٥ هنّ مغنّيات.
٦ هم حرّاس.
٧ هي محامية.
٨ هم أطِبّاء.

Exercise 3

١ يعمل أخي حارساً في فندق كبير.
٢ تعمل سميرةمحامية في وزارة الزراعة.
٣ يعمل أحمد مهندساً في مصنع سوري.
٤ أعمل بنّاءً في شَرِكة صغيرة.
٥ يعملون سائقين في السفارة البريطانيّة.
٦ تعمل خالتي مراسلة في الكويت.

Exercise 4

a٣; b٥; c١; d٦; e٧; f٢; g٤

Exercise 5

See page 42 for answer.

Exercise 6

١ أحياناً استيقظ قبل الساعة السابعة.

٢ أنام في النهار نادراً.

٣ كلّ يوم أنظّف المائدة قبل العشاء.

٤ عادةً أُعدّ الفواتير قبل الساعة السادسة.

٥ أنا دائماً أُغلق بيتي قبل أن أقود سيّارتي إلى المكتب.

٦ لا آكل في الصباح أبداً.

Exercise 7

The answer to this exercise depends on your personal circumstances. Try to check your answer with an Arabic-speaker.

Exercise 8

1 مُؤَهّلات 2 جنسيّة 3 عنوان 4 جنس

5 مَهارات 6 خبرة عمليّة 7 تاريخ ميلاد

Exercise 9

السيرة الذاتية

الاسم: هاشم سعيد الجنس: ذَكَر

تاريخ الميلاد: ٥/٥/١٩٨٥ الجنسيّة: مغربي

العُنوان: شقّة ١٦، ٧٨ شارع ماينز، فرانكفورت، ألمانيا.

المُؤهّلات:

كلية فنون التصميم بالكمبيوتر، جامعة فرانكفورت: التقدير: جيّد جدًا

الخِبرة العمليّة:

٢٠٠٧- : مصمّم - مجلة "Videoman Express" للشباب، فرانكفورت

المَهارات:

اللغة الألمانية: جيّد جدًا اللغة الفرنسيّة: جيّد

إجادة برامج التصميم و"Photoshop"

Exercise 10

١ كلّ يوم تقود سميرة السيّارة إلى مكتبها.

٢ إن العُمّال ينظّفون المطبخ بعد العشاء.

٣ أنا ومساعدي نعدّ الفواتير كلّ يوم خميس.

٤ يعمل أخي محامياً لدى الحكومة.

٥ أنا لا أشتري أبداً جريدة في الصباح.

٦ هل أنتَ ترتّب غرفتك كلّ يوم؟

٧ إن البنات يستيقظنَ دائماً الساعة السابعة.

٨ هل أنتم تُقفلون مكتبكم قبل الخروج؟

٩ عادةً أمّي وأبي يُعدّان العشاء معاً.

١٠ هل أنتِ تنامين قبل الساعة التاسعة ليلاً؟

Exercise 11

1 Nadia is most suited to the position of assistant to the manager of an engineering company in Baghdad *(top right)*. Nadia is a qualified engineer, has good English and has more than three years' work experience. She lives in Basra and is Iraqi.

2 Hashim is most suited to the job of designer for a German magazine *(bottom left)*. He went to Frankfurt University and is a qualified graphic designer.

3 The answer depends on your own qualifications and experience.

Exercise 12

(Model answer. Yours may vary.)

مطلوب في دمشق

مساعد للمحاسب الرئيسي في فندق خمسة نجوم في دمشق. خبرة لا تقلّ عن ٣ سنوات. متخرّج من الجامعة. إجادة الإنجليزيّة تحدّثًا وكتابةً. طموح في عمله.

نظرة على سوريا *(A look at Syria)*

Arabic in Syria: transcript and translation, page 52

مرحبا. أنا سحر من سوريا. ساكنة بدمشق القديمة بحارة الزيتون مع الماما والبابا ببيت عربي. والبابا متقاعد من الجيش.

أختي الكبيرة ملك مجوزة وعندها صبي وبنت. سليمان الكبير كثير شاطر بالمدرسة وبيحب يلعب فوتبول والصغيرة شذى هي المدللة، حبيبة قلبي. أختي ملك كانت مبرمجة كمبيوتر بس تركت بعد ما جابت سليمان.

أنا باشتغل دليلة سياحية. درست أدب فرنساوي وسويت دورات انكليزي. هلا مسجلة دورة روسي – سمعت انها مطلوبة كتير.

عمري خمسة وعشرين سنة ولسّاني عزابية متل ما بيقولوا لسة ما اجا النصيب، ما بافضى حك رأسي! يلا خاطركم.

Hello. I am Sahar from Syria. I live in the old City of Damascus in Zaytoum quarter with my mother and father in a [traditional] Arabic house. My father is retired from the army.

My oldest sister Malak is married and has a boy and a girl. Suleiman, the oldest, is very good at school and he likes playing football. The youngest, Shaza, is the spoiled one ['loved by everyone'], the love of my heart [term of endearment]. My sister, Malak, was a computer programmer but she left work after having Suleiman.

I work as a tourist guide. I studied French Literature and followed English courses. Now I am doing a Russian language course. I heard it is in demand.

I am 25 years old and still single, as they say my number hasn't come up yet. I'm too busy ['I don't have time to scratch my head!']. See you soon.

Questions on passage, page 53

١ SAWA ISP شركة تطلب مصمّماً.

٢ الوظيفة في الإمارات هي مندوب مبيعات.

٣ هناك ١٢٥ وظيفة في سوريا.

٤ هناك ١٦ وظيفة في لبنان.

UNIT 4

Exercise 1

رياضات فرديّة	رياضات جماعيّة
السباحة	كرة القدم
التنس	كرة السلّة
الجولف	كرة اليد
ألعاب القوى	الكرة الطائرة
الملاكمة	
الإسكواش	
الجودو	
تنس الطاولة	

Exercise 2

☹	☺	😐	😐	☹	☺	☺	جمال
☹	☹	☺	☺	☺	☹	😐	نورة

Exercise 3

١ جمال
٢ جمال
٣ نورة
٤ نورة
٥ نورة
٦ جمال ونورة

Exercise 4

The answer to this exercise depends on your personal preferences. Try to check your answers with an Arabic-speaker.

Exercise 5

(Model answer. Yours may vary.)

لا تحبّ نورة التنس كثيراً ولكنّها تفضّل ألعاب القوى لأنها مسلية جدًّا في رأيها. تحبّ نورة أيضاً السباحة وتنس الطاولة ولكنّها لا تشاهد الجولف لأنّه مملّ والكرة صغيرة جدّاً! كما أنّها لا تحبّ الملاكمة بسبب العُنف. وأما كرة القدم فهي تَكره هذه الرياضة لأنّها في رأيها لا فائدة منها.

Exercise 6

Form	*Present verb*	*Verbal noun*	*Active Part.*	*Passive Part.*
II	يُصَوِّر *(photograph)*	تَصوير	مُصَوِّر	مُصَوَّر
I	يذهَب *(go)*	ذَهاب	ذاهِب	مَذهوب
III	يُشاهِد *(view/watch)*	مُشاهدة	مُشاهِد	مُشاهَد
I	يَركَب *(ride)*	رُكوب	راكِب	مَركوب
IV	يُرسِل *(send)*	إرسال	مُرسِل	مُرسَل
II	يُفَضِّل *(prefer)*	تَفضيل	مُفَضِّل	مُفَضَّل
I	يقرأ *(read)*	قِراءة	قارِئ	مَقروء
II	يُخَيِّم *(camp)*	تَخييم	مُخَيِّم	مُخَيَّم

Exercise 7

Exercise 8

١ يحبّ القراءة. /يحبّ أن يقرأ.

٢ تفضّل الذهاب إلى المسرح.

٣ يحبّون أن يشاهدوا البرامج الرياضيّة.

٤ إن هوايتها هي صيد السمك.

٥ يفضّلون أن يخيّموا على الشاطئ.

٦ يحبّ كثيراً ركوب الخيل.

٧ يحبّون الذهاب إلى النادي للعب التنس.

٨ إن هوايتهم هي التصوير.

Exercise 9

	اليوم	الساعة	المكان	النشاط
محمود وجاك	الجمعة	٤	النادي	إسكواش
نجيبة ولوسي	الأحد	٥:٣٠	الإسطبل	ركوب الخيل

Exercise 10

Activity	Day	Venue	Suitable for
Ramadan tent	*Thursday 12*	*Palace hotel*	*family*
Horse riding	*Thursday 5*	*Al-Jawaad club*	*children*
Exhibition of Iraqi artist	*Wednesday 4*	*Arts house*	*adults*
Children's library	*Tuesday 10*	*Arts house*	*children*
Exhibition of drawings from children's books	*Saturday 7*	*Culture centre*	*children*
Comic play	*Sunday 1*	*Al-Hussein theatre*	*family*
Children's Ramadan party	*Friday 13*	*Airport hotel*	*children*
History of European art	*Monday 9*	*Arts house*	*adults*
Bird Show	*Wednesday 11*	*Al-Malik Garden*	*family*
Yoga	*Sunday 8*	*Mecca mall*	*mothers*

نظرة على المغرب *(A look at Morocco)*

Arabic in Morocco: transcript and translation, page 70

السلام عليكم... كيفاش عاملين؟ بخير؟ كل شي لابأس؟ الصحة لابأس؟ العائلة لابأس الحمد لله.

أنا سميتي مراد الديوري. متزوج والحمد لله. أنا مغربي، الأصل ديالي من الشمال من مدينة طنجة. طنجة هي أصلاً مسقط رأس الرحالة المشهور إبن بطوطة والمغاربة كيسموها عروسة الشمال.

أنا أستاذ جامعي للتعليم الإلكتروني للغة العربية في جامعة ادنبرة.

أفضّل مشروب عند المغاربة هو التاي الأخضر بالنعناع وعادةً كيكون مشحر على حقه وطريقه.

مرحباً بكم عندنا في المغرب في أي وقت إن شاء الله. وخليتكم على خير والسلام عليكم ورحمة الله تعالى وبركاته.

Assalamu Alaykum [Peace be on you]. How are you keeping? Fine? Is everything OK? Is your health OK? Is the family OK (thanks to God)?

My name is Mourad Diouri. I'm married (thanks to God). I'm Moroccan, originally from the North, from the city of Tangiers. Tangiers is the original birth place of the famous traveller Ibn-Battouta. The Moroccans call it the 'Bride of the North'.

I am a university teacher in e-learning for the Arabic language at the University of Edinburgh.

The favourite drink of the Moroccans is green tea with mint, which is usually brewed in a particular way ('according to its right and method').

You are all welcome with us in Morocco at any time, God willing. Take care. Peace be upon you and God's mercy and blessings.

Questions on passage, page 71

١ تاريخ المقالة ١٤ مارس ٢٠٠٧.
٢ العدّاء في الصورة هو هشام الكروج.
٣ وقّعت الحكومة الاِتّفاق مساء الثلاثاء ٣ مارس.
٤ الاتّحاد المغربي لألعاب القوى.
٥ المبلغ ٦٥ مليون دولار، ٥٥٠ مليون دِرهَم.

UNIT 5

Exercise 1

١ محطّة القطار
٢ محطّة البنزين
٣ مركز الرياضة
٤ مكتب الطيران
٥ مكتب السياحة
٦ مركز التسوّق
٧ مركز الشرطة
٨ مكتب البريد
٩ محطّة الباص

Exercise 2

١ أين محطّة القطار؟
٢ هل هذا هو الطريق إلى مركز الرياضة؟
٣ كيف أصل إلى المسرح؟
٤ أين أقرب مركز تسوّق؟
٥ كيف أصل إلى مكتب السياحة؟
٦ أين أقرب محطّة باص؟

Exercise 3

١ إشارة المرور
٢ محطّة القطار
٣ محطّة الباص
٤ مكتب البريد
٥ مركز الرياضة
٦ الميدان
٧ مكتب السياحة
٨ مركز التسوّق
٩ مركز الشرطة
١٠ محطّة البنزين

Exercise 4

a١٠; b٣; c٦; d٨; e٧; f٤; g١; h٢; i٥; j٩; k١١

Exercise 5

٦ أَخَذنا الباص من جدّة إلى مكّة المكرّمة.

٢ اِشتَرينا تذاكر السَفَر من مكتب السياحة.

١ قَرَّرنا أنا وأبي وأمّي أن نُؤَدّي فريضة الحجّ هذا العام.

٥ رَكِبنا المركب إلى جدّة.

٨ رَجَعتُ ومعي ثلاث زجاجات ماء من بِئر زمزَم.

٣ ذَهَبتُ إلى السِفارة السَعوديّة لآخذ تأشيرة.

٧ أَدَينا فريضة الحجّ وَزُرنا الكَعبة والمَسجِد الحَرام.

٤ أعدَدتُ حقائِبي للسَفَر.

Exercise 6

plane ✔ *boat* ✘ *camel* ✔ *donkey* ✘ *fort* ✔ *stars* ✔ *palm trees* ✔
beach ✘ *cinema* ✘ *well* ✔ *shopping* ✘ *tent* ✔ *mountains* ✔
flowers ✘

Exercise 7

Paragraph 1:
غادَرَت it [our plane] left; وَصَلنا we arrived; كانَت it was [an hour]; كان it [the wind] was; كنتُ I was; شَعَرتُ I felt; رَكِبنا we took/rode; زُرنا we visited; ذَهَبنا we went

Paragraph 2:
كانَت it [our room] was; كان it [the air conditioning] was; لم يَعمَل it [the air conditioning] didn't work; كانَت it [the cafeteria] was; كان it [the tea] was; كانَت it [the cola] was; لم نَجِد we didn't find; أعدَدتُ I prepared; ذَهَبنا we went

Paragraph 3:
غادَرنا we left; تَوَجَّهنا we headed; شاهَدنا we saw; زُرنا we visited; شرِبنا we drank; أكَلنا we ate; كانوا they [the Bedouin] were; رَكِبتُ I rode; ذَكَّرَتني it [the movement] reminded me; نِمنا we slept; كانَت they [the stars] were

Paragraph 4:
أحبَبتُ I liked

Exercise 8

١ الشاي كان باردا
٢ الكولا كانت دافئة
٣ البدو كانوا كراماً
٤ تكييف الهواء كان مضحكاً
٥ كنتُ خائفة
٦ النجوم كانت عجيبة
٧ غُرفتنا كانت صغيرة وحارّة جدّاً
٨ الريح كان شديدًا جدّاً

Exercise 9

(Model answer. Yours may vary slightly.)

السيّد مدير فندق الشمس، القصير

تـحية طيِّبة،

نزلنا، أنا وعائلتي، في فندق الشمس في الشهر الماضي في رحلتنا. للأسف غرفتنا رقم ٥١٢ في الدور الخامس كانت باردة جدًّا وتطلّ على محطّة الباص.

كان الطقس بارداً، ولكن المدفأة لم تعمل أبداً، رغم أنها كانت كبيرة جداً!

في المساء ذهبنا إلى الكافيتريا ولكن للأسف كانت القهوة باردة والبيتزا صغيرة. رجعنا إلى غرفنا ولكنّا لم نَجد صابوناً في الحمّام.

أرَدتُ أن أُخبِرك حتى تَحِلّ هذه المشاكل،

وشكراً،

(اسمك)

نظرة على تونس *(A look at Tunisia)*

Arabic in Tunisia: transcript and translation, page 88

السلام عليكم.

صباح الخير. أنا اسمي عبد الحقّ، تونسي، عمري ٣٤ عام. نخدم أستاذ جامعي في كليّة العلوم بتونس، العاصمة. ولكن أصلي من جنوب تونس.

نحبّ السباحة والمطالعة والشطرنج وكرة القدم.

عندي ٣ أولاد، هم معزّ وأحمد ومحمّد. أنا نحبّ المأكلة التونسيّة كما الكسكسي والبريك وشوربة الشعير.

بلادي باهية برشة وهي يقصدوها السياح والمستثمرين من كلّ البلدان. بصفة خاصة شطوطها وجبالها والصحراء الكبيرة اللي فيها في الجنوب يجوها السياح من على طول العام. وكذلك عندنا صناعات تقليديّة ياسر متنوّعة.

Assalamu Alaykum [Peace be on you].

Good morning. My name is Abdelhaq. I am Tunisian, aged 34. I work as a university professor at the Faculty of Sciences in Tunis, the capital city. But I'm originally from the south of Tunisia.

My hobbies are swimming, reading, playing chess and football. I have three sons: Moez, Ahmed and Mohammed. I like Tunisian food such as couscous, brik [Tunisian pastry parcels], and barley soup.

My country is very beautiful and tourists and investors from every country head for it. In particular, tourists come to its beaches and mountains and the large desert that is in the south throughout the year. We also have very varied traditional handicrafts.

Questions on passage, page 89

١ المغنّي اسمه صابر الرباعي.

٢ الأغنية اسمها «خلوني» ('Let me be').

٣ يصوّر الكليب في الجنوب التونسي.

٤ سيقيم صابر الحفلة في ٢١ يونيو القادم.

٥ الحفلة في قصر القُبة بالمنزه.

UNIT 6

Exercise 1

bread	خُبز	tomatoes	طَماطِم	milk	حليب
bananas	مَوز	yoghurt	زَبادي	apples	تُفّاح
lemons	لَيمون	eggs	بَيض	butter	زُبدة
water melon	بَطّيخ	juice	عَصير	rice	أَرُزّ
figs	تين	cheese	جُبن	oranges	بُرتُقال
chicken	دَجاج	meat	لَحم	potatoes	بَطاطِس
sugar	سُكَّر	oil	زَيت	cake	كَعك
biscuits	بَسكويت	coffee beans	بُنّ	fish	سَمَك

Exercise 2

أَرُزّ بَيض عَصير زَيت بُنّ سُكَّر	تُفّاح بُرتُقال بَطاطِس طَماطِم مَوز لَيمون بَطّيخ تين	كَعك خُبز بَسكويت	سَمَك	لَحم دَجّاج	حليب زُبدة زَبادي جُبن

نشتري الحليب (الزبدة/الزبادي/الجبن) من اللبّان.

نشتري اللحم (الدجّاج) من الجزّارة.

نشتري السمك من السمّاك.

نشتري الكعك (الخبز/البسكويت) من المخبز.

نشتري التفّاح (البرتقال/البطاطس/الطماطم/الموز/الليمون/البطيخ/التين) من الخضريّ.

نشتري الأرزّ (البيض/العصير/الزيت/البنّ/السكّر) من البقّالة.

Exercise 3

a٥; b١٢; c٢; d١; e٩; f٧; g١٠; h١١; i٣; j٦; k٨; l٤

Exercise 4

١ كيس بنّ
٢ علبة طماطم
٣ ربع كيلو تين
٤ كوب زبادي
٥ كيلو دجاج
٦ رغيف خبز
٧ علبة سمك صغيرة
٨ زجاجة العصير الكبيرة

Exercise 5

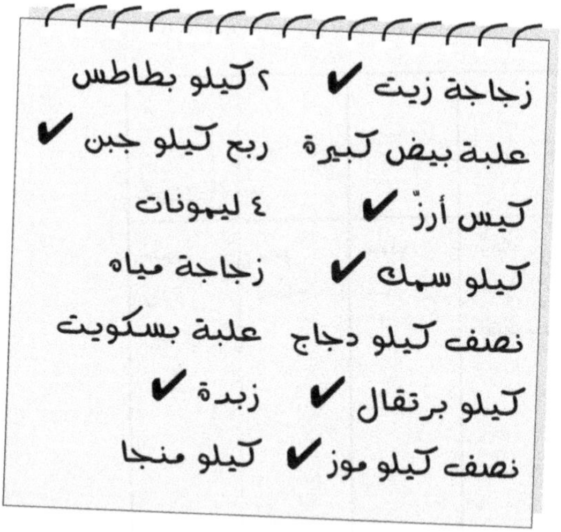

(Model sentences. Yours may vary slightly.)

تَذَكّرَت ليلى الزيت ولكنّها نَسِيَت البيض.

تَذَكّرَت ليلى الأرز ولكنّها نَسِيَت الدجاج.

تَذَكّرَت ليلى البرتقال ولكنّها نَسِيَت البطاطس.

تَذَكّرَت ليلى الجبن والزبدة ولكنّها نَسِيَت البسكويت والماء.

تَذَكّرَت ليلى الموز لكنّها نَسِيَت الليمون والمنجا.

Exercise 6

1 ✗ 2 ✓ 3 ✗ 4 ✓ 5 ✓ 6 ✗ 7 ✓ 8 ✓

Exercise 7

	اسم الزبون *customer name*	عدد الأشخاص *number of people*	اليوم *day*	الساعة *time*
١	بركات	٢	الجمعة	٨:١٥
٢	فهيم	٤	السبت	١:٣٠
٣	فارس	٩	الأحد	٦:٠٠

Exercise 8

٤ بركات.

١ مساء الخير!

٧ طبق اليوم كفتة مشوية مع سلاطة الزبادي.

١٠ أنا سآخذ الكفتة. ونريد زجاجة مياه من فضلك.

٥ أهلا وسهلا يا سيّد بركات. تفضّلوا. مائدة رقم عشرة.

١١ طيّب... واحد سمك مقلي، واحد كفتة مشوية وزجاجة مياه.

٦ شكراً.... من فضلك، ما هو طبق اليوم؟

٨ كفتة مشوية؟ أنا أفضل السمك. هل عندكم سمك؟

٣ الاسم من فضلك؟

٩ نعم يا سيّدتي. عندنا سمك مقلي ممتاز. وحضرتك يا سيّد بركات؟

٢ مساء النور. حجزنا مائدة لشخصين.

Exercise 9

a٥; b٧; c٦; d٢; e٣; f١; g٤

Exercise 10

Mr Barakat ordered the kofta (minced meat skewers), but was charged for kebab and chips.

ـ يا متر! أعتقد أن هناك خطأ في الحساب!

ـ خطأ في الحساب؟ أنا آسف جداً يا سيدي.

ـ أنا طلبتُ كفتة مشوية وفي الحساب كباب بالبطاطس المحمرة!

ـ آسف جداً يا سيدي! الكباب خطأ.

ـ بسيطة يا متر! كانت وَجبة ممتازة!

Exercise 11

Present verb	يَختَلِف	يَتَناوَل	يَلتَقِط	يَستَهلِك
Past verb	اِختَلَف	تَناوَل	اِلتقط	اِستَهلَك
Root letters	خ / ل / ف	ن /و / ل	ل / ق / ط	ه / ل / ك
Form	VIII	VI	VIII	X
Meaning	to differ	to eat/partake	to shoot (a film)	to consume
Verbal noun	اِختِلاف	تَناوُل	اِلتِقاط	اِستِهلاك
Active Part.	مُختَلِف	مُتَناوِل	مُلتَقِط	مُستَهلِك
Passive Part.	مُختَلَف	مُتَناوَل	مُلتَقَط	مُستَهلَك

Exercise 12

١ ✓   ٢ ✗   ٣ ✗   ٤ ✓   ٥ ✓   ٦ ✓

نظرة على لبنان *(A look at Lebanon)*

Arabic in Lebanon: transcript and translation, page 106

مرحبا. أنا اسمي فؤاد حدّاد وعايش بِبيروت حي الأشرفيّة. أنا أصلاً من مواليد الخنشارة المتن، ضيعة بالجبل على علو ١٠٠٠ متر فوق سطح البحر. لهجتي لهجة سكّان بيروت الوافدين من المناطق النائية.

أنا متزوّج وعندي ولدين: واحد عمره ١٦ سنة والتاني عمره ١٢. خليل الكبير بحبّ الموسيقى وبيلعب البيانو وسمير الصغير بيحبّ الرياضة وبيلعب فوتبال وباسكتبال.

تخرجت من الجامعة الأمريكيّة بِبيروت وباشتغل مُبَرمِج بشركة كومبيوتر. بتبعَتني الشركة لانفذ مشاريع بكلّ البلاد العربيّة خاصةً بالخليج. بِأوقات فراغي وخاصةً بالويكند، باخذ العيلة بالشتة ليلعبوا سكي بالجبل، وبالصيف منحبّ نروح نسبح بالبحر.

Hello. My name is Fouad Haddad and I live in Beirut, the district of Achrafieh. I am originally from Khencharah Metn, a village in the mountains, 1000m above sea level. My accent is the accent of Beirut residents who originally came from remote areas.

I am married and have two boys, one 16 years old and the other 12. Khalil the eldest likes music and plays the piano and Samir the younger one likes sports and plays football and basketball.

I graduated from the American University of Beirut and I am working as a programmer for a computer company. The company sends me to work on projects all over the Arab world, especially the Gulf. In my spare time, and especially during the weekend, I take the family – in winter – to ski in the mountains. During summer we like to go to the beach and swim in the sea.

Questions on passage, page 107

١ الوجبة لثلاثة أشخاص.

٢ ملعقة شاي

٣ كوب زبادي

٤ ثلاث أرغفة خبز

٥ سيخان (ستة بين ثلاثة أشخاص)

UNIT 7

Exercise 1

الاسم ......نجيبة بدران..................

تاريخ الميلاد ..٦. فبراير ١٩٨٦..................

مكان الميلاد حلَب..................

العنوان ......١٨. شارع الحسين، برزة، دمشق..

الجنسية ......سورية..................

جنسية الأب سوري..................

جنسية الأم ..فلسطينيّة..................

المهنة ......مندوبة مبيعات..............

الشركة ......شركة النجمة الشرقية.............

(Model paragraph. Yours may vary slightly.)

وُلِدَت نجيبة بدران يوم ٦ فبراير عام ١٩٨٦ في مدينة حلب فهي سورية. أبوها سوري أيضاً. أما أمّها فهي فلسطينية، أصلا من مدينة رفح. يُقيمون الآن في دمشق وعندهم شقّة في عمارة حديثة، العنوان ١٨ شارع الحسين، برزة، دمشق. تعمل نجيبة مندوبة مبيعات لشركة دولية في وسط العاصمة اسمها «شركة النجمة الشرقية».

Exercise 2

الكلمة Word	الجَمع Plural	المَعنى Meaning
نَجم	نُجوم	*stars*
كرسيّ	كَراسي	*chairs*
مَحطّة	مَحطّات	*stations*
حفيد	أحفاد	*grandchildren*
مُصمِّم	مُصمِّمون/ين	*designers*
حمّام	حمّامات	*bathrooms*
مَركَز	مَراكِز	*centres*
غُرفة	غُرَف	*rooms*
كوب	أكواب	*glasses/cups*

١ في هذه المدينة هناك أربعة مراكز تسوّق.
٢ كانت النجوم لامعة في ليل الصحراء.
٣ لي سبعة أحفاد – خمس بنات وولدان.
٤ نحتاج إلي ثلاثة أكواب أرزّ للعشاء.
٥ هل توجد غُرَف تطلّ على البحر؟
٦ استأجرنا فيللا بأربع غرف نوم وثلاثةحمّامات.
٧ يعملون مصمّمين في دار أزياء إيطالية.
٨ رأينامحطّات بنزين كثيرة في الطريق.
٩ هل رأيتم الكراسي التقليديّة القديمة في بيت جدّي؟

Exercise 3

يزور متاحف
يلعب كرة القدم
يعمل مساعداً للمدير العام
يَركب الخيل
يُعدّ العشاء للعائلة
يكوي الملابس

يرتِّب الأوراق على المكتب
يشتري الخضروات من السوق
ينظِّف المطبخ
يستيقظ قبل الساعة السابعة
يشاهد التليفزيون

Exercise 4

١ أحياناً نلعب كرة السلّة في النادي.

٢ تساعد في الطبخ نادراً.

٣ عادةً يقود المدير سيّارته إلى المكتب.

٤ دائماً نفطر قبل الساعة السابعة.

٥ كلّ يوم أعمل حتى الساعة الخامسة والنصف.

٦ لا يرتّبون غُرَفهم أبداً.

Exercise 5

١ مرحباً بكم في مطعم الصيّادين!

٢ مساء الخير يا متر. حجزنا مائدة لأربعة أشخاص. الاسم بدران.

٣ أهلا وسهلا ياسيدة بدران. تفضلوا. مائدة رقم خمسة.

٤ شكراً.... من فضلك، ما هو طبق اليوم؟

٥ طبق اليوم سمك تونة مشوي مع أرزّ أحمر.

٦ سمك مشوي؟ أنا أفضل الدجاج. هل عندكم دجاج؟

٧ نعم يا سيد بدران. عندنا دجاج مقلي ممتاز. وحضرتك يا مدام؟

٨ أنا وبنتاي سنأخذ السمك. ونريد أربعة عصير ليمون.

٩ إذاً... واحد دجاج، وثلاثة سمك وأربعة ليمون...

١٠ ...يا متر! الحساب من فضلك!

١١ الحساب؟ تفضلوا.

١٢ شكراً! كانت وَجبة ممتازة!

Exercise 6

1 Hisham's father and mother; **2** Athens and Marseilles; **3** delicious sweet things and beautiful Lebanese apples; **4** visit the mountain; **5** the Acropolis by bus; **6** on the ship - they both like photography; **7** the Greek minced meat skewers; **8** talking to Adnan; **9** they ate fish in the old port of Marseilles; **10** by train

Exercise 7

(Model paragraphs. Yours may vary.)

في اليوم التالي وصلت السفينة إلى اليونان. أخذ الركّاب الباص من الميناء لزيارة الأكروبوليس والحيّ القديم في أثينا. وقال هشام أن الكفتة هناك ذكّرَته بمصر رغم أنه في أوروبا. على المركب قابل هشام طالباً سورياً اسمه عدنان. إنه يدرس الهندسة في دمشق وهوايته التصوير مثل هشام. في المساء غادروا اليونان في الطريق إلى مرسيليا في جنوب فرنسا.

أثناء الرحلة إلى مرسيليا جلس هشام مع صديقه الجديد عدنان على سطح المركب بعد العشاء وتكلّموا حتى الفجر ولم يشعروا بالبرد إطلاقاً. بعد شروق الشمس وصلوا مرسيليا. ثمّ زاروا المدينة القديمة وأكلوا سمكاً مشوياً في مطعم شهير في وسط الميناء فكانت وجبة ممتازة. بعد الزيارة رجعت السفينة إلى الإسكندريّة وأخذ هشام القطار من المحطّة هناك إلى بيته.

Exercise 8

١٩٧٩	Visit of former president Jimmy Carter to Egypt
١٩٨٧	Death of Egyptian businessman, Mohammed Ahmed Farghali
١٨٨١	Birth of British foreign minister, Ernest Bevan
٢٠٠٧	Crash of Indonesian Boeing 737
١٩٤٥	Allied occupation of Cologne
١٩٨٣	New Delhi summit of non-aligned states
١٩٧٤	East and West Germany recognition of each other's sovereignty

Exercise 9

1 cotton king ملك القطن
2 passenger plane طائرة ركاب
3 for the first time لأول مرة
4 non-aligned states دُوَل عدم الانحياز
5 of the make/type من طراز

UNIT 8

Exercise 1

ج	ف	ش	م	ا	ز	ح	ي	ع	م
ي	ص	غ	ط	ن	ر	ب	س	ك	د
ب	ق	ح	خ	ء	ا	ذ	ح	ش	ب
ة	ر	ت	س	ض	خ	ر	ث	ا	ن
ف	د	ن	ا	ذ	ه	ق	ا	ف	ط
ت	ع	و	ف	ط	ع	م	س	د	ل
ي	ذ	ر	ص	غ	ة	ي	ش	ك	و
ط	س	ة	ق	ء	ا	ص	م	غ	ن
ة	ع	ب	ق	ك	ض	ق	ة	ح	ث
ن	ف	ش	ر	ن	ا	ت	س	ف	ح

belt حزام dress فستان coat معطف skirt تنورة hat قبعة
jacket سترة trousers بنطلون shirt قميص shoes حذاء

Exercise 2

١ بلوزة blouse
٢ جينز jeans
٣ جاكيت jacket
٤ بلُوفِر pullover
٥ بِيجامة pyjamas
٦ بوت boots
٧ سويتر sweater
٨ شال shawl

Exercise 3

١ (woman) تلبس المرأة تنّورة طويلة وبلوزة وحجابًا.
٢ (man) يلبس الرجل بدلة وربطة عنق مع قميص أبيض.
٣ (girl) تلبس البنت شورت وتي–شيرت مع صندل جلد.
٤ (boy) يلبس الولد بنطلون وسويتر ومعطفاً كبيراً.

Exercise 4

١ ليمونيّ
٢ برتقاليّ
٣ مشمشيّ
٤ ذهبيّ
٥ بنفسجيّ
٦ عسليّ
٧ فضّيّ
٨ رصاصيّ

Exercise 5

(Model descriptions. Yours may vary slightly.)

تلبس أميرة بلوزة زرقاء مع حجاب وردي. أما تنّورتها فهي رمادية وصفراء.

تلبس فيفي تي-شيرت مشمشي وبنطلون أصفر مع حزام أخضر. تلبس أيضاً قبعة خضراء وأما صندلها فهو بنّي.

Exercise 6

	First item	Second item
Type of clothing	*summer shirt*	*sun hat*
Size information:	*16.5 collar*	*wide*
Colour offered:	*green (with orange pocket)*	*purple*
Colour preferred:	*grey (with red collar)*	*dark blue*

Exercise 7

يلبس/تلبس *wearing*	قريب أميرة *relation to Amira*	الاسم *name*	
فستان أبيض	زوجة الأخ	هيلينا	١
بدلة رمادية	الأخ	شكري	٢
شال	الأخت	زينب	٣
سويتشيرت أبيض	ابن الأخت	أشرف	٤
نظارة وبنطلون أبيض	زوج الأخت	فوزي	٥
جلابيّة تقليديّة وحجاب	الأم	فضيلة	٦
بدلة وربطة عنق سوداء ورمادية	الأب	سامي	٧
فستان أسود	بنت الخال	أمل	٨
صُدَيرية وقميص أبيض	ابن بنت الخال	ميدو	٩

Exercise 8

١ المرأة التي تلبس الفستان الأبيض هي زوجة أخي، هيلينا.
٢ الرجل الذي يلبس البدلة الرماديّة هو أخي، شكري.
٣ المرأة التي تلبس الشال هي أختي، زينب.
٤ الولد الذي يلبس السويتشيرت الأبيض هو ابن أختي، أشرف.
٥ الرجل الذي يلبس النظّارة والبنطلون الأبيض هوزوج أختي، فوزي.
٦ المرأة التي تلبس الجلابيّة التقليديّة والحجاب هي أمّي، مها.
٧ الرجل الذي يلبس البدلة وربطة العنق السوداء والرماديّة هو أبي، سامي.
٨ المرأة التي تلبس الفستان الأسود هي بنت خالي، أمل.
٩ الولد الذي يلبس الصُديريّة والقميص الأبيض هو ابن بنت خالي، ميدو.

Exercise 9

١ أين القبّعة السوداء التي كانت في الخزانة؟
٢ اشترَيتُ الفستان الذي تلبسه ابنتي.
٣ هل خرج الأولاد الذين كانوا في السينما.
٤ اجتمع الوزير مع البنات اللاتي أرسلنَ خطاباً للجريدة.
٥ ذهبنا إلى مدينة ليس فيها فندق.
٦ لم أتذكّر الأرقام التي كتبتُها على ورقة صغيرة.

Exercise 10

A شادية (Shadya) B سمر (Samar) C جميلة (Jamila) D هند (Hind)

Exercise 11

a٦; b٥; c١; d٩; e٨; f١٠; g٣; h٢; i٤; j٧

Exercise 12

A١٠ B٩ B٨ A٧ D٦ C٥ B٤ D٣ C٢ A١

نظرة على العراق *(A look at Iraq)*

Arabic in Iraq: transcript and translation, page 132

اسمي علي من محافظة البصرة، جمهورية العراق. مدينة البصرة جميلة تقع في جنوب العراق.

الحالة الاجتماعية أعزب. لدي أخ واحد اسمه محمد.

أعمل حاليا كمدير لمكتب دار النشر العالمية ماكميلان في دولة الامارات العربية المتحدة.

أحبّ ممارسة الرياضة. كنت لاعب تايكواندو وأني حائز على الحزام الأسود.
حاليا أكمل دراسة الماجستير في ادارة الأعمال الدولية في الجامعة الاسترالية، جامعة وولونغوغ.

أحب قراءة الكتب المتعلقة بمجال الاعمال. أعتبر الدراسة من الامور المهمة في حياة الانسان. أطمح للحصول عى شهادة الدكتوراة.

My name is Ali. I'm from the municipality of Basra [in the] Republic of Iraq. Basra is beautiful city and is located in the south of Iraq.

[My] marital status is single. I have one brother called Muhammed.

I work as the country manager for Macmillan Publishers Worldwide in the United Arab Emirates.

I like sport. I used to play Tae Kwon Do and I achieved a black belt.

I am studying for my Masters in International Business at the Australian University of Wollongong. I enjoy reading business books. I think studying is important in a person's life. I aspire to have a PhD.

Questions on passage, page 133

١ لون الملابس التقليدية في الصيف هو أبيض.

٢ تكون الملابس فضفاضة صيفاً لِتَسمَح بحركة الهواء.

٣ جو الصحراء بارد جدّا خاصّةً في الليل.

٤ لا. ملابس الشتاء مصنوعة من الصوف.

٥ ملابس النساء مُحتَشِمة وفضفاضة.

UNIT 9

Exercise 1

السنة/الصفّ *class/year*	المدرسة/الجامعة *school/university*	العمر *age*	الاسم *name*	
السنة الأولى	الجامعة	١٩	سعيد	١
السنة الثالثة	المدرسة الثانوية	١٧	منيرة	٢
السنة الثانية	المدرسة الإعدادية	١٣	كمال	٣
السنة الخامسة	المدرسة الابتدائية	١٠	خالد	٤
السنة الأولى	الروضة	٤	سارة	٥

Exercise 2

١ منيرة عمرها ١٧ سنة وهي في السنة الثالثة من المدرسة الثانوية.
٢ كمال عمره ١٣ سنة وهو في السنة الثانية من المدرسة الإعدادية.
٣ خالد عمره ١٠ سنين وهو في السنة الخامسة من المدرسة الا.بتدائية.
٤ سارة عمرها ٤ سنين وهي في السنة الأولى من الروضة.

Exercise 3

history التاريخ
geography الجغرافيا
music الموسيقى
drawing and art الرسم والفنون
mathematics الريّاضيات
religious education التربيّة الدينيّة
Arabic (language) (اللغة) العربيّة
algebra الجَبر
physical education التربية الرياضية
English (language) (اللغة) الانجليزيّة
(science of) biology (عِلم) الأحياء

(science of) physics (عِلم) الفيزياء
(science of) chemistry (عِلم) الكيمياء
medicine الطبّ
law الحقوق
engineering الهندسة
philosophy الفَلسَفة
business studies/commerce التِجارة
literature الآداب
economics عِلم الاِقتصاد
sociology عِلم الاجتِماع
phsychology عِلم النَفس

Exercise 4

أكمل		منيرة	
سلبي	إيجابي	سلبي	إيجابي
الرياضيات	الموسيقى	الإنجليزية	الرياضيات
الجبر	الرسم	العربية	العلوم
علم الفيزياء	التاريخ	التاريخ	
	اللغات		

Exercise 5

١ أنا لا أجيد علم الأحياء.
٢ ذهبَت أختي إلى الجامعة في باريس لدراسة الأدب الفرنسي.
٣ هل أنتم تدرسون اللغة العربية؟
٤ حضر اليوم وزير التعليم لزيارة مدرستنا.
٥ يبدأ اليوم المدرسي الساعة الثامنة صباحاً.
٦ الطلبة يدرسون الكيمياء والفيزياء في قِسم العلوم.
٧ وكالة «ناسا» فيها مجموعة كبيرة من العلماء.
٨ أبي علّمني ركوب الدراجات في سن السابعة.

Exercise 6

1 chemistry; 2 because she is weak in English; 3 civil engineering
4 father: thinks engineering will suit her because she's good at maths and science; mother: thinks it is "all dust and sand" and does not suit girls, thinks economics or business studies would be better; 5 to work in an international construction company, to travel, to build houses for the poor.

Exercise 7

١ اِقرأوا الأسئلة كلها جَيِّدا.
٢ ضعوا الهواتف المحمولة في حقائبكم.
٣ استَمِعوا إلى هذه التَعليمات المُهمّة.
٤ لا تتكلّموا إطلاقاً أثناء الامتحان.
٥ رَكِّزوا على أوراقكم.
٦ لا تقلبوا ورقة الأسئلة.
٧ اُكتبوا التاريخ.
٨ لا تنظروا إلى أوراق زملائكم.
٩ ابدأوا بالأسهل.

Exercise 8

	Past	*Present*	*Instruction*	*Negative*
draw	رسم	ترسم	ارسم!	لا ترسم!
mention	ذكر	يذكُر	اُذكر!	لا تذكُر!
study	درس	يدرُس	اُدرُس!	لا تَدرُس!
explain	شرح	يشرَح	اِشرَح!	لا تَشرَح!
fill	ملأ	يملأ	املأ!	لا تملأ!
use	استعمل	يَستَعمِل	استَعمِل!	لا تَستَعمِل!
complete	أكمل	يُكمِل	أَكمِل!	لا تُكمِل!
colour	لوّن	يُلَوِّن	لَوِّن!	لا تُلَوِّن!
describe	وصف	يَصِف	صِف!	لا تَصِف!
close/switch off	أغلق	يُغلِق	أَغلِق!	لا تُغلِق!
stop	وقف	يَقِف	قِف!	لا تَقِف!

Exercise 9

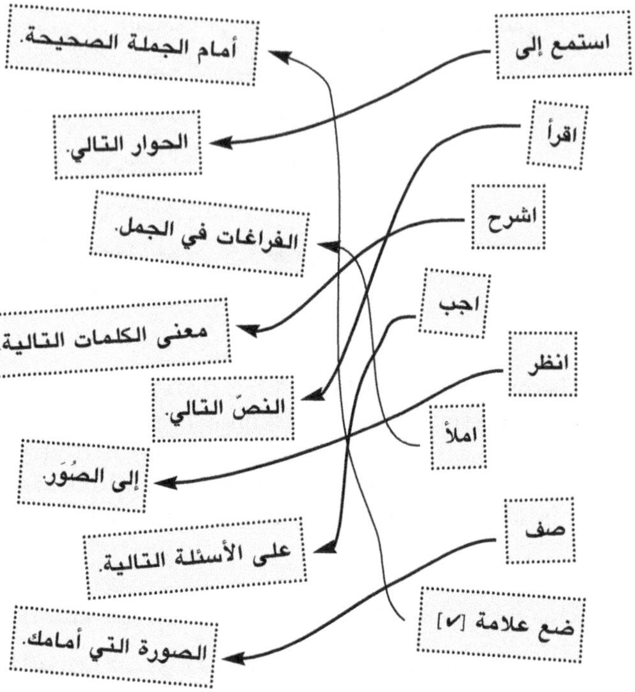

Exercise 10

١ اِقلب الصورة.
٢ اِقرأوا هذه الكُتُب.
٣ أغلقي التليفزيون.
٤ اِرسموا صورة للغرفة.
٥ أرسلي لي إيمايل.
٦ لا تستعملوا الهواتف المحمولة.
٧ اُكتب كلمة مناسبة في الفراغ.
٨ اِستمعوا إلى المحادثة.
٩ قُل لي معنى الكلمة.
١٠ لا تُجيبي على هذه الأسئلة.

نظرة على الجزائر *(A look at Algeria)*

Arabic in Algeria: transcript and translation, page 150

أهلا بكم، واسمني راضية وانا عايشة في الانجليز مع اختي الصّغيرة. والديّا مازالهم في الجزائر، يسكنو في الأبيار. اختي الكبيرة تانيك مازالها في البلاد. بابا وهراني من قديل وماما من قسنطينة. يمّا ماتخدمش قاعدة في الدّار وبابا يخدم في شركة تاع البترول. هو مهندس.

اختي الكبيرة طبيبة واسمها أمينة وهي مزوجة بصّح ماعندهاش الدراري. ماتسكنش بعيد ممّواليّا. هي ساكنة في حيدرة والوالدين في الأبيار. تروح تشوفهم كلّ يومين بصّح تيليفوني لماما كلّ يوم. راني متوحشة بزّاف لفاميليا وناوية نروح نشوفهم في الصّيف. مانقدرش نروح دوك على خاطر نخدم فلمسيد نقرّي لعربيّة فيها. والعطلة تاعي حتى لأوت.

نحبّ نقرأ الكتابات ونحبّ نروح السينما. نحبّ الرّقاد ونحبّ ناكل بصّح نعجز نطيّب. علابيها نصرف الدّراهم بزّاف في المأكلة برّا.

Hello, my name is Radia and I live in England with my little sister. My parents are still in Algeria. They live in El-Biar [a suburb of Algiers]. My oldest sister is still back home. My father is Oranese from Gudyyel and my mother is from Constantine. My mother does not work. She's a housewife and my father works in a petroleum company. He is an engineer.

My oldest sister is a doctor. Her name is Amina. She's married but has no children. She doesn't live far from my parents. She lives in Hydra [on the outskirts of Algiers] and my parents [live in] in El-Biar. She visits them every two days but calls my mother every day. I miss my family a lot and I intend to go and see them in summer. I can't go now because I work in a school as an Arabic teacher and my holidays won't be until August.

I like reading books and like to go to the movies. I like sleeping and eating but I'm lazy about cooking. That's why I spend a lot of money eating out.

Questions on passage, page 151

١ سيبدأ تعليم الأمازيغية في العام الدراسي المقبل.

٢ من السنة الرابعة ابتدائي.

٣ وزير التربية الجزائري اسمه بوبكر بن بوزيد.

٤ لا، سيطبّق في الولايات النموذجية.

٥ لا، يعتقد أن تعليم الأمازيغية شيء جيّد.

UNIT 10

Exercise 1

١ الرياضة
٢ الثقافة والفنّ
٣ الطبّ والصحّة
٤ المجتمع
٥ الطبّ والصحّة
٦ الطقس المناخ
٧ المجتمع
٨ العلوم والتكنولوجيا
٩ الاقتصاد والمال
١٠ السياسة
١١ الثقافة والفنّ
١٢ الطبّ والصحّة
١٣ السياسة / الأخبار الدُوَليّة

Exercise 2

١ الكولسترول الضارّ
٢ النوم المبكر
٣ السينما الصامتة
٤ قانون المرور
٥ احتياجات المرأة
٦ الانفجار العظيم
٧ الكأس الايطالي
٨ نسبة الرطوبة
٩ السنة الماضية
١٠ التوتُّر في العلاقات
١١ نجاح كبير
١٢ أسعار الفائدة

Exercise 3

1 the first column is Greenwich (mean)time (غرينتش), the outside column is Mecca time (مكة); **2** ten; **3** إعادة ; **4** 14:55 (GMT): Palestinian villages (in) 1948; **5** four; **6** summary; **7** 18:30 (GMT); **8** *Eye on the World* (على العالم عين) is recorded, *Without Limits* (بلا حدود) is live; **9** *The Economy Today* (الاقتصاد اليوم); **10** 15:15 (GMT); **11** 16:57 (GMT); **12** the name means *More than One View,* so the programme is likely to be a live discussion; the programme is broadcast on Friday at 19:05 GMT.

Exercise 4

					✔		عنوان ١
		✔					عنوان ٢
				✔			عنوان ٣
	✔						عنوان ٤
			✔				عنوان ٥

Exercise 5

أيها السادة المستمعون مرحباً بكم في موجزِ أخبارِ الساعةِ السادسةِ.

البرلمانُ يوافقُ بالإجماعِ على قانونِ الهجرةِ الجديدِ، ورئيسُ الوزراءِ يصفُ التصويتَ بأنه نَصرٌ تاريخيٌّ للديموقراطيةِ.

سفينةُ الفضاءِ الروسيةُ تبعثُ بأوّلِ صورٍ للكوكبِ الجديدِ، والعلماءُ حولَ العالمِ يحتفلونَ بهذا الاكتشافِ الرائعِ.

قمةُ المجموعة الاقتصادية تطلب من البنوك المركزية التعاون معها في مكافحة التضخم في أفريقيا وآسيا.

يوم ذهبي للعرب في الدورة الأوليمبية: ذهبية لمصر في الجودو وللإمارات في الرماية وللمغرب في العدو ولتونس في السباحة.

طبيب يمني يكتشف علاجاً لسقوط الشعر باستخدام زيت الزيتون وأوراق شجر التين.

والآن، إليكم الأخبار بالتفصيل....

Exercise 6

١ أعمَق	٤ أكثر تَضَخُّماً	٧ أحدَث
٢ أغنَى	٥ أكثر إيداعاً	٨ أكثر احتشاماً
٣ أكثر تَحديداً	٦ أكثر تَحليليةً	٩ أكثر تسليةً

Exercise 7

Daily newspapers	✔	Radio	☐
Weekly newspapers	☐	Terrestrial TV	✔
Weekly magazines	✔	Satellite TV	✔
Mobile phones	☐	Internet	✔

Exercise 8

The answer to this exercise depends on your choice of news story. Try to check your report with an Arabic-speaker.

نظرة على الخليج واليمن *(A look at the Gulf and Yemen)*

Arabic in the Gulf and Yemen: transcript and translation, page 166

السلام عليكم. انا اسمي محمد اليافعي من اليمن. عايش في بريطانيا مع ابي وامي واخواني. ابي يشتغل تاجر في بقالته وامي كانت تشتغل في الزراعة والآن ربة بيت وهوايتها اكتشاف طبخات جديدة.

اخواني واحد في الجامعة يدرس هندسة معمارية والثاني في الكلية يدرس محاسبة.

اما أختي الصغيرة وأخي الصغير، في المدرسة مع ابني الأوّل.

اما انا متزوج ومعي اثنين عيال – ولد وبنت، شغلي نجار أركب مطابخ، أبواب وطوق واي شي يتعلّق في النجارة.

في أوقات فراغي أحبّ أخرج مع أصحابي وأدرّب في النادي وأروح المسبح.

Assalaamu alaykum [Peace be on you]. My name is Mohammed Yafai from Yemen. I live in Britain with my father, mother and siblings. My father is a shopkeeper in a grocery and my mother used to work as a farmer but now [she is] a housewife and her hobby is discovering new recipes.

My brothers are studying, one of them is at university studying architecture and my second brother is at college studying accountancy.

As for my little sister and brother, [they are] in school with my eldest son.

I am married and I have two children, a boy and a girl. I work as a carpenter installing kitchens, doors, windows and anything connected with joinery.

In my spare time I like to go out with my friends, train in the gym ['club'] and go swimming.

Questions on passage, page 167

١ المصدر الوحيد أثناء حرب الخليج هو قناة سي إن إن (CNN)

٢ بدأت الدول الخليجيّة البثّ الفضائيّ باستئجار قنوات فضائية خاصة بها على الأقمار الصناعية المتاحة.

٣ فوائد القنوات الفضائية للدُوَل الخليجيّة هي تطوير أنشطة كثيرة مثل المهرجانات والمعارض وزيادة كبيرة في زوّار هذه الدُوَل.

UNIT 11

Exercise 1

Exercise 2

١ ٣٣ درجة
٢ ٢٦–٣٢ درجة
٣ ١٨ كم (كيلومتر)
٤ شماليّة غربيّة
٥ ٣٢ درجة
٦ ٣٨٪
٧ ٢٥–٤٠ درجة
٨ ٣٦٪

Exercise 3

١ معتدل
٢ منخفضة
٣ جافّ ومشمس
٤ على الجبال
٥ عواصف
٦ ٢٥ و٣٠

Exercise 4

The answer to this exercise depends on the climate where you live. Try to check your comparisons with an Arabic-speaker

Exercise 5

(Model answer. Yours may vary slightly.)

Advantages		Disadvantages	
coast الساحل	desert الصحراء	coast الساحل	desert الصحراء
short journey	*peaceful*	*crowded*	*long journey*
luxury hotels	*see oases*	*no hotel rooms*	*very cold at night*
great seafood	*sleep under stars*		*have to sleep in tent*
	drink well water		

Exercise 6

١ سيكون الطقس حارّاً غداً.

٢ سيكون ممطراً يوم السبت.

٣ سأجد لنا غرفة في فندق.

٤ سنذهب إلى الساحل.

٥ سوف تستغرق الرحلة ست ساعات.

٦ لن ينام قبل الساعة التاسعة.

٧ لن تصِل أختي قبلنا.

٨ ألن يأكلوا اللحم؟

Exercise 7

١ إذا ذهبنا إلى الساحل، فسنأكل سمكاً كلّ يوم.

٢ إذا ذهبتِ إلى الصحراء، فستشربين الماء من البئر.

٣ إذا زارت المتحف، فسترى التِمثال الشهير.

٤ إذا وصلوا قبلنا، فسيحجزون غرفة لنا.

٥ إذا قُدتُ السيارة، فلن أصل قبل الساعة التاسعة.

٦ إن لم تشترِ التذكرة اليوم فلن ترى المسرحية.

Exercise 8

١ المياه المعدنيّة

٢ الطاقة الشمسية

٣ الليمون العُضوي

٤ يمكن إعادة تدويرها

٥ صديقة للبيئة

٦ مَنعاً للتلوُّث.

Exercise 9

- The company's activities began 20 years ago.
- The machines in the factory are operated by solar energy because it is natural energy and environmentally friendly.
- The mineral water is extracted from wells in the far reaches of the desert.
- As for the juice, it is squeezed from organic lemons ...
- ... and added to some of our drinks.
- The drinks are packaged in cartons that can be recycled, preventing pollution.
- Finally our drinks are transported to the market and sold to the public.

Exercise 10

١ صُنِعَ	٤ أُستَخلِصَ
٢ أُستَخدِمَ	٥ أُضيفَ
٣ قيل	٦ عُبِّئَ

Exercise 11

الآلات في المصنع أُديرَت بالطاقة الشمسية لأنّها طاقة طبيعية وصديقة للبيئة.

أُستُخرِجَت المِياه المَعدِنيّة من الآبار في أعماق الصحراء.

أما العصير فاُستُخلِصَ من الليمون العُضوي...

وأُضيفَ إلى بعض مشروباتنا.

عُبِّئَت المشروبات في عُلَب يمكن إعادة تدويرها منعاً للتلوُّث.

وأخيراً نُقِلَت مشروباتنا إلى السوق لتُباع للناس.

نظرة على ليبيا *(A look at Libya)*

Arabic in Libya: transcript and translation, page 182

السلام عليكم.

كيف حالكم اليوم؟ إن شاء الله بخير كلكم. شن أخباركم؟

أني أخوك عبد الرحيم من طرابلس، الطرابلسي من ليبيا. اسمي عبد الرحيم عبد الحميد بن ضو.

طبعاً أني متزوّج وعندي ثلاثة أطفال. هي زوجتي طبعاً نجوى، ملاك ونوران وأحمد وكلهم ما شاء الله يمشو للمدرسة وفرحانين.

وأني طبعاً نشتغل في الأعمال الحرة وتساعد فيّ نجوى في أعمالي. وأني من هواة الرياضة، نحبّ السباحة، نحبّ العومان، نحبّ البحر، نحبّ الكرة، نحبّ جميع الرياضة.

Assalamu Alaykum [Peace be on you].

How are you today? God willing, all of you are well. How are things with you?

This is your brother, Abdul Rahim from Tripoli, the Tripolitanian, from Libya. My name is Abdul Rahim Abdul Hamid ibn Daw. Naturally I am married and I have three children. [Naturally] my wife is Najwa, [and my children are] Malak and Nuran and Ahmad, and all of them [thanks for God] go to school and are happy.

I am self-employed and my wife Najwa helps me with my work. I'm a fan of sport. I like swimming, I like going for a swim; I like the seaside; I like football; I like all types of sport.

Questions on passage, page 183

١ بدأ المشروع عام ١٩٨٤.

٢ حُفرت الآبار في الصحراء الجنوبيّة.

٣ قُطر الأنابيب أربعة أمتار وطولها سبعة أمتار.

٤ طول النهر الصناعي أربعة آلاف كيلومترا

٥ تستغرق رحلة المياه تسعة أيام.

٦ تُجمع المياه عند وصولها في خمس بحيرات صناعية.

UNIT 12

Exercise 1

١ بطن (stomach)
٢ صدر (chest)
٣ رأس (head)
٤ رجل (leg)
٥ ذراع (arm)
٦ أنف (nose)
٧ إصبع (finger)
٨ عين (eye)
٩ أسنان (teeth)
١٠ أذن (ear)

Exercise 2

g٨ e٧ b٦ d٥ f٤ h٣ a٢ c١

Exercise 3

1 What's wrong exactly? Do you have a headache?
2 pains in his legs and arms and a bad pain in his stomach.
3 because he is a traffic poiiceman.
4 sunstroke (ضَربة شمس).
5 because he is allergic to parecetamol.
6 to consult a doctor as soon as possible.

Exercise 4

See page 189 for answer.

Exercise 5

ـ صباح الخير. ممكن أُساعِدِك؟
ـ أنا أشعر بالمرض.
ـ وماذا بكِ بالضَبط؟ هل عندِك صُداع؟
ـ نعم، وأيضاً عندي آلام في رجليّ وذراعيّ.
ـ همم... هل تشعرين بأعراض أخرى؟
ـ عندي ألم شديد في بطني. لا أستطيع أن آكل.
ـ الطقس حارّ جداً. هل كُنتِ في الشمس؟
ـ طبعاً، أنا شرطيّة مرور!
ـ أشُكّ أنكِ مصابة بِضَربة شمس. جَرِّبي هذا الدَواء، اشربي ماءً كثيراً ولا تقفي في الشمس.
ـ عندي حساسية من البراسيتمول. هل هناك براسيتمول في الدواء؟
ـ نعم، نعم، لا تأخذي هذا الدواء إذاً. أنصَحِك باستشارة الطبيب في أسرع وقت.

Exercise 6

ضارّ بالصحّة harmful to health	مُفيد للصحّة beneficial to health
التدخين	أكل الخضروات
تلوّث الهواء	التمرينات الرياضيّة
التوتّر	السعادة
البدانة	تقليل الملح
	الهواء الطلق

(Model sentences. Yours may vary slightly.)

التدخين ضارّ بالصحّة في حين أن تقليل الملح مُفيد.

التوتّرِ ضارّ بالصحّة في حين أن السعادة مُفيدة.

البدانة ضارّة جداً بالصحّة في حين أن التمرينات الرياضيّة مُفيدة.

تلوّث الهواء ضارّ بالصحّة في حين أن الهواء الطلق مُفيد.

Exercise 7

١ من المفروض أن يُقلع عن التدخين.

٢ من الضروري أن نأكل الخضروات كلّ يوم.

٣ من اللازم أن تمارس التمرينات الرياضيّة كلّ يوم.

٤ من المفروض ألاّ تأكلي الطعام الدهني. من المحتمل أن يضرّ بصحّتك.

٥ من المرجَّح أن تلوُّث الهواء سيضرّ بصحّتنا.

٦ من اللازم ألا تَضَعوا ملحاً كثيراً على الطعام.

Exercise 8

(Suggestions only. Yours may vary.)

١ من الضروري أن تُقلع عن التدخين. التدخين ضارّ جداً بالصحّة ويسبّب الأمراض وارتفاع ضغط الدم.

٢ من المفروض أن تمارسي التمرينات الرياضية وأن تأكلي الخضروات كلّ يوم. البدانة ضارّة بالصحّة في حين أن الخضروات والهواء الطلق مفيدة.

٣ من الضروري أن تقلّلوا من الملح في الطعام لأنّه ضارّ بالصحّة ومن المحتمل أن يسبّب ارتفاع الضغط في المستقبل. كما أن من المفروض ألا تأكلوا الطعام الدهنيّ.

٤ التوتّر ضارّ بالصحّة في حين أن السعادة مفيدة. من اللازم ألا تعمل كلّ يوم من الفجر حتى الساعة الثامنة بالليل.

Exercise 9

1 high blood pressure.
2 take pills and give up smoking.
3 He doesn't feel unwell at all.
4 He doesn't want to take pills or give up smoking.
5 because he's young and wants to enjoy his life.
6 Hamdy thinks he's stubborn and stupid and should listen to the doctor.

Exercise 10

a٣; b٦; c١; d٧; e٢; f٤; g٥

Exercise 11

(Model letter. Yours may vary)

عزيزتي نادية،

أهمّ شيء في الحياة هو الصحّة. إنك لَستِ غبيّة كما قالت سارة ولكنّك عنيدة! من اللازم أن تسمعي كلام الطبيبة.

أنتِ لا تشعرين بالمرض الآن، ولكن من المرجّح أن البدانة ستسبّب لك المشاكل في المستقبل، مثل مرض السكّر أو ارتفاع ضغط الدم.

ينبغي عليك يا صديقتي أن تُقلعي عن الطعام الدهني وأن تأكلي الخضروات والأكل الخفيف. وأخيراً من الضروري أن تمارسي التمرينات الرياضية كلّ يوم وبعد ذلك من الممكن أن تستمتعي بحياة طويلة وصحّة جيّدة!

المخلص/المخلصة، (اسمك)

نظرة على السودان *(A look at Sudan)*

Arabic in Sudan: transcript and translation, page 198

السلام عليكم، اِزيكم؟ أنا اسمي أشرف وعايش حسع في ادنبره في اسكتلندا وانا أصلا في السودان من مدينة دنقلا في شمال السودان لكن اتربيت في الخرطوم عشان كده للاسف ما برطن. واللهجة الانا حسع بتكلمها دي هي واحدة من لهجات الوسط والسودان فيهو كمية من اللهجات العربية يعني ما لهجة واحدة زي ما الناس بتفتكر.

أنا ما متزوج والزول الماتزوج عندنا في السودان بقولوا عليهو عزابي. شغلي باحث اكاديمي قريت لغويات في جامعة الخرطوم. هواياتي لو في وقت بحب العب كورة بحب اتفرج على التلفزيون وبالذات الاخبار وبرضو بحب العب كوتشينة.

الجو عندنا في السودان بصورة عامة سخانة. طبعا السودان هو اكبر دولة افريقية من حيث المساحة وهو صورة مصغرة لافريقيا وفيهو كمية من اللغات والثقافات والعادات والأديان والأثنيات وده في رايي اللي بيخلي السودان دولة جميلة جدا. شكراً لكم.

Assalamu Alaykum [Peace be on you]. How are you? My name's Ashraf, and I am currently living in Edinburgh in Scotland. I'm originally from Sudan from the city of Dongola, in the north of Sudan, but I was brought up in Khartoum, that's why unfortunately I do not speak its [Dongola's] language, and the dialect which I speak now is one of the dialects of central Sudan. There are many Arabic dialects in Sudan, not one dialect as people might think.

I'm not married, and an unmarried person in the Sudan is called 'A'zabi' ['batchelor']. My job is an academic researcher. I read linguistics at the University of Khartoum. My hobbies, if there is enough time: I like playing football, I like watching TV and specifically the news, and also I like playing cards.

The weather in the Sudan is generally hot. Of course Sudan is the largest country in Africa, area-wise, and is a microcosm of Africa. There are many languages and cultures and customs and religions and ethnicities, and this, in my view, is what makes Sudan a very beautiful country. Thank you.

Questions on passage, page 199

١ كانت الحملة ضد الحصبة بين الأعوام ٢٠٠٠ و٢٠٠٧.
٢ كان شعار الحملة «لَقّحوا الأطفال ضد الحصبة».
٣ حوالي ٤,٥ مليون طفل.
٤ عمر أصغرهم ستة أشهر.
٥ عمر أكبرهم ١٥ سنة.

UNIT 13

Exercise 1

(Model answer. Yours may vary slightly.)

شعر	أوبرا	رقص	مسرحية	قصّة	أغنية	فيلم	رواية	
	✔		(✔)		✔	(✔)		مغنٍّ
✔	✔		✔	✔	(✔)	✔	✔	مؤلّف
	(✔)	✔	(✔)		(✔)	(✔)		راقص
	(✔)		✔			✔		ممثّل
	✔	(✔)	✔		(✔)	✔		مخرج
✔			(✔)		(✔)			شاعر
	✔	(✔)			✔	(✔)		موسيقي

Exercise 2

The answers to this exercise depend on your personal preferences. Try to check your sentences with an Arabic-speaker.

Exercise 3

١ فيلم رعب　　٣ فيلم خيال علمي　　٥ فيلم غرامي　　٧ فيلم هزلي

٢ فيلم حرب　　٤ فيلم تاريخي　　٦ فيلم تسجيلي

Exercise 4

يوم السبت	يوم الجمعة	
٦،٠٠	٧،٣٠	ليلة في قَصر الأشباح
٨،١٥	٩،٠٠	مَعرِكة فوق بحر النار
١٠،٣٠	١٠،٣٠	نابليون بونابرت
—	٥،١٥	مشمش في وادي الأسود

Exercise 5

١ رِسالة من الكَوكب الأزرق

٢ قُلوب في العاصفة

٣ مِشمِش في وادي الأُسود

٤ الحياة مع الرِمال

٥ ليلة في قَصر الأشباح

٦ مَعرِكة فوق بحر النار

٧ نابليون بونابرت

Exercise 6

١ كنتُ أذهب إلى السينما كثيراً.
٢ كان يستمتع بأفلام الخيال العلمي.
٣ كانَت قد قرأَت الرواية.
٤ كانوا قد شاهدوا الفيلم.
٥ كنّا سَنَذهَب إلى السينما.
٦ كنتِ سَتَستمتِعين بالشعر.

Exercise 7

The answer to this exercise depends on your choice of film, play or performance. Try to check your review with an Arabic-speaker.

نظرة على الأردن وفلسطين *(A look at Jordan and Palestine)*

Arabic in Jordan and Palestine: transcript and translation, page 214

مساء الخير. أنا اسمي يوسف، فلسطيني من الناصرة. أبويا عنده ثلاث محلات تصليح ساعات وذهب. كلّ العيلة، كلّنا... كلّ العيلة، ١٢، كلّهم بيصلّحوا ساعات... حتى امّي بتصلّح ساعات.

أنا حلاق للستات وللرجال. عندي هوايتي لُعب الشدّة، بالعب «بريدج» وكمان هواية كمان السباحة وبافضّل البحر أحسن من البرَك.

متجوّز، عندي ثلاث بنات: ياسمين ٢٦ سنة، نادية ٢٤ سنة، ايلا ٢٢ سنة... (وأيش كمان؟)

شكراً، مع السلامة.

Hello. My name is Youssef, [I'm] Palestinian from Nazareth. My father has three shops for repairing watches and gold. All the family, all of us... all the family, twelve [people], all of them repair watches... even my mother repairs watches.

I'm a hairdresser for women and men. A hobby I have is playing cards, I play Bridge, and also a hobby is swimming. I prefer the sea to [swimming] pools.

[I'm] married. I have three girls: Yasmeen is 26 years old, Nadia is 24 years old, Ella is 22 years old... (and what else?)

Thank you. Goodbye.

UNIT 14

Exercise 1

الكلمة	المَعنى
أخبار	news
صحيفة	newspaper
إذاعة	broadcasting
مصدر	source
قناة	channel
بثّ	transmission
إعادة	repeat
مستمعون/ين	listeners
مشاهدون/ين	viewers
جَدوَل	list/schedule
مدوَّنة	blog/journal
تغطية	coverage
فضائية	satellite (channel)

١ أحبّ أن أشتري صحيفة «الأهرام» كلّ يوم.
٢ أفضّل أن أستمع إلى موجز الأخبار في الراديو.
٣ كلّ أسبوع يكتب أخي المدوَّنة على الأنترنت.
٤ أيها السادة المستمعون، مرحباً بكم في راديو الشمس.
٥ نرحّب بكم في هذا البثّ الحيّ من البرلمان.
٦ إن «الجزيرة» فضائيّة شهيرة في قطر.
٧ المشاهدون من الرجال يفضّلون القنوات الرياضيّة .

Exercise 2

١ هي تلبس تنّورة حمراء.
٢ أنا دائماً ألبس بدلة زرقاء للمكتب.
٣ يلبس معطفاً رمادياً وقبّعة سوداء.
٤ لَبِسَت ابنتي الحذاء الورديّ للحفلة.
٥ لَبِستُ معطفي البنّي قبل الخروج.
٦ يلبس دائماً جدّي النظّارة.
٧ يلبس أخي ربطة عنق حريرية للزفاف.
٨ المرأة التي تلبس القبّعة الخضراء هي خالتي.

Exercise 4

	المفقودات lost items	اللون colour	المادة material
١	فستان	أحمر	حرير
٢	معطف	أسود	صوف
٣	بوت	بنّي	جلد
٤	قلادة	-	فضّة
٥	بلوزة	صفراء	قطن
٦	بنطلون	أزرق فاتح	جينز

Exercise 5

١ الطقس صحو ومشمس.
٢ الطقس غائم وممطر.
٣ الطقس مثلج.
٤ درجة الحرارة ٣٥ درجة.
٥ الريح شديد جدّاً.
٦ الضباب كثيف.

Exercise 6

١ هو ضعيف في التاريخ واللغات.
٢ إن أختي متفوّقة في العلوم.
٣ ابني في السنة الأولى من الروضة.
٤ قال المدرّس إنّك موهوب في الموسيقى.
٥ أغلق الطلبة الهواتف المحمولة قبل الامتحان.

Exercise 7

٣ أخرِج البطاريّة.
١ أغلق الهاتف المحمول.
٦ أعِد البطاريّة.
٢ افتح الغِطاء في ظهر الهاتف.
٤ امسك السيمكارت بأطراف الأصابع.
٥ ضع السيمكارت في مكانه.
٧ أعِد الغطاء.

أوّلا يُغلَق الهاتف المحمول. بعد ذلك يُفتَح الغِطاء في ظهر الهاتف وتُخرَج البطاريّة. ثمّ يُمسَك السيمكارت بأطراف الأصابع ويوضَع في مكانه. أخيراً تُعاد البطاريّة والغطاء.

Exercise 8

1 yesterday; 2 Ayman Lutfi from Kuwait; 3 Amal Halabi from Syria; 4 she is struck down by an unknown illness; 5 her millions; 6 a young doctor; 7 car chases; 8 *River of Blood* and *Storm of Love*; 9 crying

Exercise 9

١ طبيب شابّ
٢ تقع في غرام
٣ مليونيرة
٤ كما رأينا
٥ مشاهد المطاردة بالسيارات
٦ سرقة ملايينها
٧ نهر الدم
٨ في فيلميها الأخيرين
٩ ينتهي بمفاجأة
١٠ إلى أن تلتقي
١١ مرض مجهول
١٢ عاصفة الحب

English–Arabic glossary

The following glossary contains the key words presented in *Mastering Arabic 2*.

The meanings given are as used in this book. There may be alternative English or Arabic meanings. For these, you will need to use a dictionary.

Plurals are given in brackets after the singular. The most common plural is listed.

Verbs are followed by *(v.)* in the English. (If a word is not followed by *(v.)*, you can presume that it is not a verb.) Both the past and present tenses are given in Arabic.

A

abandoned	مَهجور
able: be able to *(v.)*	اِستَطاع، يَستَطيع
absence	غِياب
according to	حَسَبَ
active	نَشيط
activity	نَشاط (أنشِطة)
address	عُنوان (عَناوين)
advise *(v.)*	نَصَحَ، يَنصَح (بِ)
afraid	خائِف
again	مَرَّة أُخرى
age	عُمر (أعمار)
agreement	اِتِّفاق (ات)
air	هَواء
air-conditioning	تَكييف هَواء
airline	خَطّ (خُطوط)
airline office	مكتب الطَيَران
algebra	الجَبر
all: all ... long	طَوال...
at all	إطلاقاً
allergy	حَسّاسيّة (ات)
allow (for) *(v.)*	سَمَحَ، يَسمَح (لِـ)
ally	حَليف (حُلَفاء)
also: and also	كَما أنّ
always	دائِماً
ambitious	طَموح
analysis	تَحليل (ات)
answer paper	وَرَقة الأسئلة
apartment	شَقّة (شُقَق)
apartment building	عِمارة (ات)
appear *(v.)*	بَدا، يَبدا
apply *(v.)*	طَبَّقَ، يُطَبِّق
apricot-coloured	مِشمِشيّ
area (district)	حَيّ (أحياء)
arm	ذِراع (أذرُع)

army	جَيش (جُيوش)
art	فَنّ، (فُنون)
artist	فَنّان (ون/ين)
as for…	أما
assistant	مُساعِد (ون/ين)
association	اِتّحاد (ات)
athletics	ألعاب القُوَى
atmosphere	جوّ (أجواء)
aunt (maternal)	خالة (ات)
(paternal)	عَمّة (ات)
autumn	الخَريف
available	مُتاح

B

baked (in the oven)	في الفُرن
bakery	مَخبَز (مَخابِز)
balcony	شُرفة (ات)
ball	كُرة (ات)
bang: the Big Bang	الانفِجار العَظيم
basketball	كُرة السَلّة
bathroom	حَمّام (ات)
battle	مَعركة (مَعارِك)
beach	شاطِئ (شَواطِئ)
beauty	جَمال
bedouin	بَدَويّ
bedroom	غرفة نَوم
begin (*v.*)	بَدَأ، يَبدأ اِبتَدأ، يَبتَدِئ
believe (*v.*)	اِعتَقَد، يَعتقِد
bell	جَرَس (أجراس)
belt	حِزام (ات)
beneficial	مُفيد
benefit	فائِدة (فَوائِد)
benefit (from) (*v.*)	اِستَفاد، يَستَفيد (من)
bill (check)	حِساب (ات)
biology	عِلم الأحياء
bird	طائِر (طُيور)
blank	فراغ (ات)
block (*v.*)	سَدَّ، يَسُدّ
blog	مُدَوَّنة (ات)
blood	دَم
blood pressure	ضَغط الدَم
blouse	بلوزة (ات)
body	جِسم، (أجسام)
boiled	مَسلوق
boots	بوت
boring	مُمِلّ
born: I was born	وُلِدتُ
he/she was born	وُلِدَ / وُلِدَت
boxer	مُلاكِم (ون/ين)
boxing	مُلاكَمة
break/be broken (*v.*)	اِنكَسَر، يَنكَسِر
bright (colour)	زاهٍ
broadcaster	مُذيع (ون/ين)
broadcasting	إذاعة
brother	أخ (إخوَة)
builder	بَنّاء (ون/ين)
bus station	محطّة الباص

business studies	التِجارة
businessman	رَجُل (رِجال) أعمال
businesswoman	سَيِّدة (ات) أعمال
busy	مَشغول
butcher shop	جَزّارة (ات)
button	زِرّ (أزرار)
buy *(v.)*	اِشتَرَى، يَشتَرِي

C

calendar (schedule)	رُزنامة (ات)
call to prayer	آذان
camp *(v.)*	خَيَّمَ، يُخَيِّم
campaign	حملة (ات)
candidate number	رَقم الجُلوس
carnival	مَهرَجان (ات)
carpets	سَجّاد
castle	قَلعة (قِلاع)
cause *(v.)*	سَبَّبَ، يُسَبِّب
celebrate *(v.)*	اِحتَفَلَ، يَحتَفِل
cellar	سِرداب (سَراديب)
centre	مَركَز (مَراكِز)
century	قَرن (قُرون)
challenge	تَحَدٍّ (تَحَدِّيات)
channel	قَناة (قَنَوات)
chase	مُطارَدة (ات)
chemist	صَيدَلِيّة (ات)
chemistry	عِلم الكيمياء
chest	صَدر (صُدور)
childhood	طُفولة (ات)
Chinese (language)	اللُغة الصينيّة
cholesterol	الكولَسترول
chopped	مُقَطَّع
civil engineering	الهَندَسة المدنيّة
class	صَفّ (صُفوف)
climate	مُناخ (ات)
climate change	تَغيير المُناخ
clip (video, etc.)	كليب (ات)
close *(v.)*	أغلَقَ، يُغلِق
clothes	مَلابِس، ثِياب، أزياء
clothes show	عَرض الأزياء
cloud	سَحابة (سُحُب)
clown	مُهَرِّج (ون/ين)
club	نادٍ (نَوادٍ)
coach (trainer)	مُدَرِّب (ون/ين)
coach *(v.)*	دَرَّبَ، يُدَرِّب
coast	ساحِل (سَواحِل)
coat	مِعطَف (مَعاطِف)
cold (illness)	بَرد
collar	ياقة (ات)
colleague	زَميل (زُمَلاء)
collective	جَماعيّ
colour *(v.)*	لَوَّنَ، يُلَوِّن
column	عامود (عَواميد)
come *(v.)*	أتَى، يَأتي
comfortable	مُريح
comic	هَزَليّ
company (business)	شَرِكة (ات)
compare *(v.)*	قارَنَ، يُقارِن

complain *(v.)* شكا، يَشكو
complete *(v.)* تَمَّ، يتِمّ
أكمَلَ، يُكمِل
composer مُؤلِّف (ون/ين)
computer حاسوب (ات)
computer programmes
بَرامِج الكُمبيوتر
concentrate *(v.)* رَكَّزَ، يُرَكِّز
concern (be about) *(v.)*
دارَ، يَدور حَول
concert حَفلة (ات)
condition (disorder) خَلَل (خِلال)
confront *(v.)* واجَهَ، يُواجِه
conserve *(v.)* اِقتَصَدَ، يَقتَصِد في
consist (of) *(v.)* تَكَوَّنَ، يتَكَوَّن (من)
consume *(v.)* اِستَهلَكَ، يستَهلِك
consumer مُستَهلِك (ون/ين)
contact *(v.)* اِتَّصَلَ، يَتَّصِل
continue *(v.)* اِستَمَرَّ، يَستَمِرّ
cooker فُرن (أفران)
cooking طَبخ
corner ناصِية (نَواصٍ)
correct صَحيح، على حَقّ
countryside ريف
course دَورة (ات)
courtyard باحة (ات)
cover *(v.)* غَطَّى، يُغَطِّي
coverage تَغطِية
crash تَحطُّم (ات)
creamed مَهروس
criticism (review) نقد
cross *(v.)* عَبَرَ، يعبُر
crowded مُزدَحِم
cry (weep) *(v.)* بكا، يَبكي
cucumber خِيار
cumin كَمّون
cunning مَكّار
curbing مُكافَحة
cure عِلاج (ات)
curtains سَتائِر
CV سيرة ذاتيّة

D

daily يَوميّ
dairy لَبّان (ون/ين)
damage *(v.)* ضَرَّ، يَضُرّ بـ
dance رَقص
dancer راقِص (ون/ين)
dark (colour) داكِن
date of birth تاريخ الميلاد
dates تَمر
daughter اِبنة (ات)
dawn فَجر
day: in the day(time) في النهار
death وَفاة (وَفَيات)
decrease اِنخِفاض (ات)
deep عَميق
defeat خَسارة (ات)

delicate رَقيق
dentist طَبيب (أطِبّاء) الأسنان
depart *(v.)* غادَرَ، يُغادِر
depths: in the depths of في أعماق
desert *(f)* صَحراء (صَحارَى)
design *(v.)* صَمَّمَ، يُصَمِّم
designer مُصَمِّم (ون/ين)
despite بالرَغم من، رَغمَ أنَّ
desserts حَلَويات
determined (to be) *(v.)* أصَرَّ، يُصِرّ
diabetes مَرَض السُكَّر
dialogue حِوار (ات)
diameter قُطر (أقطار)
die *(v.)* ماتَ، يموت
differ *(v.)* اِختَلَفَ، يَختَلِف
difficult صَعب
dig *(v.)* حَفَرَ، يَحفِر
dining room سُفرة (ات)
direct مُباشِر
direction اِتِّجاه (ات)
director مُخرِج (ون/ين)
discovery اِكتِشاف (ات)
disembark, get off *(v.)* نَزَلَ، يَنزِل
dish of the day طَبَق اليَوم
disorder خَلَل (خِلال)
district حَيّ (أحياء)
divide *(v.)* قَسَّمَ، يُقَسِّم
divorce طَلاق (ات)
doctor طَبيب (أطِبّاء)
documentary تَسجيليّ
dress فُستان (فَساتين)
drive *(v.)* قادَ، يقود (السيّارة)
driver سائِق (ون/ين)
drown *(v.)* غَرِقَ، يَغرَق
dry جافّ
due to بِسَبَب
dust تُراب

E

ear أُذُن (آذان)
early مُبَكِّر
eat *(v.)* تَناوَلَ، يَتَناوَل
eat breakfast *(v.)* أفطَرَ، يُفطِر
economics عِلم الاِقتِصاد
editor رَئيس (رُؤَساء) التَحرير
education تَعليم، تَربِية
educational تَعليميّ
effect تأثير (ات)
elegant أنيق
elevator مِصعَد (مَصاعِد)
embroidery تَطريز
employ (use) *(v.)* اِستَعمَلَ، يَستَعمِل
encourage ، شَجَّعَ، يُشَجِّع
energy طاقة (ات)
engineering هَندَسة
enjoy *(v.)* اِستَمتَعَ، يَستَمتِع بـ
enjoyable مُمتِع
enquire *(v.)* استَفسَرَ، يَستَفسِر

enrol *(v.)* سَجَّل، يُسَجِّل
entertaining مُسَلٍّ
entrance مَدخَل (مَداخِل)
environment بيئة (ات)
environmentally friendly صَديق للبيئة
equivalent to ما يُعادِل
error خَطأ (أخطاء)
event حَدَث (أحداث)
exactly بِالضَبط
examination اِمتِحان (ات)
examination hall صالة الاِمتِحانات
excellent مُمتاز
excelling (in) مُتَفَوِّق (في)
excessive زائِد
exciting مُثير
exercise(s) تَمرينات رِياضيّة
exhibition مَعرِض (مَعارِض)
experience خِبرة
experiment تَجرِبة (تَجارِب)
explain *(v.)* شَرَحَ، يَشرَح
explore (study) *(v.)* تَعَرَّفَ، يَتَعَرَّف على
explosion اِنفِجار (ات)
extract *(v.)* اِستَخرَجَ، يَستَخرِج
eye عَين (عيون)

F

face وَجه (وُجوه)
face *(v.)* واجَهَ، يُواجِه
face (towards) *(v.)* تَوَجَّهَ، يَتَوَجَّه (نَحو)
fall (autumn) الخَريف
family عائِلة (ات)
famous شَهير
fast(ing) صَوم
fatality وَفاة (وَفَيات)
father أَب (آباء)/ والِد (ون/ين)
father-in-law حَم (أَحماء)
fatty دُهنيّ
favourite مُفَضَّل
feel *(v.)* شَعَرَ، يَشعُر بِـ
fellow (student, etc.) زَميل (زُمَلاء)
festival مَهرَجان (ات)
fever حُمّى
field حَقل (حُقول)
(sphere) مَجال (ات)
fill *(v.)* مَلأَ، يَملأ
finance المال
finger إصبَع (أصابِع)
finish *(v.)* تَمَّ، يَتِمّ
fire نار (نيران)
first floor الطابِق الأوّل
fishing صَيد السَمَك
fishing rod سَنّارة (ات)
fishmonger سَمّاك (ون/ين)
floor (storey) طابِق (طَوابِق)
flowers وَرد
flowing فَضفاض

fog	ضَباب
food	طَعام (أطعِمة)، غذاء (أغذية)
foot	قَدَم (أقدام)
on foot	ماشِياً
football (soccer)	كُرة القَدَم
for that reason	لِذالِك
forbidden	مَمنوع
forecast	تَنَبُّؤات
forget *(v.)*	نَسِيَ، يَنسَى
former	أسبَق
fort	قَلعة (قِلاع)
forum	مُنتدَى(مُنتَدَيات)
found: can be found	يوجَد/توجَد
fountain	نافورة (ات)
free time	وَقت الفِراغ
fresh air	الهَوا الطَلَق
fresh water	مياه عَذبة
fridge	ثَلاّجة (ات)
fried	مَقلي
frightened	خائِف
funeral	جِنازة (ات)
funny	مُضحِك

G

gap	فراغ (ات)
garage	جَراج/كَراج (ات)
garden	حَديقة (حَدائِق)
garlic	ثوم
gender	الجِنس
general application	تعميم
generous	كَريم
get up *(v.)*	اِستَيقَظ، يَستَيقِظ
ghost	شَبَح (أشباح)
give *(v.)*	أعطَى، يَعطي
give up *(v.)*	أقلَعَ، يُقلِع عَن
glass	كوب (أكواب)
glasses	نَظّارة (ات)
gold *(adj)*	ذَهَبيّ
golf	جولف
good: be good at *(v.)*	أجادَ، يُجيد
good idea	فِكرة جَيِّدة
graceful	رَشيق
grade (class)	صَفّ (صُفوف)
granddaughter	حَفيدة (ات)
grandfather	جَدّ (أَجداد)
grandmother	جَدّة (ات)
grandson	حَفيد (أحفاد)
grass	عُشب
grated	مَبشور
Greece	اليونان
greengrocer	خُضَريّ (ون/ين)
grey	رَماديّ
grilled	مَشوي
grocery	بَقّالة (ات)
ground floor	الطابق الأرضيّ
group	مَجموعة (ات)
guard	حارِس (حُرّاس)
guest (hotel, etc.)	نَزيل (نُزَلاء)
gulf: the Gulf	الخَليج

H

habit	عادة (ات)
hall	صالة (ات)
hand	يَد (أيادٍ)
handball	كُرة اليَد
handmade	مَشغول باليَد
happiness	سَعادة
happy	سَعيد
harmful	ضارّ (بـِ)
hate *(v.)*	كَرِهَ، يكرَه
head	رَأس (رُؤوس)
head (towards) *(v.)*	تَوَجَّهَ، يَتَوَجَّه (نَحوَ)
head of the family	رَبّ الأُسرة
headache	صُداع
headline	عُنوان (عَناوين)
headscarf (hijab)	حِجاب (ات)
health	صِحّة
health insurance	تأمين صِحّي
height	طول (أطوال)
hero	بَطَل (أبطال)
hesitate *(v.)*	تَرَدَّدَ، يتَرَدَّد
historical	تاريخيّ
hobby	هِواية (ات)
hold *(v.)*	مَسَكَ، يمسِك
honey-coloured	عَسَليّ
horror	رُعب
horse riding	رُكوب الخَيل
house (home)	دار (دِيار/دور) مَنزِل (مَنازِل)
house (residence)	مَسكَن (مَساكِن)
huge	ضَخم
hungry	جائِع
husband	زَوج (أزواج)

I

ice	ثَلج (ثُلوج)
illness	مَرَض (أمراض)
immigration	هِجرة
incline (towards) *(v.)*	مالَ، يَميل (نحو)
increase	اِرتِفاع (ات)
increase *(v.)*	زادَ، يزيد
individual	فَرديّ
inflation	تَضَخُّم
inform *(v.)*	أخبَرَ، يُخبِر
innoculate *(v.)*	لَقَّحَ، يُلَقِّح
instruct *(v.)*	عَلَّمَ، يُعَلِّم
instructions	تعليمات
instructor	مُعَلِّم (ون/ين)
instrument	آلة (ات)
intelligent	ذَكيّ
interactive	تَفاعُليّ
interest (on money)	فائِدة (فَوائِد)
international	دُوَليّ
invoice	فاتورة (فَواتير)
iron *(v.)*	كَوَى، يكوي

J

jacket	سُترة (سُتَر)، جاكيت (ات)
jeans	جينز (ات)
job seeker	طالِب عَمَل
join *(v.)*	اِنضمَّ، يَنضمّ
journalist	صُحُفيّ (ون/ين)
journey	رِحلة (ات)
judo	جودو

K

kilometre(s)	كيلومِتر
kindergarten	رَوضة (رِياض)
kitchen	مَطبَخ (مَطابِخ)
know *(v.)*	عَلِمَ، يَعلَم

L

lake	بُحَيرة (ات)
lamb	ضأني
law	قانون (قَوانين)
(subject)	الحُقوق
lawyer	مُحامٍ (ون/ين)
lazy	كَسول
lead grey	رَصاصيّ
learn *(v.)*	تَعَلَّمَ، يَتَعلَّم
leave *(v.)*	غادَرَ، يُغادِر
leg	رِجل (أرجُل)/ساق (سيقان)
leisure	تَرفيه
lemon-coloured	لَيمونيّ
length	طول (أطوال)
library	مَكتَبة (ات)
life	حَياة (حَيَوات)
lift (elevator)	مِصعَد (مَصاعِد)
light (colour)	فاتِح
like (similar to)	مِثل
like *(v.)*	أحَبَّ، يُحِبّ
likely to	من المُرَجَّح أن
limit *(v.)*	حَدَّ، يَحِدّ
lion	أَسَد (أُسود)
list	قائِمة (ات)
listen *(v.)*	اِستَمَعَ، يَستَمِع
listener	مُستَمِع (ون/ين)
literature	الآداب
live	حَيّ
live (reside) *(v.)*	سَكَنَ، يَسكُن أقامَ، يُقيم
living room	غرفة مَعيشة
local	مَحَلّيّ
location	مَوقع (مَواقِع)
lock *(v.)*	أغلَقَ، يُغلِق
look (onto) *(v.)*	أطَلَّ، يُطِلّ (على)
loose	واسِع
lost	ضائِع
loyal	وَفيّ
luxurious	فاخِر

M

machine	آلة (ات)
majority	أغلَبيّة
make the beds *(v.)*	رَتَّبَ، يُرَتِّب الفِراش

manage *(v.)* أدارَ، يُدير
manager مُدير (مُدَراء)
manmade/manufactured صِناعيّ
marble رُخام
mark (e.g. tick) علامة (ات)
marketing تَسويق
mashed مَهروس
masterful بارِع
meal وَجبة (ات)
meaning مَعنى (مَعانٍ)
measles الحَصبة
measure كَمّية (ات)
media وَسائِل الإعلام
medicine دَواء (أدوية)
(subject) الطِبّ
meet *(v.)* اِلتَقى، يلتَقي
قابل، يُقابِل
member (of family/club, etc.) عُضو (أعضاء)
mention *(v.)* ذَكَرَ، يَذكر
method أُسلوب (أساليب)
metre مِتر (أمتار)
middle (school) إعدادي/مُتَوَسِّط
milkman لَبّان (ون/ين)
million مِليون (مَلايين)
minced مَفروم
mine (coal, etc.) مَنجَم (مَناجِم)
mineral water مِياه مَعدِنيّة
mint نَعناع
mirror مِرآة (ات)
mistake خَطأ (أخطاء)
mix *(v.)* خَلَطَ، يخلِط
mobile phone هاتف محمول
model *(adj)* نَموذَجيّ
modern حَديث
modest مُحتَشِم
mother أُمّ (أُمّهات)/والِدة (ات)
mother-in-law حَماة (حَمَوات)
mouth فَم (أفواه)
move (house, etc.) *(v.)* اِنتَقَلَ، يَنتَقِل
moving (affecting) مُؤَثِّر
musician موسيقيّ (ون/ين)
must من اللازِم أن
mutton ضأني

N

narrow ضَيِّق
natural طَبيعيّ
need اِحتِياج (ات)
need to من الضَروريّ أن
negative سَلبيّ
nervousness عَصَبيّة
neutral مُحايِد
never لا... أبَداً
news item *(pl* = news) خَبَر (أخبار)
news summary موجَز الأخبار
next (coming) مُقبِل
Nile Delta دَلتا النيل

non-/not	غَير
non-alignment	عدم الانحِياز
nose	أنف (أُنوف)
not less than	لا يَقِلّ/تَقِلّ عَن
novel	رِواية (ات)

O

oasis	واحة (ات)
obesity	بَدانة
obtain *(v.)*	حَصَلَ، يحصُل على
occupied (busy)	مَشغول
occupy (land, etc.) *(v.)*	احتَلّ، يَحتِلّ
office	مكتَب (مكاتِب)
opera	أُوبرا
operate *(v.)*	أدارَ، يُدير
orally	شفاهةً
orange *(adj)*	بُرتقاليّ
organic	عُضَويّ
originally	أصلا
ought to	يَنبَغي على
outfit	طَقم (طُقوم)

P

pace	إيقاع
package *(v.)*	عبّأ، يُعبّئ
pain	ألَم (آلام)
palm tree	نَخلة (نَخيل)
pan-fried	مُحَمَّر
paper	وَرَق (أوراق)
park	حَديقة (حَدائِق)
participation	مُساهَمة (ات)
party	حَفلة (ات)
pass (over) *(v.)*	مَرَّ، يمُرّ (فَوق)
passenger	راكِب (رُكّاب)
password	كَلِمة مُرور
penicillin	البنيسيلين
people	ناس
percentage	نِسبة
perform *(v.)*	أدّى، يُؤدّي
person	شَخص (أشخاص)
petrol station	محطّة البَنزين
pharmacy	صَيدَليّة (ات)
philosophy	الفَلسَفة
phone	هاتِف (هَواتِف)
photograph *(v.)*	صَوَّرَ، يُصَوِّر
photography	تَصوير
physics	علِم الفيزياء
pickled	مُخَلَّل
pilgrimage	حَجّ
pill	حَبّة (حُبوب)
pink	وَرديّ
pipe	أنبوبة (أنابيب)
planet	كَوكَب (كَواكِب)
play	مَسرَحِيّة (ات)
player	لاعِب (ون/ين)
pocket	جَيب (جُيوب)
poet	شاعِر (شُعَراء)
poetry	شِعر (أشعار)

point: no point to it
لا فائِدة منه/منها
police الشُرطة
police station مركز الشُرطة
policeman شُرطيّ (ون/ين)
politics السِياسة
pollution تَلَوُّث
pop songs أغاني الشَباب
popular (loved) مَحبوب
(public) شَعبيّ
port *(f)* ميناء (مَوانٍ)
position (job) وَظيفة (وَظائِف)
positive إيجابيّ
post office مكتب البَريد
postcard بِطاقة (ات) بَريديّ
power طاقة (ات)
prayer صَلاة (صَلَوات)
prefer *(v.)* فَضَّلَ، يُفَضِّل
preparation تَحضير
prepare *(v.)* أعَدَّ، يُعِدّ
pressure ضَغط
prevent *(v.)* أوقَفَ، يُوقِف
preventing مَنعاً لِـ...
price سِعر (أسعار)
primary اِبتِدائيّ
private خاصّ
problem مُشكِلة (مَشاكِل)
profound عَميق
project مَشروع (ات)
proportion نِسبة
protection حِماية
publish *(v.)* نَشَرَ، يَنشُر
pullover بُلوفر (ات)
put (place) *(v.)* وَضَعَ، يَضَع
put on (clothes) *(v.)* لَبِس، يَلبَس
pyjamas بيجامة (ات)
pyschology عِلم النَفس

Q

qualification مُؤَهِّل (ات)
quantity كَمّية (ات)
question سُؤال (أسئِلة)
question paper وَرَقة الإجابة
quiet هادِئ

R

rain مَطَر (أمطار)
rainy مُمطِر
rarely نادِراً
ray شُعاع، أشعّة
really! فِعلاً!
recognition اِعتِراف
recorded مُسَجَّل
recycling إعادة تَدوير
reduction تَقليل
reflect *(v.)* عَكَسَ، يَعكِس
remember *(v.)* تَذَكَّرَ، يَتَذَكَّر
remind *(v.)* ذَكَّرَ، يُذَكِّر
rent: for rent لِلإيجار

rental/renting اِستِئجار
repeat إعادة (ات)
representative مَندوب (ون/ين)
requirement اِحتِياج (ات)
residence إقامة (ات)
resident ساكِن (سُكّان)
rest: the rest of... باقي...
result نَتيجة (نَتائِج)
resumé سيرة ذاتيّة
rhythm إيقاع
ride *(v.)* رَكِبَ، يَركَب
right (correct) على حَقّ
rise اِرتِفاع (ات)
road طَريق (طُرُق)
robe (traditional)
جَلابيّة (ات)، عَباية (ات)، ثَوب (ثِياب)
romantic غَراميّ
roof سَطح (سُطوح)
room غُرفة (غُرَف)
routine عادة (ات)
runner عَدّاء (ون/ين)

S

salad سَلاطة (ات)
salary راتِب (رَواتِب)
sales مَبيعات
salt مِلح
sand dune كَثيب (كُثبان) الرِمال
sandals صَندَل (صَنادِل)
sapphire ياقوت

satellite *(adj)* فَضائيّ
save (conserve) *(v.)* اِقتَصَدَ، يَقتَصِد في
(rescue) *(v.)* أنقَذَ، يُنقِذ
scene (film, etc.) مَشهَد (مَشاهِد)
schedule رُزنامة (ات)
scholastic مَدرَسيّ
science عِلم (عُلوم)
science fiction الخَيال العِلميّ
scientific عِلميّ
scientist عالِم (عُلَماء)
search بَحث (بُحوث)
Second World War
الحَرب العالَميّة الثانية
secondary ثانويّ
security أمن
see *(v.)* رَأَى، يَرَى
seem *(v.)* بَدا، يبدا
segment فَصّ (فُصوص)
send *(v.)* أرسَلَ، يُرسِل
sentence جُملة (جُمَل)
sex (gender) الجِنس
shawl شال (شيلان)
shining لامع
shirt قَميص (قمصان)
shoes حذاء (أحذِية)
shooting (gun, etc.) رِماية
(film, etc.) اِلتِقاط
shop مَحَلّ (ات)
shopping centre مركز التَسَوُّق

short-sleeved	بِنِصف كُمّ
should	من المَفروض أن يَنبَغي على
show (exhibition)	مَعرِض (مَعارِض)
show (the way) *(v.)*	دَلّ، يَدُلّ (الطريق)
shower	دُش
sign *(v.)*	وَقَّع، يُوقِّع
silent	صامِت
silver *(adj)*	فِضّيّ
similar to	مِثل
simple	بَسيط
sing *(v.)*	غَنّى، يُغَنّي
singer	مُغَنٍ (ون/ين)
sink	حَوض (أَحواض)
sister	أُخت (أَخَوات)
sitting room	غرفة جُلوس
size	مَقاس (ات)
skewer	سيخ، (أسياخ)
skilful	بارِع
skill	مَهارة (ات)
skirt	جيبة (ات)، تَنّورة (ات)
sleeve	كُمّ (أكمام)
slogan	شِعار (ات)
smart (elegant)	أنيق
smile *(v.)*	اِبتَسَم، يَبتَسِم
smoker	مُدَخِّن (ون/ين)
smoking	تَدخين
snow	ثَلج (ثُلوج)
snowy	مُثلِج
society	المُجتَمَع
sociology	عِلم الاِجتِماع
sock	جَورب (جَوارِب)
sofa	كَنَبة (ات)/أَريكة (أَرائِك)
soldier	جُنديّ (جُنود)
solve *(v.)*	حَلَّ، يَحِلّ
sometimes	أحياناً
son	اِبن (أَبناء)
song	أُغنِية (أغانٍ)
sorry	آسِف
sought	مَطلوب
source	مَصدَر (مَصادِر)
spacious	واسِع
speed	سُرعة (ات)
spend (time) *(v.)*	أَمضَى، يُمضي
spoon	مِلعَقة (مَلاعِق)
sports centre	مركز الرِياضة
spring	الرَبيع
square	ميدان (مَيادين)
squash	إسكواش
squeeze (juice) *(v.)*	اِستَخلَص، يَستَخلِص
stage	مَرحَلة (ات)
stairs	سُلَّم (سَلالِم)
starring	من بُطولة
starting with	بَدءاً من
station	مَحَطّة (ات)
statistics	إحصائيات
statue	تِمثال (تَماثيل)

stolen items	مَسروقات
stomach	بَطن (بُطون)/مِعدة (مِعَد)
stop *(v.)*	وَقَفَ، يَقِف
(prevent)	أوقَفَ، يُوقِف
storage	خَزن
store (shop)	مَحَلّ (ات)
storey	طابِق (طَوابِق)
storm	عاصِفة (عَواصِف)
story	قِصّة (قِصَص)
straight on	على طول
stress	تَوَتُّر
stubborn	عَنيد
student	دارِس (ون/ين)
studying	دِراسة
stuffed	مَحشي
stupid	غَبيّ
sturdy	مَتين
style: in the style of...	بطِراز...
subject	مادّة (مَوادّ)
success	نَجاح (ات)
suffering (from)	مُصاب (بـ)
suit	بَدلة (بِدَل)
suit *(v.)*	ناسَبَ، يُناسِب
suitable	مُناسِب
sum (of money)	مَبلَغ (مَبالِغ)
summer	الصَيف
(adj)	صَيفي
summit	قِمّة (قِمَم)
sunny	مُشمِس
sunset	شُروق الشمس
supervision	إشراف
support *(v.)*	دَعَمَ، يَدعَم
surprise	مُفاجَأة (ات)
sweater	سويتر (ات)
sweets (desserts)	حَلَويات
swimming	سِباحة
swimming pool	حَمّام سِباحة
switch off *(v.)*	أغلَقَ، يُغلِق
symptom	عَرَض (أعراض)

T

table tennis	تَنِس الطاوِلة
take (pills) *(v.)*	تَناوَلَ، يَتَناوَل
talented	مَوهوب
teach *(v.)*	دَرَّسَ، يُدَرِّس
teacher	مُعَلِّم (ون/ين)
teaching	تَدريس
technology	التكنولوجيا
teeth	سِنّ (أسنان)
tell *(v.)*	أخبَرَ، يُخبِر
tennis	تَنِس
tennis court	مَلعَب تنس
tension	تَوَتُّر
terrestrial	أرضيّ
test	تَحليل (ات)
	تَجرِبة (تَجارِب)
test *(v.)*	جَرَّبَ، يُجَرِّب
text	نَصّ (نُصوص)
thanks to	بِفَضل

thick	كَثيف
thing/something	شَيء (أشياء)
think (believe) *(v.)*	ظَنَّ، يَظُنّ
thousand	ألف (آلاف)
ticket	تَذكِرة (تَذاكِر)
tidy *(v.)*	رَتَّبَ، يُرَتِّب
tie	رَبطة (رِباط) عُنُق
tight	ضَيِّق
tired	تَعبان
toilet	دَورة (ات) مِياه
tooth	سِنّ (أسنان)
topic	مَوضوع (مَواضيع)
torture	عَذاب
tourism	سِياحة
tourist office	مكتب السِياحة
towards	نَحوَ
traditional	تَقليديّ
traditionally	تَقليديّاً
traffic	المُرور
traffic lights	إشارة (ات) المُرور
train *(v.)*	دَرَّبَ، يُدَرِّب
train station	محطّة القِطار
trainer	مُدَرِّب (ون/ين)
training	تَدريب
transient	عابِر
transmission	بَثّ
transport *(v.)*	نَقَلَ، يَنقُل
transportation	نَقل
travel	سَفَر
trilogy	ثُلاثيّة (ات)
trousers	بَنطَلون (ات)، سِروال (سَراويل)
try on *(v.)*	جَرَّبَ، يُجَرِّب
tube	أنبوبة (أنابيب)
turn over *(v.)*	قَلَبَ، يَقلِب

U

uncle (maternal)	خال (أَخوال)
(paternal)	عَمّ (أعمام)
underground train	قِطار الأَنفاق
undertake *(v.)*	أدَّى، يُؤَدِّي
unfortunately	لِلأَسَف
union (association)	اِتِّحاد (ات)
unknown	مَجهول
unsettled	مُضطَرِب
until *(+ verb)*	إلى أن
upbringing	تَربِية
use *(v.)*	اِستَعمَلَ، يَستَعمِل
useful	مُفيد/نافِع
usually	عادةً

V

vary *(v.)*	تَراوَحَ، يَتَراوَح
	اِختَلَفَ، يَختَلِف
victory	نَصر
view	مَنظَر (مَناظِر)
view *(v.)*	شاهَدَ، يُشاهِد
viewer	مُشاهِد (ون/ين)
village	قَرية (قُرىً)

violence عُنف
violet *(adj)* بنَفَسَجيّ
visa تأشيرة (ات)
visitor زائِر (زُوّار)
volleyball الكُرة الطائِرة
vote *(v.)* صَوَّتَ، يُصَوِّت

W

waistcoat صُدَيريّة (ات)
wanted (sought) مَطلوب
war حَرب (حُروب)
warning إنذار (ات)
washing machine غَسّالة (ات)
watch (view) *(v.)* شاهَدَ، يُشاهِد
way (road) طَريق (طُرُق)
wear *(v.)* لَبِسَ، يَلبَس
weather (atmosphere) جوّ (أجواء)
weather forecast النَشرة الجَويّة
wedding party زِفاف
weekly أُسبوعيّ
weight وَزن (أوزان)
welcome *(v.)* رَحَّبَ، يُرَحِّب
well (water) بِئر (آبار)
wholesale market سوق الجُملة
wide عريض
wife زَوجة (ات)
win (a prize, etc.) *(v.)* حَصَلَ، يحصُل على
wind *(f)* ريح (رِياح)
winter الشِتاء
wise حَكيم
wish أُمنِية (ات)
witness *(v.)* شَهِدَ، يَشهَد
woman امرَأة (نِساء)
wonderful عَجيب
wool صوف
worker عامِل (عُمّال)
Worldwide Web الشَبَكة العالميّة
writer مُؤلِّف (ون/ين)
written by من تَأليف

Y

year عام (أعوام)/سَنة (سِنين)
young boy صَبيّ (صِبيان)
young/youthful شابّ

Grammar index

The following index contains the key Arabic structures and grammar in *Mastering Arabic 2*, referenced by page number.

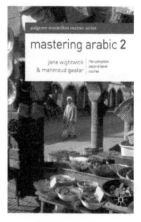

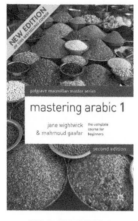

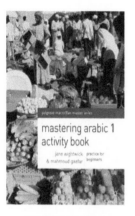

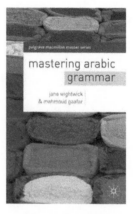

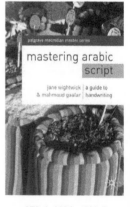

Printed and bound by CPI Group (UK) Ltd, Croydon, CR0 4YY